What's happening to our boys?

Maggie Hamilton is a publisher and writer, regular media commentator and keen observer of social trends. Her books have been published in Australia, Italy, Holland, Brazil, Lithuania and Saudi Arabia, and include *Coming Home: Rediscovering Our Sacred Selves; Love Your Work; Reclaim Your Life; Magic of the Moment; A Soft Place to Land; What Men Don't Talk About* and *What's Happening to Our Girls?*

www.maggiehamilton.org

MAGGIE HAMILTON

What's happening to our boys?

VIKING
an imprint of
PENGUIN BOOKS

that is playing havoc with not only our children's wellbeing but also our own. This book provides a formula for parents to get back to basics with boys, doing the things with them that build strong emotional bonds.

Rick Wilson, Vice President, NSW Parents Council

Maggie Hamilton's new book, *What's happening to our boys?*, is informative and readable. Perhaps most importantly, this book takes a positive view of boys: it sets out to build on what is good about being a boy and to strengthen that side. It also looks at the pitfalls facing boys in today's world. It gives insights to parents and concerned adults about how they can walk alongside boys on their journeys.

Professor John J Macdonald, Foundation Chair in Primary Health Care, Co-Director Men's Health Information and Resource Centre, University of Western Sydney

What's happening to our boys? is a must-read book for all parents with boys. Full of great ideas and practical solutions.

Warwick Marsh, Dads4Kids Fatherhood Foundation

VIKING

Published by the Penguin Group
Penguin Group (Australia)
250 Camberwell Road, Camberwell, Victoria 3124, Australia
(a division of Pearson Australia Group Pty Ltd)
Penguin Group (USA) Inc.
375 Hudson Street, New York, New York 10014, USA
Penguin Group (Canada)
90 Eglinton Avenue East, Suite 700, Toronto, Canada ON M4P 2Y3
(a division of Pearson Penguin Canada Inc.)
Penguin Books Ltd
80 Strand, London WC2R 0RL England
Penguin Ireland
25 St Stephen's Green, Dublin 2, Ireland
(a division of Penguin Books Ltd)
Penguin Books India Pvt Ltd
11 Community Centre, Panchsheel Park, New Delhi – 110 017, India
Penguin Group (NZ)
67 Apollo Drive, Rosedale, North Shore 0632, New Zealand
(a division of Pearson New Zealand Ltd)
Penguin Books (South Africa) (Pty) Ltd
24 Sturdee Avenue, Rosebank, Johannesburg 2196, South Africa

Penguin Books Ltd, Registered Offices: 80 Strand, London, WC2R 0RL, England

First published by Penguin Group (Australia), 2010

1 3 5 7 9 10 8 6 4 2

Cover and text design by Tony Palmer © Penguin Group (Australia)
Cover photograph by Anthony Marsland/Getty Images
Typeset in 12.25/16.5pt Perpetua by Post Pre-Press Group, Brisbane, Queensland
Printed and bound in Australia by McPherson's Printing Group, Maryborough, Victoria

National Library of Australia
Cataloguing-in-Publication data:

Hamilton, Maggie.
What's happening to our boys / Maggie Hamilton.

ISBN: 978 0 67 007393 1

A823.4

penguin.com.au

Contents

Appreciation   ix

Introduction   1

Billion-dollar babies   8

What baby boys need to thrive   16

Shrinking childhood   21

A tween's world   30

Tween boys, food and fashion   36

Losing tween boys to virtual worlds   42

Reclaiming childhood   46

Engaging tween boys   50

Young boys in need of good blokes   53

The impact of the stories we tell   57

Early sexualisation   64

Puberty sucks   73

Boys and their need for possessions   80

Why looks matter   87

Worries about body image   91

Peer pressure   102

The bullying thing   109

Stressed-out boys   119

Understanding a boy's feelings   126

Mums and their boys   135

Why boys love their computers   145

Not enough sleep   153

The weird world of cyberspace   158

The secret lives of boys   166

Addicted to gaming   173

The alcohol generation   182

The drug scene   191

Boys and cars   201

The sex lives of teen boys   206

Boys into porn   216

Camboy   229

When sex becomes sexual assault   232

Mental health issues   238

Living in a violent world   243

When boys are vulnerable to violence   253

Why dads matter   257

Role models and rites of passage   267

When boys push the boundaries   272

Building resilience   277

Where to now?   285

Further reading   290

Notes   294

Appreciation

This has been a big research project and would not have been possible were it not for the huge support I received from so many. Firstly I must thank all the boys who so generously and willingly shared so much of themselves and their world.

A special thanks to the many experts in child and adolescent health, teachers, child psychologists and counsellors, and law enforcement and medical personnel, whose professional observations and years of experience have been invaluable.

A special thanks to my wise, ever-insightful publisher Julie Gibbs; to managing editor Ingrid Ohlsson for her warmth and continual support; to my tireless publicist Shelley McCuaig, designer Tony Palmer, and perceptive editor Jocelyn Hungerford, for their ongoing love and commitment, as well as Dan Ruffino, Sally Bateman, Anne Rogan and Peg McColl.

A big thanks to my family and dear friends, who have never failed to encourage. To Derek, my beloved, whose unwavering belief in all I do sustains me, and to the Great Spirit, who inspires me to look at how life is, and dare to dream about how it yet may be.

Introduction

Twenty-first-century life is exhilarating and challenging. So too is bringing up boys, as our children are at the forefront of the many changes that have taken place in a few short years. Children see so much more than adults. They're very aware of the distinct differences emerging within their generation. They know that what they did five or six years ago is not what their younger friends and siblings are now into. Many teenagers express concern for younger boys, particularly regarding their values, pressures and risk-taking.

The current generation gap is possibly greater than it has ever been. Boys are acutely aware of this and find it frustrating. That's why they go to their peers, or to the media and the internet for answers. While the information they get may be misleading or inaccurate, it's accessible and immediate. Adults tend to be less available, so boys are less likely to approach us for advice.

This information generation does not like to be kept waiting. Today's boys don't have to rely on parents or teachers to find out about life. In many ways popular culture has become the new parent. It's where boys go for education and entertainment, for comfort and social connection.

A boy living in Sydney, Ontario, Dubai, Auckland, London or Singapore can often access the same material, and form the same aspirations, especially around teen consumer and celebrity values.

Access to a world of information also means that marketers can contact boys directly. Until recently boys have been relatively free of their attention. But with the endless drive to increase market share, corporations now have boys firmly in their sights. 'Stealth marketing', advergames, 'relationship marketing', focus groups, 'sensory marketing', 'symbolic advertising', 'integrative marketing', 'product placement', and 'neuro marketing' are just a few of the means now used to hook boys in. Increasingly boys are being targeted by the entertainment industry, fashion houses and toiletry manufacturers, to name but a few. Unless we act, the resulting pressure on boys will only intensify.

The already overwhelming levels of marketing to our kids comes at a time when mental health issues amongst teen and tween boys are on the rise. Shrinking childhoods, less family and community support, and the focus on consumption above all else is creating a new fragility amongst our young. As a result, boys judge themselves and each other by the only criteria they know – their looks, their popularity and their possessions. These developments have proved a boon for the corporate bottom line. American kids alone now spend an estimated $US40 billion per year, and influence a further $US700 billion of adult spending, which equals the GDP of the world's 115 poorest countries.[1] How did we come to be in this place?

It's not just the addiction to possessions which is of concern, but the degraded values and rampant self-interest this relentless marketing encourages. The continual pursuit of material possessions does not serve boys well. As media critic Robert McChesney points out, it 'promotes the sort of world in which you don't think anything matters unless it serves your material gain. Why be honest? Why have integrity? Why care about other people?'[2] The thousands of expertly crafted messages that bombard our kids daily encourage them to believe that such essentials as happiness, friendship and security can be bought. Buying the promise, increasing numbers of boys are becoming lost in carefully packaged fantasy worlds created by advertisers. How can we prepare boys for adult life when their whole focus is on the next purchase and the next?

In the short time since the publication of my book *What Men Don't Talk About*, which examines the lives of men and boys, I believe boys have become more vulnerable in a number of key areas. Thanks to the rampant consumerism of our culture, they too are increasingly concerned about body image and presentation. It's depressing to hear of boys aged ten and under preoccupied with their hair and clothing, with how they look and come across, and with worries about getting a girlfriend, just so they won't be seen as a loser. Teen boys talk of not wanting to take off their shirts, or to strip down to their shorts, because they don't have the 'right' body. What kind of world dictates that wearing the same T-shirt twice in a week, or pants from K-Mart, risks social suicide?

Now our boys are targeted by marketers within months of birth, and their days are filled with branded junk and related DVDs. Instead of fresh air, spontaneous play, and an endless curiosity about the world around them, they're experiencing life through the TV or computer screen. These changes come at the expense of boys' mental, physical and emotional development. Kids need to experience the world *directly* for their brain pathways to grow. When their essential life experiences are narrowed, it is hard for boys to value their individuality and to have a rich inner life, an active imagination and a genuine sense of self.

Neuroscientist Susan Greenfield warns that contemporary lifestyles, and particularly the exposure to computers, may be keeping boys childlike – in need of constant reassurance and instant gratification, and assuming the world revolves around them. This prolonged immaturity amongst our young comes at a time when they have ready access to a world of information, including the worst kinds of material imaginable.

This immaturity makes them doubly vulnerable to the multi-million-dollar campaigns that target them daily and dictate how a boy should look and behave if he wants to be cool. Susan Greenfield also questions how adult life will be for a generation who have the same packaged childhood experiences, think the same way and hold the same values.

Parental authority is constantly being eroded by market forces. This leaves many parents uncertain of their roles, and their boys ever more vulnerable to sometimes overwhelming commercial influences. This trend is of growing concern to professionals in child and adolescent health, because the only value boys have to corporations is in their contribution to the bottom line. As media critic professor Mark Crispin Miller puts it, 'The official advertising worldview is that your parents are creeps, teachers are nerds and idiots, authority figures are laughable, nobody can really understand kids except the corporate sponsor.'[3]

Against this backdrop are additional challenges. Boys are wonderfully, sometimes challengingly physical. But with the contained lives they frequently lead, they have few options other than to turn to computer games for excitement and adventure. Often violent, these video games are addictive, and in no time many boys find these virtual worlds more appealing than the real world, as they have so little room to move in everyday life. Inside and beyond some of our schools we're seeing an escalation in violence, from groups of boys ganging up against others and assaulting them, boys carrying weapons to school, and the appearance of underground fight clubs, to growing violence towards parents and teachers. Yet what can we expect, when violence is treated as entertainment?

As a society we have become used to men and boys getting hurt, so give it little thought until it touches us personally. It's critical we face up to the fact that boys are vulnerable to violence, random assaults, dating violence and rape. They need to know how to handle these situations.

It's curious that while we're so fearful of strangers, we sometimes allow children almost unlimited access to cyberspace, where they can bully, gamble, take on other identities, and view live sex acts and the worst kinds of violence imaginable. With some online communities now in their millions, there are literally vast worlds within worlds on the net. While we wouldn't dream of allowing a young boy to take off on his own in a foreign country, some parents think nothing of allowing these freedoms on the net, where a boy's access to material is often limited only by his imagination.

With the growth in new technologies, virtual worlds have become extremely alluring to boys. There are now more texts sent and received in a day than there are people on the planet. Every month Google hosts 31 billion searches. Real-life activities and relationships can take a poor second place. It's not only exercise and face-to-face interaction boys miss out on when they lose themselves in these new technologies. Too many boys suffer sleeplessness and physical and emotional issues as a result.

Sometimes we fail to see where boys can be at risk. We are naturally concerned about girls being vulnerable to sexual assault, but rarely do we consider the impact that growing up in a hyper-sexualised world has on young boys trying to come to terms with their emerging sexuality. We also need to be more aware of what it's like for a boy to be surrounded by aggressive, over-sexualised young girls. This is not something we talk about, yet it is a very real concern of many of the parents I meet.

Popular culture encourages girls to behave sexually in ways that place them at risk. Young girls often do so because they want to look cool. Boys respond in kind, because they too want to be seen to be where it's at. Or, as one boy described it, 'It's a vicious circle where no-one wins.' It's essential we recognise how much more complex the sexual landscape has become.

One of our biggest challenges is how to deal with boys' growing access to porn, as porn is so accessible and supported by big business and very powerful lobbies. Studies show that repeated exposure to porn shuts down a boy's feelings, and may even lead him to become a sexual abuser.

Scratch the surface and you see just how many boys are viewing porn. It's crucial parents realise a boy doesn't have to be at home to download porn. He can do so on his mobile, or at a friend's place. This isn't just an activity high school boys are into. Increasingly primary school boys are getting into porn, and boys are also watching it together. Porn gives them a new language and a new way of relating which does no-one any favours.

The capacity for kids to lead secret lives is perhaps greater now than at any other time. With this new development come additional challenges. It's not only adults who are predators online and in the real world. With the new technologies, and increased access to adult content, we now have boys grooming other kids for sex. And, as teens now have their own secret language and can assume hidden identities and enjoy covert friendships, increasingly parents are being marginalised. That's why it's vital parents get up to speed with the furtive aspects of teen life. Parents also need to be aware of where their boys retreat for solace when they're feeling sad or lonely, and the likely consequences of the new level of isolation many boys are experiencing.

Sometimes we let boys down because we fail to understand what they need to thrive. Much work still needs to be done to support the emotional lives of boys and help them early on to be confident communicators and readers, as these are invaluable life skills. We also need to pay greater attention to the stories we tell about men and boys. Too often we see boys as troublesome and problematic. We tend to focus on a handful of men who are dangerous and abusive, ignoring the massive, ongoing contribution countless good men make. This leaves our boys feeling as if they have to apologise for being boys.

Some of the material covered in this book is shocking, but it's important to realise this is the toxic atmosphere many of our children encounter daily. It's vital we don't shrink from what lies before us, but take note, then act. Not all boys are into the risky behaviours canvassed here, but as they now grow up in a 'performance culture', where 'out there', often harmful behaviour is seen as cool, most boys are highly aware of what their peers are up to, which soon normalises their worrying behaviour.

In my quest to represent the lives of twenty-first-century boys from their unique perspective, I immersed myself in the world of boys from birth to the end of their teens. I also spoke with teachers and child psychologists, law enforcement and medical personnel, and experts in childhood and teen health, and to support services. In addition, I examined the latest trends in consumer culture, to see where advertising and marketing is heading. Where possible I used the best of local research, but as this area is so new, often the studies I refer to are from international research. While statistics vary from country to country, as our boys have access to the same technologies and popular culture I suspect there are fewer variations than there would have been even a decade ago.

In many ways our boys are struggling. Yet these many challenges are also wonderful opportunities for them to learn strength and resilience and to connect to their families and communities in new and empowering ways. When we understand what they're up against, we can help bring about much-needed change and support our boys in appealing, meaningful and relevant ways.

Billion-dollar babies

It's an exhilarating time for today's boys. With access to more information in a day than previous generations had in a lifetime, greater spending power and more career choices, better health care and education, and more opportunities to travel and work in different parts of the world, they seem to have it made. Most boys will have several careers during their lifetime. Many of their jobs haven't been invented yet, and nor has the technology they'll work with.

With these wonderful opportunities come new challenges. Boys have only had access to the internet, and to camera- and video-enabled phones, for a handful of years, yet these and other innovations have forever changed childhood and teen life. What your 13-year-old son did when he was 6 is not what your 6-year-old is now up to. To support our boys through these major changes we need to understand their world intimately.

So, what is going on with boys right now? Why do they want so much? And what's so crucial about having a mobile phone? Why are they so concerned about presentation, body issues and what their peers think? Why the attraction to alcohol, underage sex, online gambling and porn? And why do video and computer games have such an appeal? If we want to do the right thing by our boys we need to know where they are vulnerable and how to help them thrive. When we track a boy's journey from birth, the answers become obvious.

'Consumer behavior patterns begin officially at 16 weeks (of age).'
James McNeal, marketing guru[1]

WHOSE BABY IS IT?

The arrival of a baby boy is always cause for great joy and excitement for mums and dads, and selecting items for him from the vast array of cute toys, clothing and nursery accessories available is part of the fun. The purchasing decisions new parents make will affect their baby boy in more ways than they might first imagine, as babies are not immune to the social changes we're now experiencing.

For some time advertisers have known very young children can retain brand logos. The big question was how to utilise this, until marketing guru James McNeal noticed that when babies sit up, they like to stare down at their dribble. He realised that if advertisers placed branded fun figures in strategic places on the front of a baby's T-shirt, bib or nappy, product placement could begin within weeks of birth. By the age of two a child would be able to make out these figures on food packets and other products. His hunch, which he named 'the drool factor', is now used by marketers the world over and has generated millions. And most parents are none the wiser.

Tragically, branded toys and cartoon figures are replacing the rich world of people, play and exploration, and of being held.

This commercial assault on our babies is a touch of advertising genius, because meaningful attachments are very important to tiny babies. They need them to feel safe and secure in their new world. Tragically, branded toys and cartoon figures are replacing the rich world of people, play and exploration, and of being held and cuddled. To our advertisers, babies are tomorrow's shoppers, nothing more. The earlier they can capture a child's attention, the more lucrative that child's relationship to specific brands is likely to be. James McNeal estimates securing the brand loyalty of a small child may well generate revenue of around $100 000 for that brand over the course of his lifetime.[2]

'[With every branded purchase], you've turned over part of your child's love to a giant corporation.' *Professor Daniel Anderson, psychologist and child media expert*[3]

SENSORY MARKETING

'Cradle-to-grave' marketing is fairly recent, but already it's taking on new forms. Drawing on a whole raft of experts from psychologists to neuroscientists, work is now underway into *sensory* branding, using taste, sound, colour and scent recognition to capture and reinforce brand awareness. So, having discovered that breast milk contains the scent of vanilla, for example, we may soon see nursery products infused with, you guessed it, a hint of vanilla.[4] Associating products with smells is very clever, for as international marketing expert Martin Lindstrom reminds us, smell is our most primal sense.[5] For most its effect is subliminal.

'Sensory marketing' isn't entirely new. Manufacturers are already aware of the power of colour, for example. Small children love primary colours, which is why they're used in everything from toys to bedroom furnishings. Advertisers are well aware of colour in reminding us of a brand. So intensive is the marketing of certain products, such as Coca-Cola, that sometimes all we need to see is the colour of the logo to want the drink. All this is powerful information in the hands of those whose only interest in our kids is how much money they can make from them.

Small babies and toddlers have no way of screening out the barrage of branded material they're now subjected to. They simply absorb it. This targeting of our little boys happens at an age when they have no sense of being separate from their environment. As far as they're concerned Bob the Builder is as much a part of them as their big toe. And so, conveniently for the marketers at least, babies willingly embrace branded toys and clothing as a natural part of their world.

'If you own this child at an early age, you own this child for years to come.' *Mike Searle, former president Kids-R-Us*[6]

SO, WHO'S THIS ALL FOR ANYWAY?

It's not just babies who are vulnerable to marketing. Parents get a huge buzz out of providing their little boys with treats, and advertisers know this. They also know that today's parents are time-poor, work long hours and often lack wider family support, so they play on these vulnerabilities. They equate buying kids mountains of branded baby gear with being a kind and loving parent. Yet as fun and cute as these products may be, they don't provide baby boys with what they need to thrive.

Advertisers have also done an effective job in undermining parents' confidence, leaving them constantly worried they're inadequate and/ or uncool unless they're buying this or that. As a nation we now spend around $1000 per child per year on toys and related products for kids aged zero to three. Already our spending on baby products has exceeded $1 billion per year.[7] This is no surprise given the rapid growth in the number of baby shops and online baby stores. The problem is, the more time and money they spend on kitting babies out, the more parents add to their child's concerns about appearance: concerns which are now affecting boys as they grow.

'Children find security in attaching themselves to an object – a pillow, a blanket, a store, a brand – that enhances their wellbeing.'
James McNeal, international marketing expert[8]

When you shop online you can buy your baby boy everything from top-of-the-range punk, hip-hop and urban wear to classic baby gear. There's a bewildering array of selections, reflecting the latest trends. The bold prints and colourful designs are pretty enticing. Quick to catch the 'cradle-to-grave' wave, established brands from Ralph Lauren to Quiksilver have expanded their ranges to include baby wear. And, alongside leading children's entertainment corporations such as Disney, which now offers its very own Disney couture, are dozens of emerging players.

This is the perfect climate in which to flog every kind of branded baby accessory imaginable. Recently Bugaboo whetted this appetite by producing fifteen exclusive all-black Marc Jacobs Bugaboos, printed with the Little Marc signature, which were briefly available in New York, Paris, Dubai, London and Amsterdam.[9] This intense marketing to our young is of concern to child health experts who worry about the effects of what is known in ad speak as Kids Getting Older Younger. For while kids appear older, they're still just very small children. However, with the availability of baby jeans, sneakers, hoodies and more, parents may be tempted to start to see their little boys as miniature versions of themselves.

GOTTA BE COOL

Does it really matter if a baby boy has 'Wanna Rock', 'Cool Tattoo' or 'Black Kiss' on his pants, or that his shoes are patterned with grey skulls or grenades? In our rush to present a new baby boy to the world in the best way possible, we can forget our little boys aren't purely miniature versions of ourselves. They need years of nurture, encouragement and discussion to mature, qualities that can easily be neglected in the rush to package our kids a certain way. This is a critical issue. With the rising levels of depression and other mental issues facing growing numbers of boys, we're now realising the importance of nurture above all else. We need to pay close and ongoing attention to what's happening for our boys *inside*. The earlier this can begin, the better.

When we lose sight of what matters, we all come unstuck. Recently, Cotton On Kids, which produces cotton clothing for children and babies, launched a range of tiny T-shirts emblazoned with such phrases as 'I'm a tits man' and 'Mummy likes it on top'. In spite of much protest the range is still out there. What was Cotton On Kids thinking of to launch it in the first place?

TAKING TODDLERS SHOPPING

Marketers are smart. They know that when we see a little boy's face light up at the sight of Thomas the Tank Engine and so on, we will willingly fork out for the jocks, socks and T-shirts. Best of all, we buy the DVD, which is played endlessly, taking a little boy's brand recognition of that trademarked figure to a level even its manufacturers had not dared hope for. What we don't realise is that children this young can't connect up the visuals of even the simplest DVD. All a little boy sees is a hypnotic barrage of images.[10] Unless someone helps interpret what he's viewing, all he's likely to remember are the branded characters.

> **'If you're a kids' retailer or marketer, and you're focused on the children's business, the next logical migration is going to be younger, not older.'** *Marshall Cohen, NPD Group chief industry analyst*[11]

SMART KIDS

Eager to give your little boy the best possible start, you may instead decide to purchase educational DVDs – *Baby Einstein*, *Sesame Street Baby* and *Brainy Baby* – to help your little boy learn.[12] Yet while you will contribute to the multi-billion-dollar success of these DVDs, their true educational value has yet to be proven. Studies show, for example, that kids learn twice as fast when parents show them what to do than when it's explained on a screen.[13]

> '**I don't think there is any established videotape or CD or computer program or type of music to play that we've shown with any scientific backing to actually help our children.**'
> *Jay Giedd, neuroscientist*[14]

The simple fact is that TV viewing isn't a good idea for very young children. For over a decade experts have been urging parents to avoid TV for under 2s, as it can affect their early brain development.[15] And though more research has to be done, there's also a suggestion that the brains of small children are in a state of low-level seizure when they watch TV.[16] Other studies suggest that every hour of TV a boy watches per day may increase his risk of attention problems.[17] While not conclusive, these findings cannot be ignored, especially as boys are more prone to attention disorders than girls. Last year the French government went so far as to ban TV programs for the under 3s, and cable channels are required to display a health warning.[18]

Baby boys are constantly absorbing information, sensations and impressions from the world around them. When they grow up in an artificial world constructed by marketers, they miss out on vital early life experiences, and end up assuming they're only as good as their latest pair of runners, their Xbox or their iPod. As we'll see, little boys need to explore the *real* world for their brains to develop and for them to thrive. No quantity of branded toys and clothing can deliver these essentials to happy, healthy little boys.

To get your little boy off to a good start:

- *Minimise the number of branded toys and clothes he has.*
- *Be aware that TV and DVD exposure is not a good idea for the under 2s.*
- *Remember that branded stuff can't replace warm, loving, engaged parents.*
- *Don't forget that children learn best when they explore the world directly.*
- *Remember that the experiences of touch, taste, sight, sound and smells helps their brains develop.*
- *Read Raising Boys by Steve Biddulph.*

What baby boys need to thrive

It's not only the overwhelming marketing to baby boys that makes them vulnerable; our assumptions can too. While we regard boys as stronger than girls, nature suggests otherwise. More baby boys than girls are miscarried or stillborn, and generally more baby boys will die in their first year. Their testosterone, which helps them to be physically strong, can also affect their immunity, making them more prone to such health problems as hepatitis, leukaemia, and lung and gastrointestinal complaints in their early years.[1] Boys are also more likely to struggle with speech and learning difficulties, as well as suffer mental health issues, attention deficit hyperactivity disorder (ADHD), and Asperger's syndrome, a mild form of autism.

NURTURING BABY BOYS SO THEY CAN BE STRONG

Once we're aware of these vulnerabilities, we realise the importance of *nurturing* little boys first up. From birth little boys need to be held, sung and spoken to, and whispered over to feel safe. This is essential. However, often baby boys are held and cuddled less, and left to cry longer, because we expect them to be more independent from the start. It's natural for baby boys to cry, get upset and be scared. Before they can be strong, boys need to feel safe, to know their feelings matter, and learn how to handle their emotions so they won't hurt themselves and others.

> **'What children need are roots that will hold fast anywhere, in any kind of weather.'** *Gerald Hüther, international expert on early experiences and the developing brain[2]*

LITTLE BOYS GET SCARED TOO

From his earliest months a baby boy begins to note how others react to him, and responds accordingly. If his basic emotional needs aren't met, he begins to shut down. He assumes he's on his own in dealing with life's situations large and small. So begins what psychologist Dan Kindlon calls the 'emotional *miseducation*' of boys. While I dealt with this vital issue more extensively in *What Men Don't Talk About*, it needs revisiting. Basically, the boys who are not allowed to express their emotions and have their feelings taken seriously are the men and boys who come unstuck. Whether or not they're allowed to express them, boys still have the full range of emotions. Sadly, many little boys are told off or smacked for being scared or crying. Or they're informed they're not frightened, when in fact they're terrified. When this happens, a small boy has little choice but to bury his emotions deep inside.

> Before they can be strong, boys need to feel safe, to know their feelings matter, and to learn how to handle their emotions so they won't hurt themselves and others.

At six months a baby boy begins to deal with his fears. International expert on early experiences and the developing brain Professor Gerald Hüther reminds us how important it is to take a small boy's fears seriously. This helps him feel secure and allows his self-confidence to develop. As a little boy grows, he watches how his parents handle scary situations. Then, later on, he sees how others cope, building up a bank of valuable experiences which one day he'll take out into the world.[3]

So, when Mum or Dad acknowledge how their little boy is feeling and help him overcome his upsets and fears, over time he becomes comfortable with his emotions. As he grows his parents can encourage this process by talking about feelings and difficult people and situations, as well as how best to deal with them. Parents who nurture their boys in this way teach them true strength. These are the boys well able to take responsibility for their emotions and to read the emotions of others.

LEARNING TO TALK

Speaking is another area where boys need support, as verbal skills don't always come as easily to them as they do to girls. Within weeks of birth babies can distinguish between slight changes in sounds.[4] By the time they are four months old, they know their own names, and are soon able to make out words in conversations. As they start to experiment with coos and gurgles, they begin to link these sounds with what their mouth is doing. Over time they're able to copy the sounds others make, and eventually whole words.[5]

Boys tend to take longer to learn to talk, so regular time spent talking with them and reading really helps. Turning the TV off where possible and keeping background noise to a minimum is also important, as babies find it hard to make out sounds when there's background noise. We also know that the baby boys in homes where music or TV are on most of the time are at a disadvantage, as it's harder for the part of their brain that governs language to develop. Children who watch TV when they're small are likely to take longer to talk, because there's less family communication and less chance for a small boy to hear and practise new words.[6] There are lots of fun ways to encourage little boys to talk. Singing nursery rhymes and talking to toy figures with him makes language fun, as does bedtime reading.

Then as he grows, you might like to teach him nursery rhymes and to move around with him as you say or sing these rhymes together.

Dads have a big role to play in encouraging boys to read.

Out of talking comes reading and stories. Making up or telling simple stories helps boys be more comfortable with words. If it's a good story you may end up telling it over and over, as small children delight in repetition. Then, as a boy grows, these simple stories can develop into made-up stories, family and local history, ghost stories and anything else that captures the imagination and makes stories fun. Dads have a big role to play in this. By reading to their little boy they show that reading is a boys' thing too. When choosing books, allow a boy to select things that interest *him*. Most boys love humour, exploration and adventure, and quirky subjects. Don't worry if they're only interested in one or two topics to begin with. Their enjoyment will keep them reading.

GROWING BRAINS
For a baby boy's brain pathways to develop, he needs to touch, taste, smell, see and hear things for himself. From these experiences he begins to build up a sense of the world around him. (To understand more about your son's brain, see www.developingchild.net) Over time he discovers that Mum is different from Dad, as is the family cat, his sister and so on.

'Our hands constitute the first relationship for the baby with the world. What a difference when gentle, patient and peaceful hands take care of him.' *Dr Emmi Pikler, The Pikler Institute Budapest*[7]

THE IMPORTANCE OF TOUCH
Touch is very reassuring for small babies, as is being held and gently rocked or massaged. Toys with a variety of textures and different sounds provide

lots of new sensations and experiences for a baby boy's brain to absorb. Help him explore his hands, tummy and feet through singing games. Squeak toys on one side then the other, above and around him, to help him begin to understand sound and space. Talk to your baby boy whenever there's something worth pointing out, so he can begin to make sense of the many impressions he's receiving. The more you engage your little boy, the more curious and responsive he'll be, and the more he can start to understand his environment, instead of being overwhelmed by it.

DAD STUFF

One of the great bonuses of being a twenty-first-century boy is that your dad is far more likely than in previous generations to be engaged in your life from birth. Dads are a crucial part of a boy's life, because they assist in a boy's development by playing in spontaneous, unstructured, often boisterous ways. While this play may alarm mums at times, the way dads interact with their boys helps them understand there's a very exciting world out there to be explored. Not all boys have fathers, but an understanding of the importance of this approach as part of interacting with boys is invaluable. And once parents understand how central they are to their little boys, it's no big deal to keep branded products out of the home.

You help your little boy thrive when you:
- *Recognise little boys need as much nurture as girls.*
- *Switch off the TV as much as possible.*
- *Be aware of your own viewing and shopping habits.*
- *Choose toys that encourage imagination.*
- *Divide toys into three and when your son is bored with what he's playing with, simply introduce the second block of toys, and so on.*
- *Spend valuable time playing, talking and reading together.*

Shrinking childhood

As little boys start to grow, a world of adventure beckons. But for too many this world is retreating as parents struggle to keep branded toys, clothing and games at bay. Unlike previous generations, who enjoyed just a handful of toys, today's boys are increasingly immersed in mountains of branded junk. This obsession with 'stuff' begins early with such trade-marked figures as Bob the Builder. There's every imaginable branded product available from books, toys, DVDs, socks and T-shirts, to pyjamas and bedding, curtains, wallpaper, night lights, phones and stationery.

DROWNING IN BRANDED JUNK

With sales in their billions, these brands have plenty of resources to ensure the dollars keep flowing. A decade ago international marketing guru James McNeal estimated around US$1 billion was spent on advertising to kids, a further US$2 billion on public relations, US$3 billion on packaging, and over US$4 billion on samples, promotions and the like.[1] With advertising and promotional agencies now specialising in marketing to kids, it's hard to gauge what the current figures might be. Certainly, the bombardment of marketing doesn't make a parent's job any easier.

Time spent watching DVDs and playing with branded toys cuts down on family time, fresh air and sunshine, social interaction, and opportunities for boys to learn directly about the world around them. Psychologist Allen Kanner talks of the 'wounding' of our children, who from a young age now feel diminished unless they have everything on offer. By addicting our boys to The Wiggles, Ben 10, Spiderman, Harry Potter, Pirates of the Caribbean and so on, we rob them of their spontaneity and their imagination. Precious time exploring and having adventures is lost when packaged, passive, screen-based entertainment is substituted. This makes it hard for preschool and kindergarten teachers to educate kids. 'Boys are very conscious of what they have,' explained Jayne, who teaches at preschool. 'They have more branded stuff. They bring it to preschool. One boy this week brought a mobile phone to school.' She went on to explain how their gross motor skills (walking, standing, sitting and rolling) were being compromised, because they weren't getting enough physical play in their lives. 'At pre-school they prefer to be on the computers, rather than being outside,' she told me. Increasingly it was becoming more difficult for her to engage boys in other ways.

> **'Children used to be good at making up their own games. Now I have to work a lot harder at providing alternative role models to the superheroes like Ben 10 seen on DVDs.'**
> *Dee, kindergarten teacher*

THE IMPACT OF MARKETING

Preschool teachers are very aware of these pressures on boys. 'It's very evident now,' one teacher told me. 'When we have show and tell boys want to bring their latest purchase – a Bob the Builder truck or whatever. The whole point of show and tell is to talk about something *interesting* that has happened, something they've found in nature, something they've made.' Trying to keep the lid on these influences isn't easy, but it's necessary, because their impact is far-reaching. As this teacher points out, when a child brings something bought to preschool, it starts a life-time of unhealthy competition amongst young boys. Sometimes it's hard to grasp the extent to which young boys are being affected by marketing until you see the research. In one study, while 70 per cent of 3-year-olds could recognise McDonald's golden arches, only half these boys knew their own surnames.[2]

> 'My little brother, like he's mad on *Pirates of the Caribbean*. It's all he's interested in.' *TJ, 10*

It's not just branded toys which challenge preschool teachers. They are now faced with seeing trademarked figures on bags, T-shirts, lunch boxes and drink bottles. As one teacher put it, our kids are now walking ads. From the age of 3, boys do love to collect things. Previous gen-erations fossicked around for feathers, insects and shells, and all kinds of weird and wonderful objects. These activities stimulated their curi-osity and helped them focus. Now this process has been hijacked, and unwary parents are run ragged trying to give their kids everything they think they want. Early childhood expert Ruth Hammond suggests the best approach for parents is simply to acknowledge a branded fun figure whenever their boy spots one, then move on. This helps put paid to the assumption that seeing means buying.[3]

GOTTA LOOK COOL

Another trend now evident in preschool and older boys is an increased anxiety about their clothing and presentation. Little boys are now com-ing to kindergarten with gelled hair and wearing branded clothes. Some kids even have their hair coloured or streaked. Sucked into the pressure to appear cool, parents don't realise that the more attention they give to appearances, the greater emphasis boys will place on how they and others look.

When you look at some of the spin behind cool clothing for kids, sometimes it's hard to get your head around the fact marketers are targeting boys who can't even read or write yet. Cackleberry Kids, which specialises in clothes for boys aged 3 months to 6 years, promises to dress boys with 'confidence and style'. What happened to just running around and having fun? When we don't protect our little boys from these influences, childhood spontaneity and unselfconscious play is lost in anxieties about looks and possessions.

> '**Kids have never before wielded the purchase power that they wield today.**' *Dan S. Acuff*, What Kids Buy and Why[4]

DECLINE IN IMAGINATION

Preschool and kindergarten teachers also talk of a worrying lack of imagination amongst today's young boys. Instead of playing at being whatever they dream up in the moment, they're following the storylines of the DVDs they watch over and over, or they are copying the martial arts moves seen in kiddie cartoons. It's essential we keep boys' imaginations alive. Imagination helps a boy see he has choices. It also helps him navigate difficult people and situations, to have a vision for himself and his world. Keeping a boy's imagination alive is getting harder, as kids aged between 2 and 12 now see more than 25 000 ads a year on TV alone,[5] but this is no time to give up.

> '**Their play is a lot different now – it's more aggressive, copying what they see on TV and in video games, pretending to be superheroes.**' *Dee, kindergarten teacher*

Jayne, a preschool teacher, explained how rare it is to see boys doing anything remotely imaginative. 'At show-and-tell recently we had one little boy who brought in a mushroom man, made purely of mushrooms. He had a book on how to make vegetable people. You just don't see this kind of thing any more. It's normally a purchased item.' Now when Jayne takes her class, she has to work a lot harder on getting kids to make things. 'If you're doing a bit of collage work, or making a puppet out of a paper bag, you've really got to work with the kids. They now have to have something to copy to be able to make things.' Getting kids to concentrate, and to stay with a little project they were working on, was also a growing issue, as they found it hard to focus.

LACK OF BASIC SOCIAL SKILLS

Teachers spoke repeatedly about how much more time was spent trying to get young boys to toe the line. 'It's changed a lot in ten years,' one teacher told me. 'They used to respect what you say, but now they take no notice. They don't have any understanding of consequences, because they lack boundaries at home.' This makes it doubly difficult as young boys are now imitating a lot of violence they've seen on cartoons. Another teacher, Jayne, spoke of the detrimental influence of Ben 10 in particular. 'You tell them, "Don't do that because you're hurting someone," but they just keep on going. They're into, like, the kick-boxing and stuff they've seen on TV,' Jayne told me. She also spoke about the difficulty she now has getting children to work together and to share. 'There are real issues around sharing,' she told me. 'They don't want to share. And if they're playing with something like a train, they have no idea of how to play with that toy together. It's really sad.'

LOSS OF CURIOSITY

When a boy's imagination takes a back seat, he becomes more impressionable and less enquiring. Recently I was in a Balinese café when a flock of small boys appeared in temple costumes, banging drums and carrying an intricately painted figure. They wove their way in amongst the tables with lots of squeals and laughter. At the next table was a 4-year-old boy with his parents. He was engrossed in his Game Boy and never even lifted his head. The moment was lost. I couldn't help but wonder whether, apart from the plane journey, he had even noticed he'd left home.

> **'I've got a brother who's four and he's really addicted to *Bob the Builder* and stuff. Mum tries to stop him getting addicted by turning off the TV, but then he just cries because he doesn't know what else to do.'** *Robin, 9*

LANGUAGE AND LORE

One of the many casualties in this new world of wall-to-wall TV, DVDs and branded products is the opportunity for stories to be told – not just for entertainment, but to help a boy understand his place in the world. Too many children are growing up with no sense of their roots, of the tragedies and triumphs family members faced, or of the unexpected and amusing family incidents that grow with each telling. Previous generations also grew up with ancient myths (such as those of the Greeks and Romans), which told of sacrifice, betrayal and loss, of the unexpected kindness of strangers, and of hard-won victories. Today's boys have simplistic stories, which help sell a lot of products, but teach little about the complexities of life. Yet in spite of this, all is not lost. According to Dee, a kindergarten teacher, 'The curiosity is still there. It's just waiting to be lit.' She sees it when they have the firemen visit. 'We play with hoses and fire hats afterwards,' she explains, 'and it starts to trigger their own imaginations.'

ROUGH-HOUSING

As young boys are very physical, they also need to test their limits and learn boundaries, and dads are perfect teachers. Time spent wrestling and mucking about with little boys helps them explore their strength, and ways of expressing it that are and are not acceptable. Getting physical is a way boys communicate with each other as they grow. Learning how to do this safely and sensibly with Dad or a good father figure is ideal. It's also the perfect way for young boys to let off excess energy. Mark Grabowski, a former athlete, enjoys rough-housing with his young son Josh. He tries to provide a safe environment for Josh to experience 'fear and exhilaration', so he can 'be cool under pressure and less afraid to take chances' in future.'[6]

> **'Rough-house play between dads and boys is so important. It teaches them boundaries. You start early before they're too small to do any damage, so they don't end up taking out a knife and hurting someone further down the track.'** *Terry Dolling, father and youth worker*

BOUNDARIES

It's important for parents to give young boys clear boundaries so they won't hurt themselves or others, and so they can feel safe. Sometimes we're reluctant to talk about boundaries for fear of seeming repressive, but without structure boys feel insecure. They're unsure of what's expected of them. Increasingly preschool and kindergarten teachers are struggling with young boys who are unable to concentrate and get the benefit of their time together. 'At kindy we talk about why we have rules, how it keeps kids safe, and is fair to everybody. Some kids have real problems with this, because I think no-one has never said no to them. In some cases it's clear the kid runs the show at home, yet when they're given structure, they settle down,' one teacher explained. Part of understanding boundaries is learning that life isn't just about us, and about being considerate towards others, learning to share, to pass on used clothes and toys.

IMPORTANCE OF REAL-LIFE PLAY

Play is instinctive. It's also an excellent way to learn – some studies suggest an absence of play can contribute to ADHD. Encourage curiosity, persistence and imagination. Show your son how sticks or leaves can become boats when floated in a bucket or bowl of water. Let him make up his own games out of whatever he finds around the home. Move with him to music to help his co-ordination.

WHAT PARENTS CAN DO

There are hundreds of ways to fire up a little boy's imagination, and most cost almost nothing. As *Dads on Air* broadcaster Ian Purdie reminds us, 'Boys learn through *doing*, through falling out of trees and mucking around.' Encourage boys to explore what they love most. Provide a home environment where boys can be adventurers. When they are little, this begins with the chance to play with what *they* discover around the home – pots, pans and cardboard boxes. Our boys also need a much stronger connection to the earth, and to begin from a young age to care for it. They can do this through recycling and an active interest in the environment. When you play with them in the garden or park, encourage them to take note of the trees, birds and seasons. Get them to look for interesting leaves, stones and insects. Visit places where they can gather stones, leaves and feathers. Wade through autumn leaves together. Explore rock pools. Look for shells. Put up a makeshift tent using an old sheet in the garden. Allow them to build forts and secret hideouts there as well. Have a wonderful collection of dress-ups that will spark the imagination. Think about glow-in-the dark stars on your son's ceiling. Take time to notice the phases of the moon, to blow seeds off a dandelion. Make regular trips to the local library. Teacher Sandy Fazio suggests keeping a bag of activity toys – a ball, kite, beach bucket and spade, ready to take with you on outings.[7]

Help nurture your son's childhood in the following ways:

- *Once your son is of viewing age (over 2), try to keep TV time to a minimum.*
- *Have your own selection of educational, wildlife and other uplifting DVDs or videos for when you do choose to view.*
- *Avoid commercial cartoon channels.*
- *Make gifts whenever possible.*
- *Donate money, goods or time to environmental causes.*
- *Encourage recycling.*
- *Donate old toys to local charities or to children in countries in need.*
- *Make bedtime, bathtime and cleaning up fun.*
- *Set up an area in the house for spontaneous play.*
- *Visit www.cybersmart.gov.au for the best sites for kids of different ages.*
- *Use safe online search engines such as Ask for Kids and Yahoo! Kids.*
- *Note the good tips on combating advertising to your kids on www.youtube.com/watch?v=f_-q0bAj6ME*
- *Reading Adproofing Your Kids by Tania Andrusiak.*
- *Subscribe (free) to Kids Free 2B Kids – www.kf2bk.com*

A tween's world

When your boy goes to school, he enters a whole new world. A decade ago there were only children and teenagers. Then marketers suddenly realised there was serious money to be made from the kids in between, the 'tweens'. These 8- to 12-year-olds plus are perfect targets for advertisers as they're very impressionable and in a hurry to grow up. Using the best expert advice money could buy, corporations began to supply tween products and services that made these preadolescents feel cool and more mature. In a few short years manufacturers have come up with countless irresistible ways for tweens to look and act more like teenagers. As they move rapidly away from the influence of their parents, young tweens now want fashionable clothes and hair, toys and high-tech gadgets. Aware of the spending power of this burgeoning market, even film-makers are using tween focus groups to fine-tune their ads, trailers and film concepts.

'Advertising at its best is making people feel that without their product, you're a loser. Kids are very sensitive to that.'
Nancy Shalek, concerned mother and former president, Shalek Advertising Agency[1]

LOTS OF MONEY TO BE MADE

Although tween boys spend billions worldwide, their purchasing power pales into insignificance when compared to that of tween girls. That's because the marketing spotlight has largely been on girls. Aware of the potential of this new, male market, major corporations are now producing a mass of new programming and products specifically for tween boys. Currently clothing, shoes and sneakers are top of the list. However, high-tech gear and entertainment is tipped to gain the lion's share of this market. On the back of the multi-billion-dollar successes of *High School Musical* and *Hannah Montana*, the Disney channel is now gearing up to launch the tween boy equivalents on its Disney XD network.[2] And keen to get their share of the action, many adult brands are also looking at ways to extend their products and services to tweens in areas as diverse as travel and home décor. With the race on to capture more of the valuable tween boy market, young boys will be under even greater pressure to behave and look a certain way.

IN THE SPOTLIGHT

With insufficient regulation here around the range of products advertised to young kids, marketers have it made. In Sweden, by contrast, there is no TV advertising to children under 12. While in Belgium and Luxembourg there is no advertising five minutes before or after children's programs. These moves are significant because, with the help of experts, advertisers know more about our children – how their brains and bodies work, and their thoughts, emotions, aspirations and fragilities – than they have ever known. Cultural anthropologists now trawl boys' bedrooms, look in their drawers, photograph their artwork and quiz them about their dreams, then hand these intimate details on to manufacturers and advertisers.

> With the race to capture the tween boy market, young boys will be under even greater pressure to behave and look a certain way.

The result? Boys are being marketed to like never before. The problem for parents, even young parents, is that everything is moving so fast, it's hard to keep up. The speed of change is challenging marketers as well. While they spend huge amounts of money studying kids in detail, as cultural critic Douglas Rushkoff points out, 'The minute a cool trend is discovered, repackaged and sold to kids at the mall, it's no longer cool.'[3] It's not just the exploitative marketing to young boys which is of concern, but the values it promotes.

'Recently the local paper ran a series of letters to Santa from kids aged 5 to 11,' explained Rebecca, a mother and child protection worker. 'What struck me was how the kids got straight down to what they wanted, and they wanted a lot. What they asked for was so similar to other kids. They were very specific about the brands, the type of bike, a T-shirt or whatever.'

YOU CAN RUN, BUT YOU CAN'T HIDE

There are endless ways marketers now get to young boys, from computer screen pop-ups to film spin-offs, advergames, premium offers and giveaways. Our boys now see ads on buses, taxis and trains, in the catalogues stuffed into our letterboxes, at sports venues, on billboards and park benches. Films are littered with branded products, as are music videos, film posters, reality TV shows and sitcoms. Companies build their databases from information gathered in 'fun' surveys, chat rooms and through invitations to special offers. This makes life hard for even the most vigilant parents – as Peta, a mother of two young boys, remarked, 'My boys aren't too bad where marketing's concerned, but they can still sing you any ad. They know the products, even products for adults. Ramesh tells me what's good for me from ads, whether it's good for me or not.'

CELEBRITY ENDORSEMENTS

Boys also see celebrities wearing or using products in films and interviews, at parties, jogging along the beach and by the pool, so they naturally want these products too. Some companies hand out products to the coolest kids to ensure they become instant 'must have' purchases amongst their peers. Others set up fake tween sites where, in amongst the chat, they casually endorse their own products. All these tactics and more are giving young boys an insatiable appetite for stuff.

Subliminal advertising is something we're likely to see more of, according to international marketing guru Martin Lindstrom. He tells of an experiment where adult smokers were shown a number of visuals that mirrored those seen in former ads for leading cigarette brands, from a blazing red sunset to two rugged cowboys on horseback. No products, packaging or logos were in sight, yet viewers still made the connection to these cigarette brands. Researchers watched as the part of viewers' brains associated with addiction and reward lit up.[4] Neuroscience is now being used to help corporations develop their products; marketers are even monitoring the number of times a child blinks to see how attractive a product is, and fine-tuning it accordingly.[5]

'Just by drinking Coke you're giving a helping hand to your community.' *My Coke Rewards for Schools*

ADVERTISING IN SCHOOLS
Advertisers have been quick to take advantage of our cash-strapped schools, offering money or products in return for product and logo placement. This direct access to our kids is ideal for them, for as the Kid Club Marketing company puts it, 'In-school promotions are a goldmine for any advertiser.'[6] The subtle ways in which products are introduced into schools can leave you thinking these companies are there just for kids, not giant corporations determined to increase their market share any which way. On the My Coke Rewards For Schools site, for example, browsers are told that 'Just by drinking Coke you're giving a helping

hand to your community' and that My Coke Rewards for drinking Coca-Cola 'give lots of little ways to make life more fun'.[7]

KIDDIE CLUBS

As tweens can't take themselves off to the shops, branded kids' clubs are the perfect solution. These aren't exactly a new idea, but now they're a whole lot more sophisticated. Now marketers can have a direct, ongoing relationship with kids without parental interference. When Burger King introduced its Burger King Kids Club, they reported a 300 per cent increase in sales of kids' meals.[8] Now when you log on to the Burger King site, there's plenty to keep boys amused. They can Simpsonise 'The King' or watch an animated chicken video. Or they can click on the Star Wars logo to enter the animated Kingon Defense Academy, set up to combat the Kingon invasion of earth. There are also plenty of kiddie clips in the Press Room, from a sighting of Burger King to a Frisbee Ambush. While these activities may seem fun, they do little for a boy's understanding of himself or his world, other than teaching him to see himself as a walking wallet.

GIFTS AND REWARDS

More and more corporations are now offering kids gifts and valued customer schemes. On the Westfield Shopping Centre site kids can click on to the We Rock Kids' Club, select their nearest Westfield, and register their contact details in exchange for a We Rock tag. This makes them eligible for exclusive competitions and special offers. At many of the Westin Hotels children get the same five-star treatment their parents enjoy. At check-in, children aged 3 to 12 receive a Westin Kids Club drawstring bag 'chock-full of great stuff'. When kids go to the Discovery Room in the hotel they are given a Discovery Pack, which includes a compass, membership bracelet, disposable camera, canteen, travel passport and snack. In isolation these gestures may seem harmless enough, but combined with all the other ways our tweens are targeted by advertisers, we can see just how intense the marketing to our young boys has become.

Help protect your tween boy from commercialisation:

- *Teach him to spot product placement and understand what it's about.*
- *Help him recognise when his personal details are being solicited.*
- *Encourage him to see why enough is never enough.*
- *Ensure he understands that self-worth isn't about what he owns.*
- *Talk about the vulnerabilities advertisers play on.*
- *Discuss why marketers target kids and how much money they make from them.*
- *Keep these conversations light and informative.*

Tween boys, food and fashion

Well aware of the value of 'cradle-to-grave' marketing, global corporations keep the revenue rolling by investing huge amounts in advertising and special promotions. Fast food is one of the areas in which boys are most heavily marketed to. Some years ago McDonald's came up with the idea of giving away a Teenie Beanie Baby with each Happy Meal. Almost overnight the sales of Happy Meals shot up from ten million to a hundred million a week.[1] Now giveaway toys are an integral part of fast food promotions.

> **'The key to attracting kids is toys, toys, toys.'** Eric Schlosser, author of Fast Food Nation[2]

In addition to TV and other forms of advertising, many food manufacturers now connect directly with kids. Relationship marketing is particularly appealing to tweens because they're eager to make new friends. On Kelloggs World Kids Club, boys can play games, take part in fun polls, or play the trivia quiz picking the oldest of the seven wonders of the world alongside such product-related questions as when William

Kellogg invented cornflakes. On Nestlé's Nesquik home page, boys are greeted with the trademark Nesquik Bunny, and the slogan 'Happiness Is As Easy As Nesquik'. Here they are invited to download images to decorate their bedroom, locker or 'any other happy places' and, you guessed it, these posters just happen to depict The Bunny or the Nesquik logo.

'Advertising is [. . .] one curriculum kids are excelling in. The ads teach kids that buying is good and will make them happy. They teach that the solution to life's problems lies not in good values, hard work or education, but in materialism and the purchasing of more and more things.' *Gary Ruskin, director of Commercial Alert*[3]

NANOTECHNOLOGY

Fast foods are being constantly refined to ensure our palates don't become bored with the flavours. The sophisticated technologies that have brought vitamin and other supplements to foods are also used to enhance a food's flavour, texture and smell. Some foods, particularly fast foods, have up to thirty-nine ingredients, and many of these ingredients have themselves undergone intensive processing.[4] Added sugar is present in everything from breads and pasta sauces to low-fat yoghurts and stock cubes. Salt is also added to make foods irresistible, but at a cost. Research revealed one Pizza Hut meal alone had four times the salt levels 6-year-olds should have.[5] So, even though most kids know fast food isn't exactly healthy, they find the taste and packaging irresistible.

Even the seductive smell of grilled food in many fast food restaurants isn't the real aroma of food cooking. It's a scientifically formulated spray, designed to capture the smell of a perfect bacon cheeseburger.[6] A lot of effort also goes into the sounds associated with food – from the distinctive pop of a soft drink can opening to the snap and crackle of certain cereals. Again this makes a parent's job harder, but it's essential we're aware of the increasingly sophisticated ways foods are produced and marketed to boys, as studies show boys are more attracted to unhealthy food than are girls.

TOILETRIES RAKING IN THE DOLLARS

Another promising area for marketers is boys' toiletries. With revenue already in excess of $2 billion, this industry recognises there's a lot more potential in tween boys, who are described by one expert as 'one of the last untapped markets'. Some manufacturers are looking at new products for tweens. Others are taking existing men's products and marketing them to younger boys. Gillette, Nivea and L'Oreal are key players. David Beckham and Ben Affleck are just two of a growing number of celebrities used to promote these products.[7] This is well worth the investment to the big corporations. As one executive put it, 'You want to impress them with performance at an early age, which will bode well for a lifetime of brand loyalty.'[8]

TWEEN BOYS ENTER THE FASHION STAKES

The fashion world is now also paying more attention to tween boys. According to Marshall Cohen of the NPD Group, as tweens are still finding their feet in the world of fashion, they rely heavily on brands to get the right look, whereas teens like to develop their own style. Columnist Tiffany B tells us boys' clothing has changed a lot in the past couple of years. 'No longer do young boys only want to wear sweatpants and T-shirts, but they are going for a more diverse style – cargo pants, military-style outerwear, graphic T-shirts, button-up cardigans and pinstripe button-up shirts.'[9]

'The current trend for young boys of wearing plaid shorts and cropped pants is definitely a cute one . . . they can be worn everywhere, dressed up for school with a polo shirt or to the beach with a muscle tee.' *Teresa,* Upscale Baby Blog[10]

This level of detail leaves everyone, including parents, anxious if not exhausted just thinking about what their tween boy should be wearing. In one chat room an exasperated mother asked what was the best choice of backpack for her 11-year-old boy, because she didn't want him to be bullied by peers. Another mum assured her that several – branded, of course – backpacks would do, as 'No kid should get picked on carrying one of these name brands since these are about as high end as school backpacks come and cannot be purchased at a Wal-Mart or Target.'[11]

ANXIOUS BOYS

This reliance on looks and possessions is now affecting young boys' self-esteem and distracting them from essential life experiences by keeping them narrowly focused on their looks and the next purchase. Too many of today's tweens are in a constant, growing state of anxiety about whether they are cool enough, and how to stay looking cool. Whereas previous generations of tween boys had several or more spontaneous, unselfconscious, adventurous childhood years, this precious time is now lost in concerns about their presentation, and to round-the-clock packaged entertainment.

> **'Economic downturns can eventually be corrected, but the damage done to our children may be irreversible.'** *David Elkind, child psychologist*[12]

CORPORATIONS CONTROLLING OUR KIDS

Corporations have now invaded almost every aspect of boys' lives from their food and bedroom décor to their clothes and leisure time. Drawing on everything from anthropology to child psychology, it's not difficult for advertisers to craft messages in such a way that kids think they're making their own choices. And having been marketed to from the time they were very small, by the time they're a tween they have no sense of life being any other way. At this age kids don't fully understand they're being sold to. They see advertisers more as friends. And advertisers have done an effective job. By the age of 10 most kids can recall between 300 and 400 brands,[13] while they struggle to name the plants and birds they see around them. Kids are encouraged to buy now, whether or not they can afford it. When our boys are portrayed purely as consumers, this is how they start to see themselves.

The result? Our boys are growing up in a sterile world where popularity is mistaken for friendship, and where happiness revolves around branded toys, clothes and shoes. Increasingly tween friendships are based on what boys have and look like. It's a fast-moving world, as what's hot this week may not be so next week. This means even young boys have to be on the lookout for the rapid changes in trends to remain popular. In this world of instant food, endless purchases and non-stop entertainment, boys lose their individuality and creativity and the joy of anticipation, becoming lost in worlds created for them by marketers. Here enough is never enough, and increasing numbers of boys simply aspire to be rich and famous. It's no surprise then that growing numbers of boys have become vulnerable to mental health issues. And in spite of having more, too many of today's tweens are insecure and depressed.[14]

HOW PARENTS CAN HELP

We need to educate boys about advertising so they can recognise when they're being sold to. When you talk to boys like 10-year-old Callum, who understand what's going on in advertising, you can see how much more self-assured they are. 'At school our teacher taught us about ads,' he told me. 'We had to make up products, then be the mean people who make up the ads to sell them. We learned how the people who make products can trick you with bright colours and interesting information to pay more for the same thing.' Many teachers are doing their bit, by making ad spotting and dissection fun. 'I talk to my kids about the ads on TV and in magazines, and get them thinking that these are to get them to buy things,' one primary-school teacher told me. 'I try to get them noticing the ads around programs.' It's vital parents reinforce this good work.

You can counteract the marketing to your son in the following ways:

- *Discuss the content of ads, TV programs and billboards.*
- *Seek out entertaining and meaningful films to watch together.*
- *Set clear rules about time on the computer and watching TV.*
- *Turn off the TV during meals and when you have guests.*
- *Limit your son's screen time.*
- *Don't allow TVs and computers in his bedroom.*
- *Make spending an occasional activity.*
- *The PBS website for kids* Don't Buy It *is also a great start* http://pbskids.org/dontbuyit

Losing tween boys to virtual worlds

Alongside the addiction to stuff and the need to look cool, our boys are spending inordinate amounts of time watching DVDs and on the computer. These habits, formed well before most boys reach school, soon become a part of life. Apart from gaming, which we'll look at shortly, one of the most seductive online experiences for tween boys are the virtual worlds of Pirates of the Caribbean, Club Penguin, Webkinz and Nickelodeon's Neopets, to name but a few.

Sold to Viacom in 2005 for $150 million, Neopets now attracts 25 million kids worldwide, and achieves over 2.2 billion page views per month.[1] For just US$7.99 per month, boys can access the pay-to-play features. Immersive ads are cleverly inserted into the advergames, so they're hard for an unpractised eye to pick. At the click of a mouse boys are informed of their local Target store's stocks of Neopet plush toys, collectors' figures and play sets. Animated ads also offer limited-edition toys or the opportunity to customise products with their favourite Neopet. Leading research companies have been known to survey site users to glean valuable information on tweens.

'There's a narrowing of what boys are curious about; their lives are more narrow as well.' *Rebecca, a mother and child protection worker*

WHO NEEDS REAL LIFE?

According to Debra Aho Williamson, an analyst with the eMarketer research company, we need to prepare ourselves for a 'total inundation' of virtual worlds. The more time boys spend in virtual worlds, the less interested they are in real life. Psychologist and father Bill O'Hehir believes this level of bombardment is cause for real concern. 'A lot of kids are coming home, not to a home as we understand it. Their bedrooms have become autonomous rooms. Kids are eating their meals in their rooms. They have their iPod, TV, and computer in their rooms.' With all this on offer in their bedroom, there's no incentive for kids to come out unless they have to.

'It's not a generation gap we're facing, it's a universe gap.'
Psychologist Bill O'Hehir

IMMATURE BOYS

While these new technologies haven't been around long enough for us to gauge their full impact, certain trends are beginning to emerge. There are concerns that the amount of time kids spend on the computer may rewire their brains, making it hard for them to concentrate or to relax without external stimulation. What we do know is that the brain needs a rich variety of real-life experiences to grow and develop. Extended time on the computer means this new generation of boys are starting to lead much narrower lives with less face-to-face interaction, fewer friendships across the generations, less spontaneous play and less time in the real world. Susan Greenfield believes that instead of nurturing the brain, computers may be keeping their brains in a childish state. So while they may aspire to more grown-up values and behaviour, inside they're more immature than kids of just a generation ago. Like little children, many boys now have a limited attention span, assume the world revolves around them, and are addicted to instant gratification.

Susan Greenfield also points out that in cognitive tests today's 11-year-olds are on average two to three years behind in maturity than 11-year-old kids only fifteen years ago. She believes that without human interaction, nourishing food and play, and being directly engaged in life, their brains don't fully develop, so their ability to make sense of their world and express themselves creatively will continue to diminish.[3] Child protection worker and mother Rebecca agrees, 'I have a sense of boys maturing at a much slower rate. By interacting mainly with each other, instead of people of different ages, they tend to stay within this limited framework, so they have a limited maturity.'

'The computer and its information cannot answer any of the fundamental questions we need to address to make our lives more meaningful and humane. The computer cannot provide an organizing moral framework. It cannot tell us what questions are worth asking.' *Professor Neil Postman, cultural critic*[4]

WHAT HAPPENED TO ORIGINAL THINKERS?

To mature, our boys need to learn to think for themselves. They also need to know how to work out whether information is correct, and see how it relates to other bits of information. To achieve this boys need to be enquiring and curious, to have time to muck around and explore, and learn to deal with boredom creatively. They need time for talk around the kitchen table, to discuss what's happened at school, in the neighbourhood and on the news. When boys are entertained around the clock there's no room for this.

WHAT PARENTS CAN DO

We need to take charge of our boys' lives early, to be fierce gatekeepers about what matters, so their imagination and curiosity are kept alive. Kids mature when they have time to think about how to solve problems and are given the chance to discuss the best way forward and fully understand the options they have, as well as their likely outcomes. They also need to understand that life has its ups and downs, and that happiness comes in thousands of ways, from a connection to nature, family and local community, to working towards a goal, sharing time with others, helping people and enjoying unexpected moments of discovery and fun. However, boys can't make this journey on their own.

Things you can do to help your son mature:

- *Find out what he's interested in and encourage him in this.*
- *Visit museums and art galleries, and take an interest in your son's responses to what he sees.*
- *Encourage a range of simple leisure activities at home and in the garden.*
- *Get out to parks and community markets.*
- *Help foster friendships across the generations.*
- *Encourage your son to feel part of the local community.*
- *Play family games – board games, sports and made-up games.*

Reclaiming childhood

How else can we counter this massive consumer pressure that is over-whelming our boys? How do we give them a greater sense of belonging? As today's boys often have a much narrower life experience, they're no longer mixing with different kinds of people, feeling part of a commu-nity or sharing projects. To mature into happy, healthy adults, it's vital boys have a bigger vision of themselves and their world, that they feel they have something *meaningful* to contribute. This sense of belonging is best nurtured during the tween years.

GOTTA HAVE IT NOW

While we'd love to have everything the moment we desire it, as adults we know this isn't possible, and why it mightn't be such a good idea. Our boys need to know this too. Some decades ago Stanford professor Michael Mischel conducted what is known as the Marshmallow Study. A group of 4-year-olds were offered a marshmallow immediately, or two marshmallows if they waited a little. Fourteen years on, he looked at how these children had developed. Those able to delay gratification and wait for the two marshmallows proved to be more persistent and self-motivated, while those who had gone for the single marshmallow were less decisive and focused.

More recently, former teacher Angela Duckworth and noted psychology professor Martin Seligman conducted a more in-depth study of more than 300 children, measuring everything from IQ, impulsive behaviour, and thoughts and emotions to academic performance and the ability to delay gratification. The children who were more self-disciplined had better grades.[1] More study needs to be done in this area, but there seems little doubt that giving a boy what he wants whenever he wants it does him few favours. The joy of waiting and planning for something far outweighs the boredom and sense of entitlement many of our boys now suffer from.

> '**It's time to look around at what's left of our neighborhoods, communities and families, and put our children first.**'
> *John W. Whitehead*, The Hostile Takeover of Childhood blog[2]

COOL GRATITUDE

Instead of being focused on the long list of things they want, it's important boys understand how lucky they already are. This is best reinforced by exposing them to the realities of life for too many of the world's kids, through casual discussions and news items – not just about the fact that kids are starving, but what it would *feel* like day after day to hunt for a meal, or scavenge rubbish dumps for your basic needs. Receiving must be balanced with giving. Having a 'one in, one out' policy on games and clothes is an excellent step. Encourage your son to recycle his toys and games for kids in need. Involve him in charity drives. Let him help on local stalls and collect for charities. Get the family involved in public clean-up days and tree planting. These activities help connect boys to their community and experience a wider sense of belonging than they get when they spend all their time with a handful of peers or obsessed with brands.

MANNERS MATTER

Manners are an extension of gratitude. By teaching boys manners we help them become aware of others. So, when your son gets a present and takes the time to say thank you, he acknowledges the fact that someone has spent time and effort doing something for him. Having attractive stationery for him to write a thank-you note (or helping make his own stationery), and seeing you make the effort to say thank you, models how he can be.

On the rare occasions when children stand up for the elderly, disabled or pregnant on the bus, often they think they're hard done by, instead of realising they've done something special. Boys need to know it's one of many ways they can behave like a hero. Sadly our kids are growing up without basic life skills. In a number of workplaces, young executives are now having to learn manners because they don't know how to behave around clients and customers. Simple acts such as helping a neighbour with their shopping or holding a door open for someone are important gestures. They help make someone else's day, leaving young boys feeling genuinely useful.

KEEP TALKING

So many of these qualities are about communication and connection, and conversation is a central part of this. There's an art to conversation. Once learned, it helps boys navigate almost any situation with ease. When we make conversation a natural part of family life, we help boys to be more confident and articulate, to relate well to others, to handle life's ups and downs and to learn from them. These skills are best learned around the kitchen table with the TV off. And when boys read books or see films, it's an excellent opportunity to discuss *their* observations, so they start to form their own opinions and learn how to articulate them.

When boys can relate comfortably to people of different ages and backgrounds, are interested in other people's lives and can put others at ease, they have powerful life skills which help them through school and into adult life, in relationships and at work. As boys can find communication more difficult than girls, it's up to us to help them bridge this gap. All these opportunities help boys express their unique selves and allow them a glimpse at what they have to offer the world, and to be honoured for it.

Opportunities you can create for your son to mature:

- *Expose him to opportunities for gratitude by modelling it.*
- *Teach him manners and why they matter.*
- *Ensure he understands he is a valuable part of his family and community.*
- *Allow him to experience the joy of giving.*
- *Help him to grow up aware of other people's needs as well as his own.*
- *Encourage him to work towards the things he wants.*
- *Help him respect those who have less than he does.*

Engaging tween boys

Many of the qualities needed for boys to experience a richer child-hood are expressed in the Kitchen Garden Program for kids aged 8 to 11. Started by chef Stephanie Alexander, the Kitchen Garden Program teaches school kids how to grow, harvest and cook their own food. According to Ange Berry, who works with Stephanie, 'The great thing for kids is getting the connection food can bring, as kids from different socio-economic groups and cultural backgrounds sit down and enjoy the food they've cooked. Teachers and volunteers are included in the meals, so the kids start to see how *everyone* can come together around food.'

The program helps kids to relate positively to their peers. 'So when a kid says to a friend, "Try this beautiful Vietnamese salad, I made it," his friend will,' explains Ange. 'You find them becoming more involved with the food, discussing whether something needs more or less chilli as they eat. They're taking this knowledge home, and discussing what ingredients should be on the shopping list. They're cooking at home. Some are starting their own gardens at home.

'Sitting down and eating the food is important. Often kids have to be taught to stay at the table and focus on the food, and how to use a knife and fork. The food's served on platters, so they learn to pass it around, and choose the portion that's right for them. The children are expanding their experiences of food. Parents often say, "My son won't eat broccoli" or whatever, but these kids are sitting down and having vegetables and salads. One school went on a camp recently and were served hot dogs. The kids said they didn't eat that kind of food. They asked if they could do some cooking and were told they couldn't. When they came back from the camp they said they didn't want to go to another camp where they couldn't cook.

'They're learning about sustainability as well as making their own fertilisers. They don't waste anything. It all goes into the compost, because they know this helps make fantastic food. We're seeing an increased level of engagement in the kids that participate – not just the kids who are naturally engaged, but those who find it difficult to engage in the classroom.

'The children are growing their own garden and creating meals they're *interested* in. Because they can see a result, it's an instant win for them. As they're working away they're expanding their vocabulary, they're doing a bit of maths as they learn about measuring. They're learning about different cultures through food. Teachers have reported back that they'd underestimated the kids' capacity to learn.

'We've found the whole scheme is a real community-building exercise. It draws in parents and grandparents, and general members of the community as volunteers – people who may not want to read to kids in the classroom. The schools are reporting that the volunteer bank from the local community is growing. And local businesses are coming on board as well, topping up with food when the harvests of certain things are low.'

Often we worry about engaging kids because we make life so complex. The Kitchen Garden Program gives us a vision of what is possible when we give boys a bigger canvas to work on. Today's boys want to be part of something meaningful. It's up to us to provide this for them.

Help your boy experience a greater sense of community by thinking about these questions:

- *What is he passionate about?*
- *Which community group or activity might help him express this?*
- *How can you create a greater sense of community in your own street or neighbourhood?*
- *Which community events can you get involved in as a family?*

Young boys in need of good blokes

As well as community, young boys need good men in their lives so they know what being a man is all about and what's expected of them. Today, sadly, many boys lack access to grown men, so they never experience a man's world first-hand. Older men also miss out, as they never get the chance to pass on a lifetime of knowledge and wisdom. One of my most poignant findings when researching *What Men Don't Talk About* was the number of older men saddened at not being able to share life's experiences with boys in the family and community for fear of being branded a paedophile. This comes at a time when boys need men more than ever.

With the increasing fragmentation of families many boys are brought up in single-parent households. Mums strive to do their best, but this doesn't lessen a boy's need for a good man in their lives. A trusted male figure can be a great support to single mums run ragged by everything they have to do, or who are facing discipline issues. Having worked closely with juvenile offenders, New Zealand's Celia Lashlie, herself a single mother of boys and the first female prison officer to work in a male prison, is also a strong advocate for the presence of good men in a boy's life.[1] 'No matter how good a solo mum you are, and I'm speaking from personal experience, you can't give them the male influence,' admitted Kath, a headmistress and a mother of boys. 'I know how hard this is. I took my son to football, we went fishing and so on, but I'm not a man.' Andrew King of *Mensline Australia* agrees. 'Many of men's values are found in incidental things, like the apprentice hanging around. Boys are learning while they're watching, getting involved. These moments give boys something they can build on, knowing one day they'll be able to do this with confidence.'

'Our detailed 20-year review shows that overall, children reap positive benefits if they have active and regular engagement with a father figure.' *Anna Sarkadi, children's health expert, Uppsala University, Sweden*[2]

If we want our boys to live up to our expectations, they need to know what being a boy and a man is all about, and be *excited* by the prospect. Ideally they will experience this excitement long before their teens. One of the most heart-warming films in recent times was *The World's Fastest Indian*, based on the life of the retired bike enthusiast Burt Munro (Anthony Hopkins), who beat the world speed record on his motorbike in the Sixties. In the lead-up to the championships Burt painstakingly modified his Indian Scout bike while Tom, the young boy from next door, spent hours in Burt's garage helping him with little jobs. Their friendship is one of the most powerful aspects of the film. You see how much Tom benefits from his time with Burt, and how much the older man is encouraged by this young boy's curiosity.

'When the key relationships in a boy's life work well this becomes an essential keel which keeps them centred in turbulent times.' *Andrew King, Mensline Australia*

BIG BUDDY

So how can we help our boys? According to Richard Aston, who heads the Big Buddy organisation in New Zealand, today's boys desperately need to identify with strong men. Set up several years ago to support fatherless boys aged 7 to 12, Big Buddy works hard to bridge this gap. 'Boys are struggling with what it means to be a man, as there are so many confusing messages. Big Buddy focuses on fatherless boys, because they don't have any flesh-and-blood reference points. Some boys without dads rarely see men. Their only references are video games and TV, so they don't learn what it's like to be a real man in the world.'

'Boys have an instinct for maleness,' explains Richard. 'Some young boys are so hungry for male company, they literally grab their mentors when they first meet them.' This can be very emotional for the boys and their male mentors. He told of one 7-year-old boy in the program, who had suffered a lot of abuse. When he first met his mentor, he rushed at him, asking, 'Are you just for me?' Many of the things boys pick up through Big Buddy happen purely by hanging out with good men. 'Boys are like sponges. They want to know how to do this man thing. There's something quite profound that happens as boys learn how to fix a tyre, for example. It's not just about learning how to fix something, but having the *confidence* to give things a go. The boy learns that he can have a go at things – fighting fires, concreting, fixing bikes.'

One of the strengths of the Big Buddy program is that boys get a firm foundation on which to build their lives. They also get to explore maleness in a safe environment. 'Grown men represent a protection for boys,' Richard explains. 'Often boys learn just by looking, seeing how we walk, watching body language, the timbre of a man's voice, how he approaches problems. The boys on the program pick up lots of little clues as they grow into young adults. They also get into their own bodies and emotions. Then as they become young adults they shape this themselves, so they can be their own person.'

Big Buddy certainly seems to be making its mark with young boys in the critical years leading up to adolescence. One boy who entered the program had lost his dad to suicide when he was 8. Over the following years his mother never discussed how his father had died, because her son was too young. When the boy was 12, she knew it was time to tell the boy his dad had hanged himself in the garage, which she did after some counselling. The boy's response was to reassure his mum they would get through this. He went on to tell her he was fine as he had his mentor. 'Over the previous four years this boy had been filled up with all this fatherly stuff,' explains Richard, 'so he was okay.'

The men who mentor the boys also get a lot out of the program. 'It's part of being a man, being a father figure, whether it's as an uncle, a grandfather, or whatever. Somewhere deep in our psyche we need to do this. The men get a deep satisfaction out of this,' says Richard. 'I had one man who was a very senior executive, whose sons had left home. When I asked him why he was interested, he said he wanted to be a boy again and muck around with boats and things. Being around young boys enlivens your own soul, and there's a deep satisfaction in seeing a boy grow and develop.'

Help your son understand what it means to be a boy:

- *Encourage one-on-one Dad time.*
- *Make sure he has access to other good men.*
- *Let him know you love him and boys in general.*
- *Allow him to feel excited about being a boy.*
- *Make time to talk about things that matter to him.*
- *As boys often don't like face-to-face contact, use time in the car and out walking to chat.*

The impact of the stories we tell

We are influenced by the stories and anecdotes we hear, and so too are our boys. How we talk about others reveals a great deal about our attitudes and values. The negative talk about men and boys has become such a habit that many of us aren't aware of it. Yet daily men are portrayed on the news, in ads and films as predators or opportunists. Or they're depicted as Homer Simpson stupid. You only have to look at popular greeting cards and fridge magnets to get a sense of the messages boys see all the time. I was talking at a school recently when a boy asked if the world would be a better place if women were in charge, seeing as men were so violent. They'd had a speaker a few days before who'd said as much. While boys have to be clear about the dark face of the masculine, these kinds of statements are misleading and unhelpful.

Sometimes it's hard to understand why we're so quick to define men as losers or violent, yet are quite happy for them to put their lives on the line whenever there's a natural disaster, car accident, chemical spill, fatal shooting, or people who are trapped or lost. We rarely, if ever, talk to boys about these unsung heroes, or recognise how hard it would be to live without electricians, plumbers, roadside assistance, garbage men and all the other valuable, often unseen roles men play. As a result, boys can grow up feeling like they have to apologise for being boys.

> **'Boys need respect before they'll give respect. And there's often a lack of authentic praise from older men particularly, which is like gold to boys.'** *Richard Aston, Big Buddy project*

CONSTANT BAD PRESS

A number of fathers, and those who work with boys, spoke of their concerns at the endless negative messages boys get about men. 'The way men are portrayed in the media is so negative. It's really, really bad,' said Martin, father of Brad, aged 9. 'I have to tell my son constantly that being a boy is a good thing.' Ashley, a dad with two teenage sons, agrees. 'There's a lot of negative talk in the media and in society about men. In ads it's like, let's make fun of the guys. It creates a lot of hopelessness, a feeling that life's unfair, because you can't do anything about it. This leaves questions in boys' minds about what they are meant to be. They wonder if there's something wrong with them, and what they can do about it.'

> **'You never see a boy on the news for doing something great.'** *Zac, 15*

BOYS NEED MORE CONSIDERATION

These messages creep into the home and become part of family conversations. Even chance comments and throwaway lines can be damaging. 'I grew up in a family of females,' Dylan, 18, told me. 'Males weren't the most popular. It's like that with everything I see, and what I saw as I grew up.' If we're honest, many of us have been guilty of unhelpful remarks. This isn't a great environment for boys to be in. As there's little they can do about it, boys are left feeling like they're a disaster waiting to happen, or that they have to try and compensate for every man who has ever done something wrong. This is an uncomfortable subject, because we have also all been in situations – at a family barbecue or a general gathering – where derogatory stories and jokes about men and boys have been exchanged. We may have been amused by them or thought nothing of it, but that's not how boys hear these comments.

UNDERSTANDING BOYS' NEEDS

In recent years men and boys have become more sensitive to the lives and needs of women and girls. This is extremely important. However, boys also need to be encouraged to explore and express *their* needs.[1] If boys don't get this opportunity, they grow up without any real understanding of themselves, which isn't a great start for adult relationships. Part of giving boys a start is in helping them understand what being a good man is all about – not just in theory – but in practical ways they can understand and emulate. Telling boys positive stories about men is a powerful way to do this.

BOYS AT SCHOOL

As the majority of teachers are now women, one of the areas of boys' lives we struggle with is how best to school them. The lack of men in teaching puts additional pressure on boys and female teachers, as boys react differently to schooling to the way girls do. Few would dispute that it's much easier to teach a class of quiet kids who sit still and are articulate when spoken to. These are qualities boys often wrestle with. Many teachers try very hard to bridge the gap. Some succeed. Many do not. This sets up a tension between boys and their teachers.

'Quite often boys get into trouble. I think teachers think boys are troublesome.' *Callum, 10*

When they're labelled as difficult and disruptive it's not surprising boys come off second best at school. There are many good initiatives to encourage boys in schools, but we still have some way to go. Watching how we refer to boys is a key part of this process as the negative jokes and stories we tell about boys can be self-fulfilling. 'We do see boys as difficult and wish they'd go away,' admitted Kath, a primary-school principal, adding, 'but because we're not helping them to deal with their issues they're crumbling.' Austin, an assistant principal, agrees. 'People are anti-boys, which makes life much harder for boys. They're branded loud and loutish. And often it's how they are. Yet underneath all that they're still really good kids.'

BUILDING GOOD RELATIONSHIPS

We need to create stronger bonds with boys that can nurture and strengthen their emerging sense of self. Andrew King of Mensline Australia agrees. 'We minimise the need to build relationships with boys. We think we just need to talk blokey talk, but it's just not so.' There are many effective ways male and female teachers can affirm boys. Andrew told me of a teacher who had remarkable success with a class of very tough boys. This woman was an older lady from an Asian background with a quiet demeanour, and not necessarily someone you'd think could cut it with a group of difficult teens. Yet she managed to get through to these boys. What she did first was to get to know the boys — their names, where they lived and what was important to them. She then used this information in her teaching, so the boys felt included and respected. The boys developed a great relationship with her because they felt heard.

BOYS CAN BE HEROES

With few real-life stories of boys doing positive, heroic things, too often our boys are set adrift in the dark world of gaming and action movies where they identify with heroes who are little more than violent, dysfunctional loners. There's great power in stories, as they can so easily colour the way a boy thinks, feels and responds. How different it might be if our boys were given a larger vision for their lives through the empowering stories we told.

Boys ache to be heroes, but don't know how. As one boy said to me, 'It's hard to be a hero today, because there aren't the opportunities.' We need to help boys join the dots and realise they have a very real role to play. The ways they can be heroic in the twenty-first century may be different from those open to boys of previous generations, but they still have something important to give. They may campaign for important causes, or play a positive, pivotal role in community or corporate cultures. But first we need to catch boys doing heroic things. In the recent Victorian fires which claimed over 200 lives, Rhys Sund, a 19-year-old boy, helped rescue his petrified family and neighbours, including a handful of kids under 10, by driving across burning fields on a small tractor to get everyone to safety.

This is a fantastic story of usefulness and everyday courage for boys. It gives them a sense of what's possible. 'You become what you're saturated in,' points out Andrew King. 'What boys are seeing in the fires is men putting their lives on the line to protect the wider community. These relationship-rich stories are what we need to be giving to boys.' Most boys are never going to be in a natural disaster. However, as we'll see, by inviting them to have a larger vision for themselves, they can enjoy a greater sense of belonging and purpose.

When a boy knows his family background and his neighbourhood, he is able to build on this to create an even richer life story.

BOYS HAVE STORIES TOO

The other side of storytelling is in creating the right environment for boys to tell *their* emerging stories. When I talk to boys I'm always surprised at how easy it is to get them talking. I'm also blown away by how articulate and perceptive they can be. At present there are precious few opportunities for boys to tell stories. Knowing who you are, where you have come from, and what you may be capable of are central to us all. When a boy knows his family background and his neighbourhood, he is able to build on this to create an even richer life story.

With the overwhelming influence of marketing, the media and celebrity culture, a boy's real sense of self can easily be diluted. His belonging comes solely from peers, movies and branded gear, and not from his own living history. We need to work hard to help restore this. Not long ago I was in a small town in Montana, where local teenagers had portrayed the stories of elderly community members on a number of walls downtown in brightly coloured murals, which also gave details of the kids who had painted each mural. How validating for a boy to be involved in this kind of project. Not every town or city can capture people's stories in such an immediate way, but with the many mediums we now have for storytelling, we have some powerful opportunities for boys to learn about the stories of their elders alongside their own. These gestures help them understand who they are and what they are capable of.

THE WAY FORWARD

Growing up feeling like you have to apologise for yourself isn't a good start. Boys need to know they have a contribution to make, to feel valued, to have a tangible sense of belonging to their community, home and school. There are many ways we can help them do this. Stories and anecdotes about good men in the family, the community and the nation offer boys something to aspire to beyond their peers, pop culture and Playstations.

So, where are the stories that help boys understand life? Where is the sharing of disappointments and failures? Luckily new possibilities are opening up. 'I took my son to Pathways, a rite of passage program,' Dave Mallard, a father, senior executive and men's group facilitator explains. 'There, boys spend time with men talking about everything from sex and women to grief and loss. Hearing older men's stories helps guide them from being boys to young men.' Stories are a powerful part of the fabric of life, and well worth working on. What inspiring stories about men and boys can you immerse your son in?

To support your son's sense of self:

- *Be mindful of the stories you relate, even in jest.*
- *Help your son develop a larger vision of himself through positive tales about men.*
- *Ensure your son has a strong sense of the male heritage within the family – for example, life in the Depression and world wars.*
- *Encourage your son to read such books as* The Dangerous Book for Boys *that celebrate boys.*
- *Talk to your son about the derogatory comments made about men and boys, and about girls and women.*
- *Encourage the local paper to include stories of boys' achievements in your community.*

Early sexualisation

Our boys need a more detailed preparation for life than they're currently getting. This is particularly true for the sexualised world they're now immersed in. Without this guidance our boys can hurt themselves and others. In one Queensland primary school recently a 7-year-old girl was sexually assaulted over two months by a boy her age. Hitting her and threatening to kill her if she spoke out, the boy repeatedly forced this young girl to perform oral sex. In another Queensland school a group of 6-year-old boys banded together and were forcing classmates to perform various sexual acts on them.[1] Hetty Johnson, a campaigner against child sexual abuse, says there are thirteen cases reported every week in Queensland. The majority involve 5- to 8-year-olds. According to Rowan, a youth worker, 'We are now seeing children grooming younger kids for sex, there's a real seduction pattern going on. A lot of this appears to be due to exposure to porn.' With the explosion of sexy ads on billboards, in magazines and on TV, sexual content in programs viewed during family time and on the net, much younger boys and girls are exposed to sexual material they would not previously have encountered so early. This affects how they see themselves and how they behave.

'We are now seeing children grooming younger kids for sex, there's a real seduction pattern going on.' *Rowan, a youth worker*

'I was appalled to hear my five-year-old singing, "My head spins right round, baby, when your head goes down," one father said. 'Then there was another song talking about "going up and down on my disco stick". Where did that come from? This stuff gets into kids' heads and normalises having sex very early.' At this age young children don't understand what they're saying or doing, but as Dr Joe Tucci, who runs the Australian Childhood Foundation, points out, it can be very traumatising for their victims. Zac, 15, agrees. 'It seems that the younger generation of boys are, like, trying to speed up their maturity. There are lots of kids in primary school trying to be teens, when they're only ten or eleven, or younger still. There's a lot more showing off, and girls and boys interacting more, all that boy/girl stuff. Now there are kids eight and nine talking about this. They're getting the idea they should be grown-up. They want to be cool like older kids.'

If international marketing guru Martin Lindstrom is to be believed, things aren't likely to get better any time soon. He believes that advertising is tipped to get edgier and more extreme, and may even become far more subliminal, so parents beware.[2] Parents need to achieve a delicate balance. At its best sex is fun, pleasurable and life-enhancing. We don't want our boys to grow up feeling uncomfortable or shamed about their sexual selves. But nor do we want them to be exposed to material which they're not ready to handle, which may propel them into situations that may harm them and others. As psychologist Steve Biddulph puts it, 'When we see our children grow into beginning adults – what we now call teenagers – we want them to experience it [sex] at its very best. To unfold it in their own time and way, and to suffer no harm.'[3]

QUESTIONABLE GAMES

There are now many ways young boys access sexual material, including through a number of questionable online games. 'There's a whole lot of games which have sexual connotations I don't think some parents know about,' Frank, a childcare and youth worker, told me. 'There's one game, for example, *Perry the Perv*. The challenge is for the central character to look girls up and down without being seen. So his eyes wander from a girl's eyes to her bum. You use the mouse to score points to look at her breasts and stuff, without her seeing what's happening. If the girl doesn't see them, the boy wins points. There are other games where the reward is to lift the teacher's dress up and see her panties, and things like that. This isn't aimed at teens, but at kids.'

'Kids come to school saying quite inappropriate sexual things, without realising what they're saying. The parents seem to think it amusing.' *Dee, an early primary teacher*

On the one hand we love the innocence and spontanaeity of childhood, yet we see nothing wrong with children being marketed to, dressed as little adults and watching TV shows and other material that is anything but innocent. Everywhere boys look they see sexual images, but unless parents help them interpret what they're seeing, boys are left to deal with this information on their own. It's very important parents don't just bury their heads in the sand, or think a filter on the computer is sufficient. Boys need open, ongoing discussion around sexual issues. They need a framework through which to better understand the material they're subjected to.

THE PRESSURE TO GROW UP

Part of the increasing sexualisation of our children is the very real pressure they're under to look and act older than they are. We see this in the depiction of young girls as sexy chicks, and in the relentless targeting of young boys and girls by advertisers, who are constantly encouraging them to behave and dress like teens. Kids pick up on this, because they want to be accepted and to belong. They work hard to be teenagers as a result.

> **'Children exposed to sexual messages too young get a cheapened idea of what love is about, before they're old enough to form better ideas.'** *Steve Biddulph, psychologist and author of* Raising Boys[4]

Primary-school boys speak of the *need* to have a girlfriend. If they don't, they fear they'll be seen as losers. When they're encouraged into behaviour they're not ready for, boys are more likely to see girls as objects, as they're too young to understand the possibilities and nuances of relationships. In our discussions it was clear young boys saw girlfriends as little more than accessories. 'Boys my age want to have girlfriends because it's cool,' Mark, 10, told me. 'My friends have a girl-friend because everybody does.'

'If you want to be accepted by your mates, it's good to say you have a girlfriend, have had so many kisses, have a photo, received text mes-sages,' explains Kath, a primary-school principal. 'It's a question of status in peer groups. There's a real pressure to participate, because if you don't there's something wrong with you.' This is not a great start to relationships when girls are viewed as accessories. It's no surprise that we're seeing a growth in voyeuristic, denigrating attitudes towards young girls by tween boys. Rebecca, a child protection worker, shares these concerns. 'The other day my partner was in the dressing room at the local gym with a group of boys aged 10 to 11. He was so shocked at the rude and demeaning way in which they were sizing up the girls that he pulled them up.'

'I worry about girls. My son told me he's got a new girlfriend, because his last one dumped him. He's nine.' *Martin, father of Brad*

One of the big challenges for parents is that sexual content and images are so pervasive, it's hard to limit the material boys see, as they may well view it outside the home. 'The whole sex thing is in your face – in music videos, TV shows,' says Dave Mallard, a father of two teenage boys. 'Attitudes have changed. I'm surprised that young kids are allowed to watch some of the shows on TV. They're so out there.' Some parents find the thought of vetting what their kids watch as invasive, or they've become so desensitised to sexual material themselves, they don't give it much thought. This leaves their young boys vulnerable, and they may well take on the unhelpful attitudes and behaviour they see.

YOUNG BOYS GETTING INTO PORN

It's not just the seduction of billboards, magazine and movie ads and video clips parents need to be concerned about. They need to be aware of how easily young boys can access porn. Rowan, who works with troubled youth, agrees. 'We're now seeing kids sexually active way under ten, because of access to porn, or their parents' own behaviour. I've seen many cases where porn is readily left around the home, where it's part of the family culture. Then you've got parents who carefully stash their porn away, and kids have a way of finding it.' As society has become more permissive, so too have some households, exposing children to behaviour that confuses and disturbs them.

The only people who are not surprised at the way life is for younger boys are teenage boys, as they live with the same pressures and access the same material. Many teen boys expressed their concern at what some younger boys were getting up to. Others simply felt it was the way things were now. 'Sex is everywhere. It's inevitable we're going to do it younger. Kids need the right information – not just from the media that glamourises sex. Kids think it's a cool thing to do,' Gary, 17, told me. Unless our young boys have good, helpful information about sexual issues much earlier, they can be extremely vulnerable. If parents won't engage with them, be open or discuss issues, they will go elsewhere.

Parents cannot afford to be naïve about how readily accessible sexually explicit material is. This exposure can affect a boy's life in ways it's hard to retreat from. Bryan Duke, a father of five who runs a regional mentoring program for young men and boys, has real concerns about porn. 'It awakens boys too soon to respond in a healthy way to sexual situations. They're too young to make commonsense decisions. It's like kids who have suffered sexual abuse. Their experiences come out in their drawings, their thinking, their perspective. Sex is now part of the perspective of a growing number of kids ten, eleven and twelve.' Studies back this up, showing that children who view porn become desensitised to this material and may then become sexually abusive towards others.[5] The sheer volume of this material is overwhelming. It's been calculated that 1000 new sites spring up every three or four weeks.[6]

'Access to pornography is greater now than it's ever been. It's hard to avoid.' Austin, assistant principal

MOBILE PHONES
The whole culture of kids taking explicit photos on their mobile phones is also happening younger. Frequently teachers express their quiet despair at being left to deal with the fallout. One primary school I learned of recently was battling a spate of 8-year-old girls photographing themselves topless, then circulating these pictures. It is concerning to see a rise in inappropriate sexual behaviour amongst such young kids, as it deprives them of essential aspects of childhood, and the powerful foundations on which they then build their adult lives. One psychologist who heads up a sexual assault unit in a major city hospital feels that as

children are now constantly photographed and videoed from the time they are very small, they have far fewer inhibitions about cameras. So, stepping across the line is less of a big deal. To help boys through these years, they need to know about 'sexting' (sending sexual images and messages by mobile phone) *before* they encounter it. They also need to understand why it's not a good idea to get involved. Discuss these issues with them. Help them form a script as to how best to say no, so they feel confident about stating their views. These early conversations can save a great deal of pain down the track.

ABUSED CHILDREN

'We're seeing a collapsing of childhood; younger and younger children becoming victims of sexual assault,' warns this psychologist, who supports sexual assault victims. One of her concerns is the constant emphasis in popular culture on kids being seen to be 'out there'. The fewer their inhibitions, the more easily they can be groomed by peers or adults to do things they may later regret. When looking at the victims she handles, this psychologist believes that the 'performance culture', where it's cool to behave in an overtly risky way, encourages sexually explicit behaviour, and that it's part and parcel of the sexual assault she now sees.

Already too many children are at risk of exploitation, and the new technologies make it so much easier to distribute. The statistics are sobering. According to the American National Center for Missing and Exploited Children, just under two out of ten people arrested in America for illegal pornography possessed images of children under 3. Over two-thirds had images of children aged between 3 and 5, while a staggering 83 per cent had images of children aged between 8 and 12.[7] At the same time we're now seeing increasing numbers of kids abusing each other, and a number of experts are concerned this is due to the material they are viewing. 'We're now seeing six-, seven- and eight-year-olds involved in coercive, manipulative sexual behaviours, because there's a confusion around what sexuality means,' said Dr Joe Tucci of the Australian Childhood Foundation. 'This can be very traumatic to the child they're doing this to.' He went on to explain how the victims often have to undergo intensive counselling to deal with their trauma.[8]

NOT-SO-INNOCENT WEBSITES

Our high-tech world brings boys many wonderful opportunities, including setting up and viewing online photo albums. However, as postings on photo-sharing sites are easy, free and anonymous, they too have become an outlet for sexually explicit photos. In 2006 the Internet Watch Foundation discovered just over 10 per cent of all URLs containing child abuse images were on photo album websites. With no geographic boundaries on the net, the ways in which explicit material can reach our kids is growing. Over 80 per cent of all domains featuring child sexual abuse material in 2006 were from servers in the US and Russia.[9] While parents need to do all they can to screen out this material, realistically most children will come across this graphic material in their own homes, at the home of a friend or on someone's phone. So, parents need to talk through the dangers and exploitation aspects of graphic material, along with how best to respond, before these incidents occur.

BOYS IN TROUBLE

When boys start to view porn, if they are not guided it's a natural progression for them to look for ways to take this further. When boys attempt to act out what they've seen, they can be in big trouble. 'Kids are bombarded from a young age about the need to be sexy,' points out Bryan Duke, himself a dad, who runs a juvenile regional mentoring program. 'Kids want to be accepted. They'll do whatever it takes to fit in. Then they get involved in a sexual situation, acting out something they've seen, and they're in trouble. This is the real loss of innocence. What they did was just an act to them. They didn't fully understand the implications of what they were doing to others.' Boys need adults to give them sensible boundaries, to be honest about consequences, and to provide them with a rich life *beyond* peers and computers. It's important for parents to know that if a boy does exhibit disturbing sexual behaviour, with good professional help he can grow out of it.

You can help your son handle the sexualised environment in which he is growing up in the following ways:

- *Be vigilant about the material he has access to.*
- *Use filters on home computers.*
- *Talk to your son about sexualised and pornographic material.*
- *Explain why pornography isn't a good idea.*
- *Talk to him about sexual issues in language he can understand.*
- *Set clear guidelines about your expectations.*
- *Encourage openness.*
- *Let him know he can come to you with questions or concerns.*

Puberty sucks

As boys enter their teens their bodies change beyond recognition, and their brains go into partial meltdown, making life exhilarating and bewildering. Years before a boy sees physical changes in his body, his brain releases the hormone gonadotropin, which triggers puberty. During puberty he will experience a tenfold increase in testosterone, stimulating growth in his muscles, body hair, skin and bones, as well as his penis. These higher levels of testosterone will give him more energy and strength. Over this time he is likely to put on around 6 kilograms of muscle and grow an additional third of his height, while his voice may drop by up to an octave.

> Previous societies actively celebrated boys' journeys towards manhood and helped channel their energy into pursuits that were helpful to the community. Boys felt useful and appreciated.

GROWING BRAINS AND BODIES

These are massive changes to come to terms with, so parents need to be firm but gentle. Adolescent boys often worry about too much or too little body hair, pimples, erections, wet dreams and body odour. Seven out of ten boys will grow extra tissue around their nipples, making them anxious about 'man boobs'. Boys need to know tissue growth is perfectly normal and unlikely to last more than a year. Concerned about the width of their shoulders, their height and the size of their penis, boys are also anxious about not looking masculine enough. Alongside these challenges are the ups and downs of sudden mood swings.

With so much going on, it's not surprising that boys often feel out of control. Earlier societies actively celebrated boys' journeys towards manhood and helped channel their energy into pursuits that were helpful to the community. Boys felt useful and appreciated. What a contrast this is with our teenage boys, who have few positive outlets. Rarely are they made to feel good about being teenage boys and, unlike their forebears only two or so generations ago, they have several years in no-man's land, where they're neither kids or adults.

It's sad that testosterone gets such a bad rap, as it's just one more thing boys are made to feel bad about. When I talk in schools, boys are amazed when I tell them testosterone is a wonderful thing. They love it when we talk about the ways men are heroic, and how awesome it is to see a fireman rescue a baby out of a burning building, to see a boy help an old person cross the street, or take care of a child who's hurt or lost. They get excited to think they too have a role to play in the community. It's important boys are aware that the way to win respect is not by endangering themselves, so much as being able to make their own contribution to the community and be acknowledged for it.

MARKING THE MOMENTS THAT MATTER
There are many special moments in a teenage boy's life that also deserve recognition, from getting his licence or first part-time job, to going away with friends for the first time. So why let these moments drift by? The best gestures are those that will live long in the memory, that money

can't buy. Why not organise a special barbecue somewhere interesting, an afternoon kayaking, or a weekend away camping? Boys need these and other markers to give them a sense of achievement in the long, often confusing years between childhood and becoming a man.

> It's sad that testosterone gets such a bad rap, as it's just one more thing boys are made to feel bad about.

THE ANGER THING

There are many sensitive areas to navigate during adolescence. One of the things that upsets parents most are the angry episodes they have with their teen boys. Often a boy's anger isn't personal. As I canvassed in detail in *What Men Don't Talk About*, when we don't allow young boys full expression of their feelings, anger is often all they're left with. While it has its place, getting angry is not the way to deal with most issues. So if your son is mad, be aware that it may not even be anger that is causing him to explode. Yet given the limited ways he has in which to express himself, it may be the only way he can let you know what he desperately wants to say. Tony, 26, summed it up perfectly, 'Anger is the first emotion that comes up as a boy. If you feel sad, the first emotion is anger. It's very rarely pure anger for young men. If you're feeling guilty or hurt or weak, then you express it with anger, because if you're angry, you're a man. It has to be aggressive anger, not latent anger, otherwise that's seen as girly.'[1] Things are changing, though. Boys and men have greater freedom to be sensitive and expressive. Parents have a big role to play in encouraging their boys to be more emotionally intelligent.

LEARNING HOW BEST TO EXPRESS EMOTIONS

Today a boy needs to be able to read people and situations quickly and accurately, and know how best to respond. This is an essential life skill in the twenty-first century. One of the greatest gifts a boy can receive from his parents is to learn how to recognise and deal with his own and other people's feelings. Creating a culture at home where issues are discussed and where everyone is honest about their failings and vulnerabilities helps boys get real about life.

When a boy has an angry outburst, he needs time to settle, so that when you do talk, he can take in what you have to say. When you do sit down for a chat, make sure you hear what he's *really* saying. Take note of what he's telling you, his body language, and what he's *not* saying. You may then discover he's behaving in a certain way because he's afraid of his peers, lack self-worth, or needs more challenges and independence. These are valuable insights that will help you help him find a positive way forward.

Your son may need assistance in recognising when he gets stressed or upset. A great technique is to come up with a phrase that will help him realise he's in overdrive. One friend used to warn her son not to 'get his ratty tail caught in the door' when he got worked up. It immediately lightened the mood and got them talking.

When the air has cleared, it's a good time to discuss the best ways to express feelings. Boys need to know they have choices around anger. They can bottle stuff up and explode now and then, or they can talk about what's bothering them and sort it out. Often parents agonise as to how to raise sensitive issues with their boys. An excellent way to do this is to talk about issues canvassed in movies and celebrity news, in casual conversation, or anywhere else where boys aren't put on the spot. Discussions while out walking, sharing a joint activity or in the car are ideal. They help boys open up, because they don't feel under the spotlight.

BRAIN STUFF

It's not just a boy's body and emotions that take a hit during teen life. His brain is rewired as well. By the time a boy is 6, his brain is almost the size of an adult's. While there's not much more overall growth, his cells and brain pathways continue to develop. Then, at around twelve, the brain goes into a kind of meltdown and rebuilding process where all the cells and connections that haven't been used are eliminated. Some refer to this as the 'use it or lose it' phase. 'If a teen is doing music or sports or academic [pursuits], those are the cells and connections that will be hard-wired,' explains neuroscientist Jay Giedd. 'If they're lying on the couch, playing video games or watching MTV, those are the cells and connections that are going [to] survive.'[2]

These changes continue through adolescence, leaving teenagers frustrated and confused at times. In one study a group of adults and teenagers were monitored while looking at a series of faces and asked to identify the emotion each face portrayed. While the adults were able to identify each emotion with ease, some teenagers read the emotions quite differently. When the brain scans were examined, the adults had used the prefrontal cortex, the thinking part of the brain, while the teenagers, especially the boys, used the anterior part of the brain, which operates on emotions and gut instinct.[3] This may help explain why teenagers tend to act more impulsively, rather than thinking things through. Neuroscientist Deborah Yurgelin-Todd, who conducted the study, concludes, '[Teenagers] may not be as mature as we had originally thought. Just because they're physically mature, they may not appreciate the consequences or weigh information the same way as adults do.'[4]

A boy may not necessarily be defiant so much as misreading what's being asked of him.

Once we understand a little more about the teenage brain, we are better equipped to support boys. Knowing what we say or do may be interpreted differently from the way we intended, we need to allow for the fact that a boy may not necessarily be defiant, so much as misreading what's being asked of him. Whenever we're tired and stressed it's easy to assume a boy has done something just to make life miserable, when in fact he may simply have behaved stupidly because he just didn't think. When giving a boy instructions, it's a good idea to write them down clearly, even if he says he doesn't need them, as boys need clear messages. Get him to summarise any discussions around behaviour and expectations. You may like to draw up a *written* agreement for key decisions such as how, when and where he can drive the family car. This helps ensure boys are clear about what's expected of them. And remember that while these strategies can be very effective, they must be treated with great sensitivity, as no-one likes to feel belittled or humiliated.

> When giving a boy instructions, write them down clearly, even if he says he doesn't need them, as boys need clear messages.

DISCIPLINE

Contrary to what we may think, teenage life doesn't have to be dysfunctional. As boys reach puberty often parents steel themselves for the turbulent years ahead, and can overreact when something goes wrong. That said, there are times when boys deliberately cross the line. One of the hardest decisions for parents is how and when to discipline their sons. It's important we help boys handle different situations, and make sure they understand the likely outcomes of inappropriate behaviour and actions. This isn't the same thing as stage-managing their lives. We need to be clear about what is and isn't permissible. If a boy goes ahead anyway, he has to understand there's a price to pay. Parents who fail to discipline their boys do them a huge disservice, setting them up for some painful realisations in adult life. It's important to be consistent and follow through with disciplinary measures.

Boys also need to know that everyone makes dumb decisions, and that no matter how bad it gets, there's always a solution, and that you still care. This approach teaches them to focus on solutions. As well as having to cope with the consequences of breaking family rules, boys also need to be praised when they do something well, whether it's working hard, helping a friend or making a good decision.

GAINING MORE RESPONSIBILITY

You can help your son be more responsible by discussing his options in any given situation. It's important he thinks the scenario through for *himself* in the first instance, rather than you simply giving him answers. This allows him to practise decision-making and to know you have confidence in his ability to choose well. Then, together, you can work out the best course of action. It also helps to have an informal chat after he's dealt with a situation, to congratulate him for having dealt with it and, if needed, to finesse his approach. Most of us don't get everything right the first time. When a boy understands we are all works in progress, it encourages him to be more open and have a sense of humour about his issues, to relax a bit and enjoy his teen years.

Tips for adolescence:

- *Make sure your son knows what to expect during puberty.*
- *Remember boys much prefer to discuss sexual issues with their dads.*
- *Encourage open discussions and access to such books as* Puberty Boy *by Geoff Price.*
- *Ensure your son realises uncertainty, frustration and confusion are part of teen life.*
- *Celebrate milestones.*
- *Continue to let him know you care.*
- *Be honest about your own teen angst, leaving out details that will embarrass him.*
- *Respect his growing need for privacy.*
- *Balance time on his own and with peers with family activities that will engage him.*
- *Never make his physical changes the subject of family comment or discussion.*

Boys and their need for possessions

If consumption is important to tweens, it's doubly so for teenage boys, who have access to more income and have more freedom to shop than younger boys. While it's tempting to criticise teens for their spending, in many ways they are simply mirroring our values. 'We've grown up in an age when we can have stuff,' Hunter, 18, points out. 'It's a reflection of the world around us. A lot of advertising is targeted to our age, and takes advantage.' Peter, a father of two boys, agrees. 'For my boys, happiness is an MP3 player, it's an XBox, which reflects our values as adults. We take note of what type of car and job someone has. Society is totally geared to getting money.'

'For some people it's clothes. For some it's technology, sporting gear, or movies for others. I think everyone's materialistic in that sense. There's something everyone wants.' *Joel, 19*

The boys I spoke with were very honest about their love of possessions. In many cases it's all they know. 'Mostly a lot of people do want a lot of stuff in my generation,' says Damian, 18. 'There's heaps of marketing to us, like with clothes and stuff on TV.' Harry, 15, agrees. 'Yeah, definitely we seem to have a lot of money and spend it constantly on gadgets, more clothes and that sort of thing. Computer games are big, movies and music.'

DISPOSABLE INCOMES

Coming out of a time of unprecedented affluence, it's natural for teens to spend the money they have rather than save. For many, getting a part-time job is more about income than on-the-job experience. 'Money is the only motivator, the only reason to go to work, because they want the stuff,' says Rebecca, mother of a teenage son. 'They have a big list of things they want.' This focus on money doesn't encourage a strong work ethic or pride in a job well done. 'The attitude is that "I can work or not work," as they can fall back on parents endlessly,' adds this concerned mum.

'If kids have money they spend it. They have no concept of saving, no understanding of the difference between need and want.'
Austin, assistant principal

TECHNOLOGY

Boys have always loved gadgets, and their love of new technology remains strong. 'I do like my technology,' explains Joel, 19. 'I always try to pick up the latest things. I'm saving up to get a new Airport Extreme for the house, so I can get better internet in my room. I'm a technology junkie. Our generation is definitely materialistic.' Computers, mobile phones, iPods and games are must-have items for boys, as these are the mediums through which they experience their world. The prices are no longer prohibitive and as technology is moving so fast, boys also feel compelled to buy the latest model on offer, so they don't get left behind. 'Everyone relies on it, I guess. There's always a bit of a list of things we want,' says Rick, 17. 'Even if I've got something, there's always the better version.'

This constant need to upgrade is often a source of frustration to parents, who can't understand why a handful of additional features are such a big deal. But marketers do their job well. They work hard to ensure the latest phones, games and iPods are essentials for teens. The more parents resist these purchases, the more boys see them as out of touch. 'I guess there's quite a dependency on this stuff as well,' reflects Joel, 19. 'It's like I've got that one, so I'm going to get the next one. Or this will match that. It all kind of adds up.'

A GROWING MARKET FOR GOODS

Realising boys are a lucrative market, manufacturers of hair products have boys firmly in their sights. Even tween boys are waxing, gelling, contouring and colouring their hair. Boys are very conscious of hair trends and the products needed to achieve each look. Shoes are also a big fashion statement now. And with a growing interest in styling, boys are taking more of an interest in how their bedroom is furnished.

DISPOSABLE INCOME

With the advent of much smaller families, and parents having children later, now there's more attention and money to go round, and far less need for kids to share clothes, furniture or gadgets. No previous generation has enjoyed such a high disposable income. Boys are no longer reliant on their parents for money either. They're very aware of their spending power and what it can deliver. 'I get quite good pay at my part-time job,' explains Rick, 17. 'My Saturday rate's great. I'm quite lucky I have money to spend.' When boys are short of cash it's no big deal, as parents and grandparents frequently make up the difference. So, this generation of boys have become accustomed to getting what they want fairly quickly, if not immediately.

'We're used to having everything just bang like that. It's hard to wait for things and not have them instantly.' *Luca, 15*

MARKETING BONANZA

The marketers put pressure on teens to keep spending, who in turn pressure their parents to get them what they want. For boys it's the big-ticket tech items that tend to be high on their wish lists. 'There is a real pressure to buy kids things,' admits Robin, father of teen boys. 'My son is hassling me for the latest PlayStation.' Many parents and teachers echoed this sentiment.

Nothing is left to chance when marketing to teens. Companies employ the best experts money can buy, from child psychologists and cultural anthropologists to animators, whose work feeds directly into the marketing effort. Even the way kids pester parents is carefully managed. Often ads give boys the perfect script to persuade time-poor parents to buy. These campaigns have a lot riding on them. When they work, the profits are huge. Recently Microsoft announced its latest Xbox 360 had already surpassed its predecessor, with sales of over 25 million.[1] The constant dilemma for parents is when and how often to give in. Kids want the latest gizmo or T-shirt because marketers link these products with the things teens most crave – popularity and success. And as our boys live in a world that comprises winners and losers, there's very little room for them to move if they want to be on the winning team.

'Kids want the newest stuff, to be popular. It's related to social status.' *Aidan, 22*

Not all boys are so vulnerable. It was interesting to see how much more the boys who have to save up for their possessions value them. These boys were also much more discerning about what they bought. 'I'm often told to save up and buy it if I want something,' says Mark, 15, 'but there are people whose parents are lenient in that sense and will contribute a lot. People I know are getting new phones and the latest iPod and that sort of thing, which is just a waste of money really.'

HIGHER EXPECTATIONS

While marketers have a huge influence over the teenage market, teen expectations have also grown in recent years. Brand loyalty is now making way for 'brand sluts' or 'promiscuous shoppers', who are constantly on the look-out for additional benefits that come with a purchase. Teen consumers expect to feel special when they make significant purchases. They want to be continually excited by a brand. Research also indicates that teens like customised products. Adidas has been quick to respond with in-store events where kids can embellish their shoes, while web-based T-shirt store Threadless.com, much sought after by guys, allows registered site users to design, review and purchase T-shirts. Only a thousand copies of each T-shirt are printed, so each item has limited-edition status for buyers.[2]

CHANGING PATTERNS OF CONSUMPTION

Unlike previous generations, today's boys are comfortable with shopping. By the time boys are teenagers, they are seasoned consumers and trend-spotters. Before they make a purchase they like to talk to peers and check out the product online. Dubbed maturiteens, boys are no longer straight in and out of a store. Shopping has become a *social* experience, so they are happy to browse. Often they'll shop with female friends whose taste they trust.[3] Part of their comfort with shopping is having fathers who now help with family shopping, and often purchase their own clothes and accessories.

However, constant shifts in what's cool means that this generation of teens spends a considerable amount of time on their purchasing choices and keeping up with trends. These trends often start on the fringes of society. For example, the 'ghetto look', with its baseball caps, baggy jeans, hoodies and bandanas, which grew out of the Brooklyn, Bronx and Queens cultures of New York has now morphed into the more mainstream 'ghetto chic'.[4] For today's teenagers brand loyalty to a whole range of products was captured before they could read or write, so some choices are unthinking. 'Marketing does affect you,' says Joel, 19. 'We're relentlessly marketed to. I watch a Coca-Cola ad and I think, "Wow, I want a Coca-Cola now." So I walk off to the fridge and grab one.'

So, where are parents in all this? Trends in teen fashion, accessories, programs and music move so quickly teens have to work hard to keep up. Boys are constantly looking out for changes in direction in magazines and movies, in sitcoms and on the net. This makes it hard for parents to pick what their kids might like at any one time. 'I refuse to buy my teen son anything unless he's there, as it may have some slight thing that is different, and so he'll discard it,' says Frank, a dad and childcare worker. 'It seems the pressure to be exactly the same as the other kids is huge.'

INFLUENCE ON FAMILY PURCHASES

Teens are doubly attractive to advertisers, because they now influence household buying decisions from plasma TVs, computers and DVD players to cars. The faster technology changes, the more parents rely on their teens to research products online. So these teenagers are almost like inhouse consultants. The problem is that all this focus on spending makes for teenage lifestyles of continual consumption. The more boys are thinking about purchases, the more spending becomes a habit. And while this may be fine for the kids with money, it's hard on the kids who can't afford all the stuff. 'The gap between rich and poor is widening,' says Austin, an assistant principal. 'In the past we all had hand-me-down clothes. Now it's the latest of everything. The poor kids get left behind. It's not just that low-income kids can't have lots of stuff. Without it they end up at the bottom of the popularity stakes.'

Most teen boys don't like cheap things. They talk about brands as they would about their valued friends, and they like to buy now and think later about how they're going to pay for it. As a result teen debt levels are growing. It's vital parents teach boys how to handle money, to budget, and to balance their purchases with savings. They also have a big role to play in helping their sons define themselves by more than what they wear and own.

You can influence your son's spending in the following ways:

- *Promote a savings culture in the home.*
- *Be aware of your own spending habits.*
- *Encourage awareness of the environmental impact of endless shopping.*
- *Educate your son about advertising and marketing so he knows when and how he's being marketed to.*
- *Discuss how many products are only made possible by the exploitation of the poor in third-world countries.*
- *Spending is often a result of boredom, so focus your son on other ways to spend his time.*
- *Encourage giving to those who are less fortunate.*

Why looks matter

Until very recently grooming and presentation weren't something teen and tween boys thought about. But now everyone is under the microscope. The way a boy presents himself can be the difference between acceptance and rejection. So, increasingly teen boys take careful note of how and when something is worn. As Rick, 17, explains, 'If you were to, like, wear the same T-shirt twice in a week, it'd affect your school life and how you feel about your parents' decisions around the clothes you have to wear.' According to Sara, a high-school teacher, 'Now boys are very concerned about their shoes. You'll often see them cleaning their shoes in the playground. Shoes are all about status. Accessories are now big. They're very conscious of fashion.' There's nothing wrong with boys taking an interest in their appearance. For years they were criticised because they didn't. The critical issue is to ensure they're not anxious or obsessive about their presentation.

> **'Boys are a bit anxious about the way they look, what their friends think and what girls think. Often people give you a heads-up about what you can wear.'** *Daniel, 12*

PRESENTATION COUNTS

'Boys are getting more into fashion and presentation,' says Zac, 15. 'Sometimes they're making as much effort as girls. There's more pressure to get dressed up more from peers and stuff.' Jacob, 17, agrees, 'Presentation in our school in particular has really influenced me. A few of my friends are gay, so they dress really well. You try to make yourself presentable, it's seen as the thing to do. So, unless you're doing something that's really, really dirty, you'd wear good jeans and a T-shirt and a nice pair of shoes whenever you're going out.' Once boys who did take care over their appearance would be victimised. It's refreshing to see them respected, as long as this doesn't become their raison d'être.

> **'What you see in magazines and on TV, is what you want to dress like, listen to, definitely.'** *Rick, 17*

Some boys clearly enjoy the fashion stakes and get quite creative. Again this can be a good thing, as long as it's not a source of worry. 'Grooming and hair styling is very important,' Angus, 17, told me. 'It's more accepted now amongst guys using foundation and stuff, sometimes a bit of eyeliner and natural-coloured lipstick. A lot of guys are very vain.' While keeping up with the latest trends can be fun, for many teen boys it can also be stressful. 'Grooming is important for sure,' admitted Toby, 16. 'I'm very self-conscious about my body and the clothes I wear. I try to look the part for the occasion. Most kids do. It's mostly about looking good.' This was the experience of Rick, 17, also. 'There's pressure from the media, male superstars, teen celebrities to wear certain clothes. That's what girls are looking for, so guys dress to fit the part,' he explained.

> **'You've got boys not wanting to come to school if they can't wear the right shoes and clothes.'** *Kayt, high-school teacher*

FASHION CUES

It's harder for boys to know exactly how they should look, as they don't have the styling magazines and TV programs girls can access. So boys glean what information they can. They're often quite inventive about how they do this. 'With hair and fashion you follow the older guys, people who are ahead of you at school,' Lyall, 12, told me. 'It definitely helps having sisters for fashion tips,' said Zac, 15. 'Really boys follow what they see in teen magazines, and with sports players and actors.' Today's boys really want to know how to get the right look. Angus, 17, echoed the sentiments of a number of boys, saying he wished there was a guys' fashion magazine. 'I look at role models on TV, like people in bands and follow them quite closely,' he told me. 'A lot of guys choose their look out of magazines about rock stars and things, like for haircuts.'

> '**I take my cues from sporting players, when you see them on ads and, like, in sporting magazines. These magazines always have what's good and what's not good to wear.**' *Toby, 16*

HAIR

Of all the fashion statements boys can make, hair seems to be a big focus. 'Hair's the main fashion icon for boys,' Zac, 15, told me. According to Jacob, 17, 'Even if you have bed hair, if you're going out you'll make a big effort to style it.' Kayt, a high-school teacher, agrees. 'Many boys are having their hair straightened, streaked or coloured to be accepted.'

According to Angus, 17, the increased interest in fashion and hair is partly because boys are now posting photos on the net. 'If you put yourself out there, you want to ensure you look good.' These teenagers now think about how they could improve their online profile. This means making detailed decisions about how they come across.

'Boys do find it hard with, like, new fashion sort of things, because it changes all the time. When you get dressed up and no-one mentions anything, then you know you're dressed okay.' *Daniel, 12*

CHANGING FASHIONS

One of the challenges in the fashion stakes is the speed at which things move. 'Fashion changes very quickly season to season,' explained Rick, 17. 'People want to keep up with that. It's a good thing to be at a school where you have to wear uniforms or it'd be a lot worse.' Increasingly boys are enlisting the help of female friends. 'I take my cues from my girlfriends. I trust their opinions,' said Toby, 16. 'When I go shopping I go with my girl-friends, as they like shopping, and they help pick out things I look good in.'

'There's a lot more pressure now for boys to be good-looking.'
Sara, high-school teacher

And just as girls worry about appealing to boys, now boys are increasingly concerned about whether or not they 'look right' for girls. 'We do think about presentation, it's good to look good for girls. It's enjoyable,' Lyall, 12, told me. Taking an interest in fashion can be fun, but with the huge emphasis on appearance and the rapid changes in styles, teens have to be constantly on the case to ensure they're up-to-date.

To help your son with the pressures to look good:

- *Respect the fact that feeling good about the way they look is important to teens.*
- *Help balance your son's interest in fashion with richer life experiences.*
- *Offer to help shop for clothes.*
- *Help him see that everyone is under pressure to keep spending.*
- *Introduce him to wonderful vintage clothing buys.*
- *Encourage him to see he's more than his clothes and hair.*

Worries about body image

Today's boys are much more self-conscious about their bodies, as they are now exposed to endless images of male bodies in ads and on billboards, in films and magazines. Many boys feel they should have prominent muscles, trim waists and fabulous abs. They want to be able to take their shirts off and look like Hugh Jackman or Brad Pitt. 'There is a worry about body image,' said Mark, 15. 'I see it around a bit, like boys getting worried about the way they look. I see them going to the gym regularly, trying to get big, so they can show off to each other and to girls.'

'Yes, absolutely there's a pressure for boys to look a certain way, just like there is for girls. They're just so young still, they shouldn't have to worry about being sex symbols, but it's all about sex.'
Sara, high-school teacher

'The whole emphasis about perfection is fuelling body image issues. There are more boys presenting with these issues than ever before,' points out clinician and researcher Roberta Honigman, based at Melbourne's St Vincent's Image Disorder Unit. 'It's like someone keeps moving the look, the fashion statement, so no-one's ever going to feel they've made it.' She is seeing a growing anxiety in guys around appearance, and points out that the more finely attuned a boy is to perfection, the less chance he'll have of being satisfied. This is driving increasing numbers of teenage boys to undergo liposuction and laser hair removal, as well as nose and ear jobs. Some go as far as pectoral and calf implants.

Other boys battle with an obsessive dislike of certain parts of their bodies, or go to extreme lengths to look pumped up, or to be skinny. According to eating disorder expert Dr Murray Drummond, often it's not even an eating disorder boys are suffering from, so much as an attitude that affects how they see themselves and what they do.[1] 'Boys worry about their figures,' said Noah, 10. The reason? 'Because they really, really want to be the best-looking, so they'll be the most popular boy in the class.'

It's only recently we have begun to focus on boys' body issues. 'For a long time we thought boys didn't have problems with body image, because we were using the wrong measures,' explains Naomi Crafti, of Eating Disorders Victoria. 'Traditionally research on body issues centred around weight loss. The numbers of boys wanting to bulk up tended to cancel out those focused on weight loss, so it was thought boys didn't have significant body image problems.'[2] We now know that the numbers of boys struggling with body image is on the rise. Just how many boys are affected is hard to gauge. As boys' issues with their bodies are rarely talked about, many parents aren't aware their boys may be vulnerable.

'There's a subconscious body image all guys try to live up to – the muscular guy with the toned body. It's seen as attractive, good for the ego, seen as tough mentally, able to prove himself, attract girls, be dominant.' *Hunter, 18*

TOO MUCH EXERCISE

A number of teachers spoke about the excessive exercise regimes many boys are undertaking at high school to get the 'right look'. 'Now, from the time puberty hits, boys want to look hot,' one young teacher told me. 'From fifteen up they're in there at the gym doing weights and stomach crunches in the lunch hour, to get those rippled abs they see in films and ads.' Many of these boys continue to exercise even when they're injured, as they regard enduring pain as the macho thing to do. Experts now recognise that over-exercising can be similar to eating problems such as purging.[3] Trying to establish how much exercise is too much can be tricky. If a boy's exercise regime is interfering with his quality of life, and there's no longer time to chill out, see friends and vary his activities, chances are he's over-exercising.

> **'Girls' concerns about their bodies are well known, but I don't think it's on parents' radar screens that their sons might have body concerns – "I'm not big enough, I'm not strong enough, I'm not buff enough."'** *Alison Field, Children's Hospital Boston*[4]

Some sports codes such as rugby can exacerbate body image issues, because they need boys to bulk up, while in other sports such as rowing and running, horse riding, swimming and wrestling, boys need to keep their weight down and so become vulnerable to eating disorders.[5] Psychology professor Linda Smolak also believes that some boys end up with eating problems because they pursue sports that do not suit their physiques.[6]

Whether he likes it or not, a boy's body type is heavily influenced by his genes. This can make life difficult for plumper boys, or for those who are small or slight. 'After one recent talk to parents an Asian lady approached me with tears in her eyes,' said Naomi Crafti. 'Her son was depressed because he was smaller than other boys. He wanted to play sports, but was physically disadvantaged because of his size. This is hard for a lot of boys, as we live in such a sports-oriented culture.'

'Guys get anxious about themselves. If you are wearing something fitting you worry people are looking at you, so I don't wear anything fitting.' *Cody, 16*

GOTTA BE A 'HOTTIE'

In previous generations boys needed to be strong for the manual work they'd do as adults. Now muscles are cosmetic. It's all about the perfect look. '[Boys] see it as strength, power and dominance, because they don't know how to be masculine in their own way,' says Dr Murray Drummond. 'They think if you look big and strong, then you'll get by. They become fixated on dominating "weaker" people – gays, women and weaker boys.'

'Boys are dealing with something that is now informally being called "The Adonis Complex" – named after the Greek mythology figure Adonis who was half man and half god – who was considered the ultimate in masculine good looks and ideal physique for men.'
Dr Robyn Silverman, child development specialist[7]

Boys desperate to bulk up, gain a 'six-pack' and get ahead use supplements – protein powders, steroids and growth hormones, amino acids and DHEA (dehydroepiandrosterone). We're now seeing boys as young as 13 getting into steroids, not to get fit so much as to look good. There are dozens of online sites where boys can make their purchases, so parents may not know what they're doing. Most get their steroids from gyms or from drug dealers. The growth in steroid use here is reflected in the sharp rise in illegal steroids seized at airports and in mail packages. In one major US survey 12 per cent of boys had used products to enhance their muscles, strength and overall appearance. Nearly 5 per cent of these boys used supplements weekly. The boys who read men's fashion and fitness magazines were twice as likely to use weekly supplements as boys who didn't read these magazines.[8]

'Yeah, I think boys are under pressure with body image. I guess probably they worry about being fat or too skinny.' *Harry, 14*

BOYS COVERING UP

Boys' concerns about their bodies affect the activities they do, and how much of their bodies they display, as Zac, 15, explains: 'There's pressure to have a good body, like have abs and big arms, to work out more. Yeah, it definitely does make boys self-conscious, and do things like keep their top on at the beach if they don't have that kind of figure.' Angus, 17, agrees, 'Now society puts a lot of pressure on guys with looks, and guys are more aware of themselves. They do judge themselves and worry about things like going to the beach if they're not tanned and muscly. I know a lot of guys who won't go to the pool or take their top off because of body hair, or no muscles, or because of their weight. Basically who don't look like they're meant to look. So they avoid clothes like singlets, which you have to be skinny to wear. They try to cover up.'

BIGOREXIA

Boys have always wanted to look strong. Now they are bombarded with endless images of the 'perfect' male body, many boys feel compelled to try to achieve the slim yet pumped-up look to get ahead in the popularity stakes. 'Definitely there's pressure,' said Rick, 17. 'While girls want big boobs and small waists, with boys it's a muscle thing, and wanting to buff up. If you're a sporty guy you're going to have that kind of body anyway. If you don't have that body you're targeted, but people mature physically at different speeds.'

Those who do get caught up in the need to bulk up may become vulnerable to muscle dysmorphia disorder, commonly known as bigorexia or manorexia, where what a boy sees in the mirror bears no resemblance to how he looks. These boys achieve the classic V shape of broad shoulders, pumped-up arms and chest, and narrow waist by taking supplements, eating a very strict high-protein diet, and exercising constantly. Yet when they look in the mirror, these boys see themselves as puny. So they exercise harder, take more supplements and become even more obsessed with their diets. Some exercise several hours a day. Ashamed of how they look, often they can't bear to see their reflections. They cover up, wearing baggy clothes, and prefer not to socialise.

> When asked to choose their ideal male body, boys as young as eleven chose body shapes that were only possible with steroids.

INTO STEROIDS

Many boys suffering bigorexia cannot resist using steroids to help buff them up. In a recent study Dr Harrison Pope of Harvard Medical School asked boys to choose their ideal male body. Boys as young as 11 chose body shapes that were only possible with steroids. As most boys procure steroids without a prescription, they're unaware they may suffer extreme acne, yellow skin, a reduced sperm count, shrinking testicles, mood swings, impotence, breast development and difficulty urinating. All they're focused on is getting the right look.

One of the most concerning side-effects of taking steroids is the sudden explosive rages users are prone to. While there are no conclusive studies linking 'roid rage' with violent attacks committed by steroid users, there do seem to be some connections. Dr Pope tells of one young boy he calls Patrick, who like many teen boys wanted to improve his body. Patrick began to work out at the gym until he was exercising seven days a week. Keen to progress, at 14 he started using steroids until he was suffering extremely high blood pressure and his hair was falling out. Before taking steroids Patrick had been a shy boy. A couple of years later he was experiencing violent mood swings, which culminated in him taking his 14-year-old girlfriend into the woods and murdering her. While not all boys on steroids end up in such a tragic situation, they do need to understand the risks.

BOYS WITH ANOREXIA AND BULIMIA

Not every boy wants to be pumped up. Some prefer to be skinny, and may end up struggling with anorexia or bulimia to achieve this. 'Anorexia is on the increase,' says Kayt, a teacher of over two decades. She now sees boys passing on treats because they're concerned about putting on weight. 'I like to celebrate birthdays with the kids in class with a chocolate cake. Quite a few boys won't eat any. One boy runs 10 kilometres every night. You see the boys in the gym at our school lifting weights at lunchtime and after school.' This makes life even harder for boys who are nowhere near the ideal body weight, as many are subjected to terrible bullying and social isolation. Seeing what happens to the overweight kids at school is sobering for any boy. Even those boys who appear to shrug off the worries about their weight don't have it easy because they're very aware they're different. 'Some take their weight good-naturedly,' Jacob, 17, told me. 'We have one nice guy. He cracks jokes about his weight all the time. People call him melon. Like, he's nice, but he's never had a girlfriend.'

'I lost complete control of everything today, from my ex to my food. After that, I ran to crackers looking at nutritional info and, like, had to do all the division in my head. I ended up eating 2 crackers – 24 calories . . . I'm sitting here sipping a Pepsi Max. This was my only meal besides a hotdog with mustard and ketchup. I threw that up though.' *Anonymous,*[9] *online teen forum*

It's no surprise that for some obese kids the pressure is too much. After being bullied because of his weight, Adam went on a crash diet and began exercising for up to four hours a day. In just four months he lost 70 kilograms. As his weight continued to plummet he had so little muscle mass left that his body began to feed on itself. The strain on his body caused the blood vessels under his eyes to burst. By the time he was 16, Adam weighed only 40 kilograms and had to be admitted to hospital. After two rounds of recovery and relapses, he ended up in a coma.[10] The more parents are aware of boys' vulnerabilities around body image, the more they can get help before they face these extremes.

INTERNET SITES

Boys suffering anorexia, bigorexia or bulimia can find consolation and coaching on how to prolong their disorders from peers on the net suffering the same issues. While many of the pro-ana (anorexia) and pro-mia (bulimia) websites have been banned from major net providers, it's not hard for boys to meet those of like mind. New sites have sprung up offering 'thinspiration', with galleries of sleek, sometimes emaciated, celebrities. Other sites, such as mostbeautifulman.com, showcase the actors, musicians, athletes, models and supermodels with the hottest bodies. And others give voice to the 'beauty and control' of starvation, mocking those who lack the willpower to resist food. 'Sometimes I am hungry. I'm always hungry. But when I don't eat I feel good. Pure. I feel empty and it's wonderful. I feel so powerful. Like I could fly,' says Pro Ana Lives.[11] As with bigorexia, it's essential parents seek help for boys suffering anorexia or bulimia.

'They say I'm too skinny. Whatever, I am a pig. They are just trying to make me even fatter than I am. They are cruel like that . . . I am a failure, why can I not tell my stomach to shut up? Why can I not be strong? No wonder I am fat. I am disgusting.' *Prince Ivar*[12]

FOCUS ON OBESITY

The growing emphasis on childhood obesity affects those already sensitive to body image issues. Increasing numbers of boys are now concerned about being fat and unlovable. As Jacob, 17, points out, 'The big pressure is not to be overweight.' Even though there's mounting evidence that weight loss is a complex journey, with many factors to consider, including genetics, constant editorials on dieting mean that many kids now view dieting as normal. Reality TV shows such as *The Biggest Loser* only serve to intensify the pressure many kids are under to look a certain way. The thought that if you have a certain body type you may die is pretty terrifying for kids. Increasingly professionals are stressing health at any size. Terms such as 'junk food' are being replaced with less judgemental phrases such as 'occasional food'.

'We have to choose to be active and we have to choose to make healthy decisions regarding our diets.' *Professor Louise Baur, Westmead Children's Hospital*[13]

THERE'S NO EASY ANSWER

With better food and healthcare, today's boys are bigger than kids of previous generations. While there are obesity issues, studies suggest that overall today's kids may not be eating more. Instead, they're eating high-calorie treats between meals. The rise in fast foods and decline in exercise are also taking their toll. But experts stress there are no simple answers. How defined a boy's muscle is depends on his genes. Even kids who look slim may have quite a lot of fat and little muscle. Our bodies do need muscle to promote bone growth. Without it, kids may be vulnerable to osteoporosis later on. In a study of children between 1951 and 2003, professor Tim Olds of the University of South Australia found that fat in children is now tending to accumulate around the stomach, which can in turn lead to diabetes and heart problems in later life.

Finding ways for kids to balance enjoyment of food with exercise and healthy diets is the way forward. One new program, KidFit, encourages parents to lead the way with healthy diets and exercise. When kids see their parents eating properly and exercising on this program, it helps these routines to become a natural part of family life. Created by child obesity expert Brodie Cambourne, the KidFit program teaches parents easy exercises. By attending these classes with their mums and dads, children start to get involved in healthy eating and exercise.[14]

TELLTALE SIGNS

There's a natural increase in concern about appearance during teen life. Many boys struggle with body issues in silence because they don't want to be discovered, and because most parents don't know what to look for. Warning signs that a boy may have problems could include no longer enjoying his favourite foods, skipping meals, and constantly weighing himself or checking himself out in the mirror. Excessive exercise, endless grooming, or rapid weight loss or gain may also indicate there are problems. In extreme cases boys may no longer want to go out, or quit school. Body image issues aren't just about food. They're a misguided way of coping, born of years of concerns. Families needn't battle these issues alone. There's plenty of professional support available.

You can support your son in the following ways:

- *Be sensitive to peer pressure and the pressure to have the perfect body and perfect grades.*
- *Teach your son how to balance personal achievement with fun times.*
- *Help your son have a good self-image by modelling a healthy self-image.*
- *Discourage magazines that focus on body image.*
- *Celebrate food by dining together regularly as a family.*

- *Be aware of throwaway comments about weight and what makes someone attractive.*
- *Don't hesitate to seek professional help.*
- *Go to http://kissmyassets.wordpress.com/body-image-articles/ for further advice.*
- *Read* Living With Your Looks *by Roberta J. Honigman and David J. Castle for help with these issues.*

Peer pressure

Today's teens and tweens are increasingly sensitive to their peers, as almost every aspect of their lives is up for scrutiny. And for boys who find it hard to express themselves, this can make peer pressure doubly challenging. As Col, 19, explains, 'Friendships are fragile, because you have to trust someone. But because you're expected to be strong and independent, you can't talk about emotions, so you have to take things on face value.'

When you talk with boys, they freely admit to the peer pressure. 'Yeah, peer pressure is totally there for everyone now,' said Angus, 17. 'Once you could just go around in a T-shirt and jeans. Now you have to wear certain things. Guys are under a lot of pressure to look good, to wear nice branded clothes, to have good hair, and to do the kinds of stuff girls do to look good. If you don't you're rejected.' Ashton, 12, agrees. 'Peer pressure can be intense, like feeling you have to do what your friends do.' He went on to explain that he often ended up doing things he'd prefer not to, to please his friends, and that most of the time he did so without realising he was being coerced.

'Boys get judged on how they look too.' *Tyler, 10*

THE COOL FACTOR

The overwhelming influence of contemporary marketing now adds to peer pressure. Being cool is essential, and the cool kids set the teen agenda. The rest of the kids follow, not because they like the cool kids, but because they fear the consequences if they don't. While cool kids have a lot of power, they're also under a lot of pressure to stay ahead. 'In the cool group things can be pretty fragile too,' said Luca, 15. 'They like to act as if nothing can touch them, and they go around in groups, so they can back each other up, but being cool and stuff can backfire.' As trends change, so too do expectations, and boys have to be vigilant so they know what's expected of them. Tommy, 12, spoke of how important it was to 'be fashion conscious, and to know how to behave and interact with others.'

> **'When bullies start bullying they don't stop to think what the victims feel like, they think more about what their friends are thinking.'**
> *Sam, community police officer*[1]

Belonging has always been important for teens and now it seems even more so. A number of boys spoke of how careful they were about what they revealed to their peers for fear of recrimination or being rejected outright. 'My group is into music,' explained Joel, 19. 'It's like a metal rock kind of music. Some people hide some of the different artists they listen to. Like there's some bands friends think suck and would get angry if they knew you listened to them. There's others who lie through their teeth to stay accepted, seem interesting and cool.'

> **'You have sub-groups, punks and lads and things, or you're in the rejects group.'** *Angus, 17*

LIFE ON THE EDGE

One of the reasons peers have such a big influence is because of the amount of time boys spend together. So when their friends encourage them to push their boundaries, boys feel compelled to play the game. A number of boys were uncomfortable about the extent they had to go to, to prove they were worthy of their group. 'Yeah, of course boys are under peer pressure, said Harry, 14. 'It's more than girls. Like, girls will berate someone and call them a loser if they don't do something. With boys it's more like egging you on to do something risky. It's like kind of supporting them to do something risky.' Toby, 16, agrees. 'Peer pressure is a reality. They pressure you to do things you don't want to do, to fit in. At the time it's really intense.' The level of coercion some boys experience can leave them feeling extremely vulnerable. Gary, 17, felt that a lot of anti-social behaviour amongst boys was due to boys wanting to look tough in front of their friends.

Sometimes it's hard for parents to get why peers matter so much. But today's teens are very different from previous generations. They're immersed in a fast-paced, ever-changing 'performance' culture, where they have to keep up with their peers by being amazing and 'out there' all the time. This winners-and-losers climate promotes a culture of shifting friendships. Today you may be where it's at, but tomorrow you could be on the outer. Teens perform to keep their friends interested, to be popular. Basically popularity helps them survive. However, as everyone else is also trying to impress, boys need to keep on coming up with new ways to keep their friends' attention and loyalty.

'People do start to drink and do drugs, and going out to fit in.'
Joel, 19

Even when boys do what their peers demand, they're not necessarily off the hook. Like many professionals, Sara, a teacher with almost a decade of experience, is concerned at the decline in boys' loyalty towards each other, as many boys seem to delight in exposing their mates in embarrassing or potentially harmful situations. 'In this voyeuristic culture there seem to be few limits,' she explained. 'Even friends can't resist the opportunity to humiliate a close friend. Boys tape each other vomiting, lying around and almost passing out. Photos are taken and circulated.'

IT DOESN'T PAY TO BE SUCCESSFUL

As peer pressure is relentless, many boys find themselves in impossible situations. They may be well able to get good grades, and be willing to toe the line at school. But under the watchful eyes of their peers, they feel obliged to act out to be accepted. 'The pressure to succeed versus having a social life, it's hard,' said Joel, 19. 'It just becomes one massive arm wrestle. It gets extremely frustrating.' Luca, 15, agreed. 'If you don't try to raise your status by acting cool or being rebellious against teachers then there can be problems.'

> Teens perform to keep their friends interested, to be popular. Basically popularity helps them survive.

Teenage life has always been a fragile time, and with the huge emphasis on appearance and putting yourself 'out there', it is more so today. Many teens have little option but simply to try and get by. They will seize any opportunity they can to take the pressure off. It is this impulse that leads some boys to drink excessively, drive too fast or take drugs. Some participate in violence, steal or make racist remarks to keep in with their friends. 'I was forced to beat up someone at school by my friends,' admits Steve, now a youth officer who bitterly regrets his actions.[2] That said, boys who have clear boundaries and a strong sense of self are more likely to make good choices, even when under pressure from peers.

WHAT PARENTS CAN DO ABOUT PEER PRESSURE

Before tackling peer pressure, parents need to understand what it's like to be a teenager now. Today's teens are terrified of being branded losers. They don't want to be rejected by their friends or disappoint their parents. Being part of their peer group gives boys a sense of safety and belonging. How parents handle the intensity of peer relationships is crucial. Trying to compete with their son's friends only forces him to choose. If there is cause for concern about peers, then naturally parents must take action, but only when there's good reason. Often teens are drawn to certain friends because they embody the qualities they are missing in their own lives. A boy may have a thrill-seeking friend because he's craving more risk and excitement. Smart parents provide *positive* ways for boys to express such needs by encouraging their boys to get involved in activities that provide these elements.

> Today's teens are terrified of being branded losers. They don't want to be rejected by their friends or disappoint their parents. Being part of their peer group gives boys a sense of safety and belonging.

If a boy's friendships seem too intense, his parents might like to encourage him to pursue a variety of interests which will give him a wider group of friends. Diluting the influence certain friends have is a much happier route than banning them outright. One friend could see her son was getting in with the wrong crowd at school, so she encouraged him to join a local theatre group. It was a big time commitment, but it turned her son around, because it gave him an opportunity to explore drama. It gave him a new sense of belonging, and made him feel acknowledged and worthwhile. Helping a boy form friendships across the generations can also be an excellent anchor. One boy told me how regular family get-togethers helped him turn the corner when he

106

was going through a rebellious phase. He enjoyed catching up with two uncles he admired and could talk to. Being with them helped ground him and give him a bigger vision of himself.

Tackling peer pressure isn't easy. What we do know is that boys with healthy self-esteem and a rich and varied life beyond school tend to cope better than boys who lack confidence and have few interests. Recently the University of Nottingham tested a group of 10-year-olds to determine how vulnerable they were to peer pressure. Each of the participants underwent a brain scan as they watched a video depicting angry faces and hand movements. The kids who were less influenced by peers showed a greater ability to plan and sort out information, and to reject behaviour they were uncomfortable with.[3] More work has to be done in this area, but this gives us some valuable clues as to how parents can support boys by helping them decipher what is going on in different social situations, as well as providing good ways to handle them.

PEER CONTACT CAN BE POSITIVE

Not all peer contact is negative. Boys have to start to find their own way in life. Healthy peer groups help boys to discover who they are and where they're heading. Boys also need the comfort and companionship of being around kids their own age. As peers are connected round the clock, good friends can make all the difference during the ups and downs of teen life. Parents who provide a welcoming home for their son's friends help keep their son close. They also get a sense of what their boys are up to and with whom.

If a boy is suffering from negative peer pressure he will rarely talk about it, as he won't want to admit he's not coping. He may also be concerned about how his parents will react, or about repercussions from his peers. As Dylan, 18, points out, 'Guys don't talk to teachers. They don't talk to their parents, and you definitely don't talk to the school counsellor. It's kind of frowned on.' So, when parents talk to their sons about peer issues it's important they understand and respect the pressure their boys are under, and how much it takes for them to speak out. Boys need to know they are their own person and have the right to say no, and that peers can only pressure them if they let them. This isn't something they will learn overnight.

You can help your son with peer pressure in the following ways:

- *Discuss where he is likely to encounter peer pressure.*
- *Encourage him to come up with plans to deal with peer pressure.*
- *Work with him on a good plan of action.*
- *Emphasise that some situations take a while to resolve.*
- *Talk things through so he's clear about where he stands.*
- *Help him come up with a script to tell his friends he doesn't want to do certain things.*
- *Work with him to find words and phrases that aren't aggressive or judgemental.*
- *Talk about your own challenges and uncertainties from time to time.*

The bullying thing

With the heightened emphasis on appearance and possessions we're seeing a new level of fragility in some boys. With fragility comes bullying,
the consequences of which can prove fatal. A few months ago 14-year-
old Alex Wildman hanged himself at home because he couldn't bear the
bullying. Around that time Abraham Biggs, also a teenager, committed
suicide in Florida over the net. Over 1000 people watched him swallow
a handful of pills. In the following twelve hours it took for Abraham to
die, some viewers encouraged him. Others accused him of just pretending to commit suicide. No-one got help until it was too late. Unable to
handle the constant threats he received on his mobile phone and the
internet from former friend Shane Gerada, 17-year-old Allem Halkic
jumped to his death from the West Gate Bridge in Melbourne. Jye How-
ell, 11, talks of wanting to die. His bullying began at kindergarten when
he was only four. He has already attended five different schools to try to
escape the bullying.[1] Bullying is not new, but in recent years we have seen
a spike in this destructive behaviour. Some put this down to the arrival of
reality TV, which is often psychologically cruel. Frequently participants
allow themselves to be humiliated to remain 'popular'. In this uneasy

world of shifting loyalties, this week you may be the winner, but next week you may well be out.

> **'Yes, there's a lot of bullying. Boys tease other boys then it turns out to be a fight. Sometimes it's scary.'** *Mark, 10*

DECLINE IN EMPATHY

Many parents and teachers talk of bullying being more cruel and intense these days. Most boys agree. The new technologies, which allow access to camera and video-enabled phones and social networking sites, as well as increasingly sophisticated tools for manipulating photos, give bullies many more ways to get at their victims and cover their tracks. 'The way people now get at each other is more extreme,' said Angus, 17. 'Like there were some kids in the year below me, and they were handing out flyers of a boy they didn't like. They'd photoshopped him doing something inappropriate that he hadn't done. It was put all around the school. Like, it totally humiliated him.'

> **'It is a winners-and-losers culture. The moment a child is on the outer, they're a loser. It's a natural part of a boy's psyche to define their status. Reality shows give kids a language for this.'**
> *Kath, principal*

One of the darker aspects of this winners-and-losers culture is that teenagers never know when they might be the loser, so they participate in situations they feel uncomfortable with, just to remain part of the group. They admit they'd like things to be different, but don't know how. Some days they bully. At other times they are the victim. 'There used to be unspoken rules for boys,' one young teacher told me. 'You don't go out with your mate's girlfriend. You don't take advantage of your best mate. Now when boys get drunk they strip them and dump them, and take photos. They think it's funny.' It's not just reality TV which has fed this new level of bullying we're seeing. The overwhelming influence the sports culture has, particularly on boys, can be totally emasculating for some, as I covered in detail in *What Men Don't Talk About*. Sadly, there are some school cultures which mistake institutionalised bullying for strength, and destroy some boys in the process.

> **'For thirteen years I was bullied every day. It was not only the students that were bullies . . . the teachers would join in. Because it was a small town, they wanted to be seen to be mixing with the "cool kids".'** *D (now an adult)*

POPULAR NO MATTER WHAT

With the constant focus on popularity no matter what, the lines between appropriate and inappropriate teen behaviour have become blurred, as kids compete with each other in the popularity stakes. This affects their behaviour and judgement. After bad boy Olympic swimmer Nick D'Arcy received a fourteen-month suspended sentence for breaking fellow swimmer Simon Cowley's jaw from ear to ear, a string of vicious comments were posted on D'Arcy fan websites. D'Arcy's actions were judged by some as 'inspiring', while Cowley was seen as 'getting what was coming to him'. The fact that Cowley sustained serious injuries didn't figure for those involved in this online popularity contest.

> **'I have a 15-year-old grandson who has just left school as the bullying was too much for him to handle. If he was not taken out of school we were afraid of having to lose a child to death.'** *Kayleen*

GOTTA LOOK GOOD

Behaving like judges on reality TV, peers openly scrutinise each other's clothes, hair, choice of music and out-of-school activities. 'Bullying can be just as bad for boys, it's just in different forms,' explains Rick, 17. 'If a boy shows more emotion he gets bullied. If he hangs around with girls too much, he'll get paid out for that. It's like anything you do they don't like, you'll get paid out for it.' The lengths to which some kids will go to stay safe shows how much pressure they feel under. Kayt, a high-school teacher, told me about a boy who left because he just couldn't cope with the terrible bullying, even though teachers had intervened many times on his behalf. 'The following year the boy came back to school,' she explained. 'He had trendy clothes and streaks and suddenly all the girls were paying attention.' As she points out, 'It's really sad that he couldn't be himself and survive.'

When you're under this level of scrutiny, the smart thing to do is to be extremely careful around 'friends'. 'You don't expose too much to your mates,' Joel, 19, told me. 'You don't want to show weakness and that. If guys see something they can pick on they will, and they'll keep going on it. Like they remember that time when you were crying in the gutter about your girlfriend, and that'll keep them going for the next couple of months. If you're feeling down, it keeps making you feel worse because of how much people keep bringing it up and keep picking on you. So, it's like let's not give them any ammunition against me.'

WORDS DO HURT

While we tend to associate verbal abuse with girls, now boys are hurting each other even more by what they are saying to each other's faces, in chat rooms and texts, and on voicemail. 'Bullying is now verbal,' explains Tommy, 12. 'It's almost worse because it sticks with you. Physical pain is short-lived. Words stay forever.' Jesse, 17, agrees. 'Bullying is pretty intense. It's physical when you're younger, but as you get older it's bitching behind your back. It's rumours and back-stabbing and threats. It's kind of hurting people mentally and emotionally, rather than physically. It's a smarter way of bullying.'

'Some boys use words to get at people. They use humour so they won't get into trouble, pretending to be funny when it's not.'
Tyler, 10

EMOTIONAL INTELLIGENCE

When boys aren't given the skills to deal with difficult situations and people, they have little choice but to fall back on flight or fight responses. 'Boys are a lot more fragile than we realise. I often find it's the boys who are the toughest are the way they are because they're protecting themselves from the softness inside,' says author and educator Amrita Hobbs who has facilitated workshops with adults and teenagers for more than three decades. Dylan, 18, agrees. 'I think that the bullying and mucking up is often guys saying they need help, but no-one's listening.'

Boys do need help in learning how to deal with difficult situations, but gaining this knowledge isn't an overnight process. Often parents can't understand why a boy will continue to strive for acceptance from those who treat him badly. But most teens are very dependent on their peers, as they're in touch around the clock. Gaining the confidence to counter bullies is a hard but necessary journey. Parents who work with their boys on their self-esteem, social skills, and the ability to problem-solve from a young age do them a huge favour.

'I too was bullied at school. I carried a knife in my school bag to deal with those school bullies. School and teachers would do nothing about it, so I was bent on dealing with it as I thought was the only way to deal with it as a teen.' *Baz (now an adult)*

UNDERSTANDING THE TEEN WORLD

Often the difficulty for today's parents is in knowing when and where their boys are vulnerable, because they're exposed to so many experiences parents have no idea of. Allem Halkic's parents thought their son was safe when he was at home with them, only to discover the intense bullying that had caused him to take his own life had taken place right under their noses. Often these new forms of bullying can be overwhelming. Today's kids can end up getting literally hundreds of threatening or nasty texts and emails.

Many adults can't understand why a boy wouldn't just turn off his phone or give the internet a miss, but for a teen their phone and social networking sites are their lifeblood. Without them, they feel cut off from the world. It's critical parents take any form of bullying seriously, and continue to monitor how their teen is tracking, as studies now suggest that the impact of peer abuse shares many of the same characteristics as that of other forms of abuse.[2]

No-one wins when someone is bullied. On the *Four Corners* program detailing Allem's suicide, his former friend Shane Gerada admitted to bullying Allem, adding that everyone bullies. Many kids are both victims and perpetrators of bullying. However, not everyone ends up dead. Ultimately Shane is also a victim, because he didn't have the skills to resolve his differences more positively. He's now had 'RIP Allem Halkic, 08/09/91 to 05/02/09' tattooed on his back, and will wear his actions for the rest of his life.

WHEN GAMING BECOMES BULLYING

Even computer gaming has its moments. Some boys now get together to plan a vicious attack on someone else in the game. Once boys enter a game they're often under pressure to keep going until it's finished. 'There's a lot of pressure to see things through,' says Kath, a mother and principal. 'If you do withdraw you may not be accepted again, or you become a loser. There can be some really nasty emails, and general cyberbullying goes on as a result.' This was the experience of Harrison, 15. 'You have a peer group egging each other on because it's over the internet. You can get caught up and lose track of time. You don't want to be the first person to break off.'

SEXUAL HARASSMENT

With the increased sexualisation of teen life, boys are now experiencing sexual harassment from teenage girls. Numerous parents and teachers have voiced their concerns to me. 'Girls are the biggest challenge for boys,' says educator Amrita Hobbs. 'I was at a school recently when a mum came up to me, telling me about a twelve-year-old girl who kept wanting to have sex with her son. Basically this girl was "messing with his head", until he finally plucked up the courage to say no.' This is not an isolated incident. The issue needs a lot more discussion than it is currently receiving as does boys hassling other boys for sex, and boys pressuring girls for sex. The bottom line is that *no-one* should be forced to do anything they don't want to do.

'Between thirteen and fifteen it's a dog-eat-dog world, and you don't get outside your friendship group. If you do you may be out of your depth. You kind of end up with the verbal bullying, or it might get physical like with the choking, and then there's the teasing.' *Luca, 15*

LINKS BETWEEN BULLYING AND HIGH-SCHOOL MASSACRES

While some bullying is short-lived, many incidents are not. Boys handle their pain in different ways. Some turn their anguish inward, and may even commit suicide. Others do whatever they can to survive. Some boys have a complete meltdown and massacre fellow students because their pain is unbearable. Seung-Hui Cho, who was responsible for the worst mass shooting in US history, had been bullied right through his high school years by classmates, who attacked him for his shyness and accent. Finally the pressure became too much. Seung-Hui Cho killed thirty-two people, wounding another twenty-five, before turning the gun on himself. His is not the only massacre triggered by bullying. While we have been fortunate enough not to experience such a massacre in an Australian school, growing numbers of boys are arming themselves with knives and other weapons to protect themselves at school. 'Bullying is rife in schools, and for some kids bullying goes on for a very long time,' says Bryan Duke, who runs a regional mentoring service for teenagers. 'Often boys have no way to deal with it. They want to stop the bullying happening, so they resort to whatever they can — a knife, a gun. It's a survival mechanism.'

'The bullying thing is big at school. It's the biggest problem boys are facing, because they don't talk about it, so they don't get the chance to process and resolve it.' *Sara, high-school teacher*

Previous generations had the luxury of escaping bullying once they got home, as long as their parents and siblings weren't bullies too. Now peers can reach boys wherever they are. And cyberspace allows bullies plenty of chances to hide their identities. The I-Safe.org survey into cyberbullying revealed that four out of ten kids had experienced bullying online. Over a third of the kids received threats while online. More than half of them had encountered mean or hurtful messages while on the computer, but did not tell their parents or any other adult.[3] In another study one in ten kids had had a photo and/or a video taken of them by mobile phone that made them feel embarrassed or threatened. Most didn't speak out because they didn't want parents limiting or preventing their access to technology.[4] This inability of teens to speak out is quite common, as many kids fear that parental intervention will only make things worse.

THE NEW TECHNOLOGIES

It's easy for tech-savvy kids to cover their tracks in cyberspace. By using temporary email accounts and adopting a different online name, they can be anonymous. It's also much easier to be nasty to someone when you don't have to front them. There are so many ways kids can humiliate each other, by setting up fake websites, posting embarrassing images and messages, excluding people from chat rooms, texting them continuously, or by using images to blackmail them.

'Some[one] has made this profile about me and its very bad, its got all my personal details on which is causing a lot of problems. This is causing me alot of stress im still studying and people keep making fun out of me.' *hi5abuse*[5]

Parents need to know what their kids are up to on their phones and the net. Vigilant older siblings can be a great help here. And to prevent mobile phone bullying, kids should have a PIN on their phones which they keep secret. Their phone numbers should only be handed out to trusted friends, as some 'friends' can also be bullies. They shouldn't answer calls from unknown people, and should keep the evidence of nasty messages. It's important parents have firm rules about the use of mobile phones, and that there's a cut-off time each night when every-one in the house places their phones in a shared area.

Bullying has real effects on boys. Kids who are consistently bullied can become anxious and depressed. As their self-esteem takes a dive, they become withdrawn, avoiding social contact or going to school. They may also suffer a range of symptoms from sleeplessness to feeling run-down. Depending on how acutely they're affected, they may be drawn into drug and alcohol abuse, or to self-harm, or they may start bullying others.

WHEN A BOY IS A BULLY

Not all boys are victims or bystanders. The uncomfortable fact is that many kids do bully. Bullies need help and firm guidance to change their behaviour. Parents can't assume their son will know how else to resolve or defuse a situation. Suggesting they give as good as they get doesn't help. Boys need to learn *positive* life skills so they can be successful adults. Sometimes bullying stems from a boy's relationship with his parents. Many boys feel intimidated by the way their parents treat them, then replicate this with their peers. If a boy is set on bullying, he may need something to focus him. I learned recently of a mother who grounded her son after he'd been a bully, only to find he'd done it again. So she took him to a local skateboard park with his new skateboard. She then asked him to pick a boy, and made him go up to this boy and give him his skateboard. Only then did her son get the message.

WHAT PARENTS CAN DO

In seeking to redress bullying, we need to be aware of how much bullying is part of adult life, from bullying coaches and parents at weekend sports events to the powerful men and women in business. Kids also pick up on the way their parents resolve issues in the neighbourhood and in the wider family as well as at work. Families that thrive on gossip and putting others down do their boys no favours.

Some approaches to bullying you may find useful:

- *When your son admits to being bullied, don't over-react.*
- *Be aware your son may feel afraid or ashamed of being bullied.*
- *Talk around the situation, then help him come up with positive solutions.*
- *Nurture your son's confidence: it's one of the best ways to combat bullies.*
- *Encourage your son to have interests beyond school with different friendship groups.*
- *Remember that kids with a stronger sense of self tend to be less vulnerable to bullying.*
- *Help provide your son with rich and varied friendships and activities.*
- *Teach your son how to get out of difficult situations.*
- *Ask him how he would handle a suggestion from a friend to have a fight with someone, and talk about better ways to resolve disputes.*
- *Go to www.StopCyberBullying.org for further advice on internet bullying.*

Stressed-out boys

While boys may benefit from some stress in their lives to help them focus and be motivated, many teens are now experiencing undue stress. According to Linda Jones, the program manager for the Community and Law Enforcement Against Narcotics, the number one concern of young people seeking their services is stress.[1] The ups and downs of relationships, bullying, peer pressure, the demands of after-school jobs, worries about school performance, and family breakdown or relocation are just some of the areas that can stress boys out.

> **'Over eight out of ten teenagers lose sleep over exams.'**
> Teen Dreams, *Channel 4*[2]

GOTTA BE AMAZING

As they're constantly plugged into celebrity culture, teens feel the need to prove they too are amazing. They need to wear the right clothes and shoes, get the perfect haircut, keep up-to-date with new music, movies and DVDs, be on top of the new technologies, watch the right TV programs and keep in touch with friends around the clock, regardless of where they might be. When you add in homework and all the other things teens do, it's not hard to see how much stress many are under.

'We have long commutes, family aspects to deal with, homework, then social time. If you're feeling stressed and needing to relax you need social interaction. Even when there's more homework and things, you keep going until you get your social fix.' *Harrison, 15*

PARENTS' EXPECTATIONS

Many parents also want their kids to be amazing. 'The pressure to succeed is quite intense,' said Joel, 19, echoing the feelings of a number of boys. 'They want you to do something to a point, it's like, "That's ridiculous, it's like so high." When you get a good mark, they want more.' Some kids rise to the challenge. Some are left feeling like losers. Others rebel, as Joel explains. 'With teens it's like, ignore it. Like, let's just go out and do what we want. The whole rebellious thing is because my parents want me to do it, so it's like, "Let's not do it," sort of style of thing, so that goes on and on.'

Naturally parents want to stretch their boys and help them reach their potential, but teenagers aren't endlessly resilient. Too much pressure can be debilitating. Boys need to know they are valued first and foremost for themselves, and not just for their performance. Undue parental pressure can erode a boy's confidence and make him doubt his worthiness to be loved. Alongside their academic and sporting prowess, boys need time to chill out and to relate to other adults who can encourage and support them. Grandparents, friends and the extended family all have a valuable role to play in enabling a boy to open up about his issues, share his successes, and enjoy support when he's feeling fragile.

TOO MUCH ON THEIR PLATES

One of the big issues for today's teens is the number of commitments they have. With mountains of homework, part-time jobs, often several extra-curricular activities and active social lives, there's little time to relax. As adults we applaud kids with a full schedule, because we love 'self-starters'. But in amongst all this activity there's often precious little opportunity to relax. And, as we'll see, many boys are not even getting a decent night's sleep. When you put all these factors together, it's not surprising some boys may be grumpy or even aggressive. There may well be other things contributing to their behaviour, such as peer pressure, school worries and body issues, or they may simply be stressed out and exhausted. When boys do finally stop, there's not a lot of time for them to 'come down' from all their activity. That's why in part alcohol and drugs are so appealing, as they allow boys to feel good and to relax.

THE MACHO THING

Although many aspects of life have changed radically in recent years, some pressures don't change. Boys are still expected to be strong and endlessly resilient, to keep their feelings to themselves, and solve their own problems. This is a tall order, especially during the teenage years. 'You're expected to be a strong-minded tough guy – an image you're meant to maintain through life,' explained Hunter, 18. 'This image is a kind of survival thing. To an extent it's fitting into the group, the pack.' Today being strong is about the way a boy looks, how good he is at sport, and how tough he acts, and often bears very little relationship to how he's feeling inside. Boys are very aware of this and, as we'll see, are working hard to prove they have what it takes. 'Peer pressure is to grow up and be big and strong,' said Col, 19. 'The fat and the weak get picked on. You have to do boy things – drink a lot, play sport and that kind of thing.'

> Unless success is supported, ultimately it can be as damaging to a boy as failure.

Boys do need to learn a level of toughness to survive in adult life, but there's a fine line between being strong and always trying to go it alone. Too many of our boys continue to take their own lives, or turn to alcohol and drugs, or to risk-taking, because they're unable to deal with the very real physical and emotional pressures they face as teenagers. Boys need to know it's strong and smart to seek help. We must help boys understand their needs and issues, to feel comfortable talking about them and dealing with them. This support begins in the home, by parents listening to boys, and being prepared to be honest about their own ups and downs. When we can teach boys these valuable life skills, we help them become genuinely strong, as opposed to simply appearing strong.

BOYS AND SPORT

Sport does offer boys the benefits of good exercise and teamwork, and learning how to win and lose. Now that sport is big business, much is made of the talented kids. There's no doubt that being good at sport is a ticket to success and popularity. But unless this success is supported, ultimately it can be as damaging to a boy as failure. There's a great deal of talk amongst sports professionals about promising athletes burning out or peaking too soon. We need to look more closely at the stress some of our young athletes are under. Even the kids who aren't going to make it big can be subjected to undue pressure at school sport.

> **'How would you like to be eight years old and told [by your father], in front of your coach, teammates [and] parents in the stands, that you're a bum and can never do anything right? Do you think this has an impact on your self-esteem, your self-worth, your relationship with your parents? I do.'** *Fred Engh*, Why Johnny Hates Sports[3]

This 'win at any cost' attitude lets boys down. At school the boys who are naturals at sports are treated as heroes. It's every boy's dream to achieve this level of adulation. But for those who succeed, there are a lot of expectations to live up to. This pressure has to have an outlet. Frequently it results in inappropriate or out-of-control behaviour. And often boys are allowed to get away with it, because they are so valuable to their team. However, sooner or later this dysfunctional behaviour will bring them unstuck, as we're now seeing throughout the sporting world with young sports stars being apprehended for acts of violence, including domestic violence, sexual assault, and destructive and abusive behaviour due to excessive drug and alcohol consumption. How parents and coaches approach a boy's participation in sports has a big impact on how boys see their game.

> **'Peer pressure is still an issue that causes grief for some kids. Boys still tend to think that if they're good at sport they're okay. Kids less able or less interested in sport do tend to be bullied.'**
> *Siobhan, high-school teacher*

Life can be hard for boys who aren't sporty. It's important for teachers and parents to emphasise that while they may not be good at sport, they still deserve respect. Countless talented boys who go on to make all kinds of valuable contributions to society have had to endure unspeakable situations at school because they weren't sports 'heroes'. Things are slowly changing, but we still have a long way to go.

BOYS FEEL PRESSURE AROUND SEX TOO

Some pressures on boys are more obvious than others. Sometimes we fail to support boys in crucial areas, because we get stuck in stereotypes such as 'all boys want is sex'. What emerged from my talks with professionals was how often boys feel pressured to be sexually active, whether or not they felt ready. Dylan, 18, agrees. 'One person in the group has sex, and that's cool, so everyone has to do it. Young teen boys want to grow up. They want to be men.' A Kaiser Family Foundation report on teens and sex indicated that boys are under the same, if not more, pressure than girls to have sex. The boys in the study also felt they had to have sex by 'a certain age'. They also indicated that they felt sex was an expected part of relationships.[4] Given the highly sexualised environment boys are growing up in, this is an issue parents need to be sensitive to, so they can support their sons and help them make good decisions.

WHAT PARENTS CAN DO

Just because a boy seems to be coping doesn't mean this is the case. Parents need to keep a close eye on their boys, especially those with a lot on, to ensure they're not burning out. If these issues are left unaddressed a boy may feel overwhelmed and start to lose interest in school, and in life in general. He may then start to withdraw, or end up battling anxiety attacks, eating problems or self-harming behaviour. If parents feel there is real cause for concern, they are best to seek professional help. One of the best ways to teach boys how to lead a balanced life is to model this balance. While this can be a challenge, experts are now recognising the need for a regular 'detox' from our manic lives, by taking time out and doing nothing. This may be a Sunday at home where the family simply relaxes, or a weekend away in nature or somewhere simple like a caravan park.

Help your son strike a balance between activity and relaxation in the following ways:

- *Make sure he knows it's fine to say no.*
- *Help him find positive ways to say no without feeling he's let others down.*
- *Keep a close eye on your son's schedule to make sure he's not over-committed.*
- *Teach him how to amuse himself.*
- *Encourage him to talk about his feelings.*

- *Set clear limits on activities and time out.*
- *Create an enjoyable, relaxed home life, which also encourages boys to have more balance.*
- *Encourage him to try the teen stress test at: http://parentingteens.about.com/library/sp/quiz/stresstest/ bl_screentest.htm*

Understanding a boy's feelings

Contrary to popular opinion, when you look at boys a little more deeply, you discover just how tender they are. Time and again this was evident in the ways boys talked about their lives. Just because boys aren't encouraged to express their emotions, it doesn't mean they don't have feelings. They do. But because they're expected to keep their emotions to themselves, boys tend to bury them deep inside. That's why they often don't have much of an emotional repertoire. Then when life gets too much, they express themselves in the only way they know how. They get angry.

'Society expects boys to be in charge of things, to be strong, not to show as much feelings. It can put the pressure on.' *Col, 19*

Boys are very aware of the straightjacket they are in. 'The big thing is you get pressured into not caring about stuff,' says Daryl, 17. 'Girls talk about feelings, but it's considered not right for boys to talk about them. So heaps of boys bottle crap up, then they explode.' Tommy, 12, agrees. 'There's a sort of stereotype about boys being strong and independent, that they can stand on their own and have no emotions. Boys can't have a cry and talk things through like girls. They end up with a whole lot more emotion. It leads to a build-up of emotions. They're prone to violence, because they can't have a cry with friends.'

'Guys have a sense of pride about themselves, so they keep themselves to themselves.' *Damian, 18*

Even though the world has changed a great deal, too many boys are at sea with emotional issues, because they are still being raised the way boys have always been raised, to be strong and silent. 'I guess guys see it as a more girlie thing to do, to talk about their emotions and stuff,' Joel, 19, told me. 'Boys just try and keep it inside. It gets tough, and you can end up quite angry for no reason, sort of explosive. You wonder why a friend was so angry about that little thing set them off. Then you realise that person has been angry for a while. I think it'd be good if guys let it out more, but I don't think that's going to happen. Guys stick with the strong silent stereotype around emotions, keep it inside.'

'It restricts you in our culture, because it's more acceptable for a girl to cry. It changes who you are as a person when you can't be yourself.' *Rick, 17*

Sometimes the build-up of a boy's emotions is relieved by a harmless outburst, but sometimes boys bury their feelings so deeply, it affects their wellbeing. 'There is a lot of sadness in boys,' says Richard Aston, who heads up the Big Buddy mentor project in New Zealand. 'Unless this is dealt with it goes inwards and comes out in other ways.' Sometimes boys get desperate and find themselves in harm's way. 'One guy at school locked himself in the changing room with a knife, threatening to kill himself, because he was so suicidal,' Dylan, 18, told me.

'On the outside boys are saying nothing. On the inside they're under pressure, but say they're fine. They don't tell anybody, because it's like a mental weakness to tell.' *Ashton, 12*

FATHERS

There are times when fathers don't help. When I was talking with boys I found it interesting to see the negative impact overly tough fathers had on boys desperate to measure up. 'My father needs to be more understanding of emotional stuff,' Gary, 17, told me. 'He's a "big boys don't cry" kind of guy.' This was Dylan's experience as well. 'It was hard for me when I was growing up. I had a father who was like "men don't cry" and stuff. He was really hard.' Like girls, boys need to feel safe, nurtured and encouraged. It is out of these qualities their strength emerges. 'A stable home is a bedrock for boys, particularly if they have a father there who's available, and both parents emotionally available,' explains Dave Mallard, a father, senior executive and men's group facilitator. 'It helps boys with how they should react, how they see themselves in the world. It's about creating an environment where there's an emotional completeness for boys.' Jim, also a dad, agrees, 'If we have an authoritarian style of parenting, by the time a boy is ten they're very aware they're not listened to, so they keep their thoughts to themselves. There's no emotional safety there. Parents have to listen, and they have to show their own feelings.'

'One of the toughest things is you think emotions have to be kept inside. You don't cry for no-one, you know. It's tough. You have to play this role. It holds you back from being totally yourself.'
Ernesto[1]

PRESSURE OF POP CULTURE

The 'whatever' mindset of popular culture also puts pressure on boys, forcing them to pretend they don't care about a whole range of things, from relationships to achieving at school and in sport, when secretly they care a great deal. 'There's pressure to be tough, funny, cool,' explained Daryl, 17. 'If there's an exam and you fail, it's like, "Well, whatever," even though you're really mad at yourself.' Boys play the game because it helps them survive. 'There's certain stuff you have to do to get by,' Daryl admitted. 'It's easier to get along with people that way.' When boys treat everything that happens to them as if it has no importance, their emotional lives take yet another hit. Not feeling becomes a way of life. It's then hard to care for a world that doesn't seem to care much about you.

Yet even though most boys keep their feelings close, they still have to deal with what is going on inside. When we encourage them to put on a front, we deny vital parts of who they are, and set them up for even greater challenges in their adult lives. Hearing boys explain what it feels like for them should be cause enough for us to rethink what we do to them. 'Almost every single boy wants to talk their emotions through with their friends,' Tommy, 12, told me. 'But that's not part of the image. Everyone doesn't want it to be like that, but that's the way it is.'

WHEN STRENGTH IS A WEAKNESS

The emotional development of boys is just as important as that of girls. Without it boys will find it much harder to navigate the socially complex, fast-paced world they will inherit. Psychologist Dan Kindlon, who works with at-risk boys, reminds us that those who lack emotional intelligence fare worst in life. It was their lack of understanding of how else to deal with threatening or unfamiliar situations that landed many of the boys he has worked with in jail.[2] Wendy, a juvenile court co-ordinator agrees. 'We don't allow boys to be emotional. Boys should be allowed to be frightened, to cry,' she explains.

'I know some people who will turn to the bottle if they have issues. Some are just by themselves, very bottled up.' *Joel, 19*

While many people now recognise the importance of emotional intelligence, we continue to neglect the emotional education of boys, and everyone pays the price. 'Boys are far more emotional and open than young girls, and sadly we stamp that out,' says Michael Waring, who has worked with men's groups for a number of years. 'I see them in men's groups from twenty-five plus, wanting to kill themselves because they can't get the pain out.'

BOYS WORRY TOO

There are many issues boys have to face as teens, from the expectations of parents and peers to concerns around school work and what they're going to do when they grow up. As boys rarely talk about these issues, they have no option other than to find their own way forward. 'You worry about growing up, and the things you have to deal with around alcohol and things like that,' Hunter, 18, told me. 'Peer pressure as well. There's the whole image thing you have to live up to, the whole male blokey thing, having to be the strong silent type. There's not much room for a sensitive side.'

'It's a real pressure not to show emotions.' *Harry, 14*

THE RELATIONSHIP THING

Relationships are another area where boys are vulnerable. We worry endlessly about girls when their boyfriends walk away but assume boys can handle break-ups without any support. 'It's not paid attention to how young guys feel,' said Dylan, 18. 'It's even harder on guys than girls if there's a break-up. Guys are expected just to get another girlfriend, but it doesn't sort out what's happening in their head. They need to talk about feelings. That's why we've got all the male suicide, because it gets too much.' Sara, a high-school teacher, agrees. 'Boys can be very vulnerable when they really fall in love and have that special girl. When

130

the relationship breaks up it's absolutely devastating for them. Many of them just can't recover. They're suicidal. Once the relationship ends it's like they just can't see they'd ever fall in love again. It's like they opened up for the first time. The boys are much sadder than the girls. It really crushes them.'

'Boys can be very vulnerable around girls. When they find a serious girlfriend, they invest everything in her. Then she dumps him, and then we get the suicides, because they can't express anything.'
Wendy, juvenile court co-ordinator

When boys are left to face issues alone, they don't have access to the support that will see them through. They're left thinking they're the only person who is hurting. As Hunter, 18, rightly points out, 'Problems don't get dealt with because they're not talked about with friends. You have to maintain the image for self-preservation – it's a huge pressure.' This is one area, if well moderated, where social networking online can help boys open up. Boys are often surprisingly open in teen forums, because it's safe to speak out anonymously about important issues. 'I feel low and selfish about it,' admits NyN. 'But my mother is going to die, sooner rather than later. If she stops her chemo, she mightn't make the end of the year. If she continues, she could have about five uncomfortable years ahead of her, and then she's most likely gone. I feel selfish for even thinking about it, but I can't help dwelling on where that leaves me.'[3]

'Boys are told to be tough, and that emotions are weakness, but it's becoming more common to express your emotions. It's a good thing because deep down a guy is going to have emotions no matter what.' *Gary, 17*

WHO DO BOYS TALK TO?

As boys no longer need parents to access a whole range of information, parents can be very easily be left out of the loop when boys have problems. This, along with much less rounded life experience, means today's teenagers have fewer skills to deal with the complex social lives they're leading. Teenage boys also see their parents struggling with technology and assume they are living in a parallel world. A lot of parents are also too busy or too distracted to support their boys properly. Boys reveal their genuine anguish about their parents in online chat rooms. 'Hey, act like they're all supportive then i come home and no-one says anything, they're burying themselves in tv,' complains Murphy. 'Personally I'd like to not rely on them, seeing as how fucking scatterbrained they are, but I just can't trust people. like why even try when your family is here to make things better, then go off and do there own thing?'[4] Although many boys struggle to express themselves emotionally, it's good to see increasing numbers opening up. It's so important we encourage this, as everyone benefits.

There's a real need in boys' lives for other good 'go to' people with whom they can talk, and who will listen to them and give good, relevant advice. Encouraging older siblings and cousins to interact with them is an excellent way to go. 'A lot of kids don't want to talk to parents,' said Harrison, 15. 'They don't want mentoring and tutoring from parents. They prefer to talk to someone you feel more comfortable with, like an older brother who tells you something, then you share that information with your friends.' Mark, 15, agrees. 'If my friends had issues, they would keep it to themselves or go to each other. There's the sense of trust if you're good friends, and you might be talking about important things so it might just come up, so you're just sharing constantly with each other.'

PARENTS DO MATTER

Parents who have good communication with their teen boys are a real anchor for them. 'I lost one of my best mates.' recalls Dylan, 18. 'I was lucky. I had a lot of people to back me up. Like don't cry, no matter what you throw at me, but when my best mate died I burst into tears in front of Mum. She's basically brought us up. It was good, and having sisters too. I can talk to them. Most guys don't have that.' While some boys may hardly seem to care about family, most actually care a great deal. They're very sensitive, too. 'My mum said that she hates me,' admits Danny in an online teen forum. 'I feel like a failure as a son as it is, without her saying so . . . I just feel like I'm at my wits' end. I don't know what to do, which way to turn, and just want someone to cry on.'[5]

'We tell our boys to stop crying, instead of asking them what's going on for them.' *Michael Waring, men's group facilitator, father and grandfather*

Boys need their parents as much as they ever did. 'The more connection a boy has with his parents, the more parents can understand how the rest of a boy's life is going,' says Ashton, 12. Rick, 17, agrees. 'It's sad when parents are oblivious or don't care. It's important to have a good relationship, and to spend time, like, talking to your kid.' This is a critical point, for as Michael Waring, who is committed to men's health, points out, 'People get hurt when they're not listened to. We tell our boys to stop crying, instead of asking them what's going on for them.'

Whenever a boy is in distress or even simply withdrawn, we need to understand what's really happening. We may well discover his acting out is in fact a cry for help. It's amazing how often boys get what needs to be done. 'You've got to talk and establish a good relationship, says Rick, 17. Robin, a father, agrees. 'People just don't hear what boys say. There need to be more people getting boys talking, opening them up, so we all understand.'

As a society we still generally encourage boys to hide their feelings. It's very unhealthy. You see this played out in the statistics on violence, in risk-taking. Even though you may have had the day from hell, don't miss that window of opportunity to talk. Listen to the messages *behind* your son's stories and comments. While he may appear nonchalant, this may not be how he's feeling.

You can help your son open up by:

- *Being aware boys don't like to be put on the spot, especially around emotional issues.*
- *Acknowledging everyone has emotions.*
- *Helping your son realise it takes strength to express emotions.*
- *Using casual time together to bring up important topics.*
- *Being approachable, relaxed and open.*
- *Not preaching.*
- *Introducing relevant issues and discussing them as a family.*
- *Talking about your own uncomfortable feelings now and then.*

Mums and their boys

Often mothers are anxious about their sons. While they want to support and nurture them, they worry that unless their sons are toughened up, they may not be able to cut it in the world of men. This leads some mums to distance themselves from their boys, or to over-compensate for the harsh realities of life. However, boys need love and empathy to become strong and capable. They also need plenty of space. And while mums might agonise about whether they have much to offer their boys, their sons are very clear about how important their mums are.

> **'Mum gives, like, comfort and kindness and care. It's looking after you day to day.'** *Lyall, 12*

BOYS DO NOTICE

Sometimes being a mother of growing boys can seem a thankless task, as boys are often boisterous, disorganised and uncommunicative. While mothers may sometimes feel like wallpaper, boys do notice what their mum does for them. One of the many things teen boys appreciate is the way their mums help keep them organised. 'Without my mum I'd lose track of everything,' Flynn, 16, admitted. 'She brings organisation and a sense of direction.' 'My mum's a big part of organising me,' said Toby, also 16. Some boys were also quick to point out that there's a fine line between helping and smothering. 'Mum looks after every aspect of me,' Daryl, 17, told me. 'It's good, but you need a relief from it.' The mothers who give their boys support and space are way ahead, as Toby explained, 'Mums need to give boys space and care, it's important for boys.'

'Mothers tend to be a lot more concerned for boys, and want to do something about things.' Ashton, 12

Every mother needs to find her own way to strike this important balance. Over time Jacob, 17, has come to appreciate the relationship he has with his mother, by finding ways to communicate without feeling overwhelmed. 'Mums do a really good job,' he told me. 'Often we take the support of all their love and encouragement for granted. I finally found it easier when I opened up a bit to my mum. She stopped nagging and trusted me more.' Most mothers yearn for their boys to be more frank. It helps when they realise that boys and men have their own ways of communicating. As boys are not encouraged to talk about their feelings and issues, it takes a lot for a boy to open up. 'It's hard for boys to talk, as boys are meant to be the strong silent types,' Jacob, 17, explains.

In the heat of the moment it can be easy to forget that boys are very different from girls. They communicate differently. Often a mum will learn as much, if not more, about what is going on with her son from what is *not* discussed. There are so many ways boys communicate. Unless mums are aware of this, precious moments can be lost. Mother, novelist, columnist and screenwriter Joanna Murray-Smith describes this brilliantly when talking of her own son. 'Unlike my other children, he does not invite physical contact. But when a loved, distant relative died this summer, he walked up to me silently and put his arms around me.'[1]

> 'In your teen years you need your mum more than ever, even if you act as if you don't need them. Because it's an extremely hard time, you need her to be there for you.' *Gary, 17*

One of the best ways a mother can nourish and support her son is by taking an active interest in his passions. This is an excellent way to encourage boys to open up. Boys need people close to them they can talk to. Finding the right moment to talk is as important as what you speak about. Though they may never say as much, having mothers who are engaged in their world is vitally important to boys. 'It's important to have a mum who talks to you and can have a good relationship with you, because it makes you feel more secure about yourself,' Zac, 15, told me. And Mark, also 15, explains, 'I value Mum's supportiveness, and coming to watch us do stuff.'

BOYS NOTICE

Boys are far more emotionally sensitive to what's going on for their mums than mothers might realise. 'Things are falling apart,' Sheebobee explains online. 'Looks like my mom wont be staying at her job for much longer. the stress is insane and last night she had to work till 3 am when she should be home by 8pm. nothing seems to be going right . . . if I do even the smallest thing to piss her off she'll explode at me . . . and I dont think I can handle that right now.'[2] The tenderness of boys cannot be underestimated either. When we ignore it, we sell our boys short. It's surprising to see just how sensitive boys can be, which may lead them to misread situations. One father told how his son had been with his mother to a meeting with their lawyer. On leaving, she'd pecked the guy on the cheek. The five-year-old came home and told his father he didn't like seeing Mummy kiss other men.

TAKING TIME TO LISTEN

As it's hard for boys to talk about personal matters, one of the best ways mums can join the dots is by listening to what their sons have to say – not just the deep and meaningful stuff, but the attitudes and concerns they reveal in jokes and offhand remarks. While boys may not be comfortable talking face to face, often they will chat during shared time together on a run, while shopping or on the way home. Unless a matter is pressing, acknowledging how a boy might be feeling, then letting the matter rest until he's ready to talk further, is likely to be more fruitful than trying to force him to open up.

The boys who felt they could go to their mothers with their issues, be heard and get good advice were very grateful for the opportunity to offload. 'I have deeper conversations with Mum than Dad because she's always intrigued about boys because she only grew up with sisters,' Mark, 15, told me. This ability to listen is doubly important around emotional issues, as there are so few places boys can share their feelings. As Gary, 17, points out, 'Mums give you the emotional support that men seem to tense up about.' Luca, 15, felt the same way, 'A lot of guys can't talk to their dads, because they're very stern, or a lot of boys can't talk to them about their emotions. She brings reassurance.'

'Mums bring stability and emotional support to a boy.' *Angus, 17*

Sadly, sometimes the way fathers react to their sons is in stark contrast to the nurture mothers give. 'Mothers tend to support a lot, whereas fathers will come out and say things that can be unsettling,' Flynn, 16, told me. Some boys were dismayed by how negative, hostile or competitive their fathers were towards them. Others felt angry and disappointed they didn't communicate well. Ideally boys should enjoy good relationships with both parents. Often they are closer to their mother because she's around more. 'With most things I go to Mum,' said Rick, 17. 'I'm around Mum more often, so we have a stronger relationship. I definitely appreciate it.'

'Mums are more understanding and interested in your world, your perceptions.' *Harrison, 15*

What was interesting was how much some boys missed the closeness to their mothers as life started to take them in new directions. 'As you get older you do more and more things on your own,' explained Rick. 'Like I now drive myself, whereas Mum used to take me. I miss talking in the car. Mum would drive and we'd just talk about stuff.'

SUPPORTING FRIENDSHIPS

As boys don't get the same opportunities as girls to learn to be socially at ease, a number of boys talked of how much they relied on their mums to help build their friendships. They appreciated having a welcoming home where friends could visit. 'Mothers are very important figures,' Angus, 17, told me. 'They give you, like, social help, and how to deal with issues like girls and friends. They do what dads can't do.' Luca, 15, agrees. 'Mums bring backbone to your life. Without them you'd feel all alone. With your mum you feel connected to everything.'

Sometimes this encouragement may be as simple as making it easier for boys to meet friends, as Toby, 16, found. 'Mum was very involved in starting my social life off, by inviting friends over from when I was, like, six.' In other cases mothers help boys feel more relaxed socially by taking an interest in their appearance and clothes and what they're up to.

A LITTLE LOVE

It was touching the number of boys who talked openly about how much their mothers' love meant, and the immense love they felt in return. 'Mums give their child nice love,' said Tyler, 10. 'Their love is really important to boys.' Tommy, 12, agreed, 'You love your mother. There's nothing can change that. It's an instinct, an overwhelming love. An unconditional love that makes you relax.' Having this level of support helps provide an anchor for boys at a critical time in their development. One way boys experience their mum's love is through her cooking. While this may seem clichéd, a meal cooked with love is so much more nourishing. 'Mum's very kind cooking and preparing things for us,' said Mark, 15. 'I see Mum's cooking as an act of kindness.'

'My mum's a good cook. Every boy likes their food.' *Lyall,12*

'It's true Mum's meals are the way to a boy's heart. Yummy home-cooked meals are tops,' Jacob, 17, told me. Toby, 16, felt the same. 'After a hard day at school it's always good to come home and have something good to eat.' While for Angus, 17, it was his Nan's cooking he liked best. 'My Nan can cook. She's like my second mum. She makes the best potato bake, second to none.'

'A mother's cooking is important to boys, because it's homemade. It certainly calms your senses, rather than when you literally buy stuff.' *Ashton, 12*

ENTRY INTO THE WORLD OF WOMEN

Mothers are also a boy's introduction to the lives of women. They have a key role in helping boys understand the joys, nuances and likely pitfalls of this world. When mothers do their job well, their boys benefit greatly from their guidance. 'Your mum's your link to the female world. If you can talk about anything to her that's a big thing,' said Zac, 15.

'From mothers you learn how to treat women.' *Robert, 17*

While it's important mums encourage boys to respect women and their needs, we don't help boys when we encourage them to focus only on the needs of women and girls, and have no sense of their own needs. When boys respect and appreciate the world of women, and understand their own needs and know how to meet them, they are well on the way to becoming strong, rounded men.

Yet in spite of all the love and support mums give, there are aspects of a boy's life they're never going to fully relate to. This is perfectly natural. When mums don't get that boys are different, it can be endlessly frustrating for their sons. Enlisting the support of good male friends and relatives can be a big help, as there are many aspects of male life even the most compassionate of women are not familiar with. This interaction with men doesn't have to be structured time out. Simply giving boys the opportunity to hang out with good blokes enhances their sense of self and helps them comprehend what will be expected of them as men.

TALKING ABOUT SEX

According to boys one of the areas where they do need some space from Mum is around sexual matters, and on the way their bodies are changing. Boys don't feel comfortable having their personal lives put under the microscope, and mums need to understand this. As Mark, 15, told me, 'I find it weird if my mum tries to talk to me about boys' issues. Like, it doesn't work when they try to get on your level, about what's happening for you as a boy.' He found his mother's constant interest in what growing up as a boy was suffocating.

However, given the sexualised world boys live in, parents do need to talk to their boys about sex. They need to do this earlier and in a wider context. It's not enough to just cover the mechanics of sex. Discussions need to include talk about feelings, boundaries and desire. Using pop culture, rather than a parent's personal experiences, as a springboard is the way to go. Boys don't want to hear about their parents' sex lives.

Harrison, 15, speaks for most boys when he said, 'It can be a little bit embarrassing parents talking about their own experiences. Like Mum dropping tidbits. You don't want to talk about it. You just want them to understand about the hormonal bit.'

MUMS ON THEIR OWN

Break-ups aren't easy for anyone. When parents split it can be incredibly hard for boys. As I covered in more detail in *What Men Don't Talk About*, this can be a more complex situation for boys living with their mum as often they feel the need to step into their father's shoes and protect her, whether or not she has asked this of them. It's an instinctive response to want to be the protective male. Sadly, however hard a little boy tries he is only a little boy. Witnessing his mother's grief can be extremely traumatic, as it only underlines for a boy that he can't be his father. Many boys talk of feeling overwhelmed at having to care for their mum, as they have few resources.

The way any subsequent relationship unfolds can also have a dramatic impact on boys as well as girls. Teen forums constantly talk about the anguish of living in unhappy step-parenting situations. 'Since my mom moved in with her boyfriend I hated him, so I ignored them whenever I had the chance,' admits Charlie B, 'but this last two years have been the toughest in my life, they had big fights like every month or week for any matter, this week they broke off and he left with everythin,' adding helplessly, 'now she's thinking of forgiving him and bringing him back in.' Charlie goes on to weigh up his options, but realises he has nowhere to go.[3]

After taking on the role of protector, whether asked or not, if his mother does end up with another partner, often a boy's heart is broken, because he assumes his mum doesn't need him any more. Mothers have a right to move on, but they need to do so with great sensitivity, because boys don't have a lifetime's experiences to help them deal with this new situation. Boys are just as vulnerable as girls at this time. And even if they're teenagers they're still young, and have the added pressure of trying to deal with their own emerging sexuality. So, where there is a new partner, boys need to know they're not being replaced, and that their mother still needs and loves them. This is an aspect of a boy's relationship with his mother most of us are unaware of. When we can take account of their love and protectiveness towards their mothers, we can save everyone a lot of angst. One-on-one time is a great way for mums to demonstrate they still care, as is continuing to stay close and to take an interest in a boy's passions.

GOALS

The journey towards becoming a man can be confusing, with the changing roles of men and women, and the rapidly changing world we live in. In amongst all this change are young boys with fledgling visions for their lives. Mothers have an important role to play in being a good sounding board for these ideas. Many boys prefer to talk with their mums about their dreams. 'I talk to my mum about my goals, about wanting to go somewhere, because I know she'll make it happen,' Harrison, 15, told me. 'She's level-headed and gives me support.' Robert, 17, agrees, 'You're more likely to confide your dreams to your mother.' Or as Mark, 10, puts it. 'If you have a dream you talk to your mum, as she likes listening to them.' So, in the midst of all the worries mothers have about their boys, they must never doubt their importance.

'Mum helps give my dreams wings.' *Harrison, 15*

A word on mothers:
- *You are very important to your son's life. Sons do, however, need space.*
- *A mother who provides a welcoming home for her son warms his life.*

- *Don't ever underestimate your son's emotional potential.*
- *You have a major role to play in helping him express his emotions.*
- *Tread gently should your relationship break down or a new relationship emerge.*
- *Set aside time for one-on-one moments.*
- *Learn to listen to what is not said as much as what is said.*

Why boys love their computers

In a short space of time the net has become central to teen life, and offers boys a wealth of possibilities. It's where they go to socialise, talk about their problems, chill out, perform, look for new friends, get answers, and keep up with celebrities and music and sports icons. When kids go into cyberspace they enter a vast, unchartered terrain, where every kind of material imaginable is available. There are an estimated 150 million users of Facebook, and Google now hosts 3 billion searches every month. MySpace now has an estimated 106 million registered users; were it a nation, it would be one of the largest countries on earth.[1]

'Technology and the internet are great advantages for our generation. There's lots more knowledge, individuality and freedom of thought.' *Hunter, 18*

At the click of a mouse boys can access a world of information, connect with other kids across the globe, and try their hands at a whole range of things from composing music and designing their own graphics to putting together a digital scrapbook. Callum, 10, told me he likes to make little movies. 'I get Lego people and move them around. You can't see your hands or anything. It's done the same way they do Wallace and Gromit.' These and many other aspects of the internet present wonderful opportunities for boys.

'It's a lot more fun doing computer things than non-computer things, like doing stuff with the family.' *Ashton, 12*

PARENTS ARE LEFT BEHIND, AND KIDS KNOW IT

Naturally parents need to keep abreast of their son's internet activity, but it's also important not to be endlessly negative about it. Boys get very frustrated with their parents constantly wondering what they're up to, and it's a world that's left some parents behind, boys don't feel there's much they can share about their online experiences. Most parents only have basic computer skills, and little idea of the huge influence online communities have on how their boys think, feel and behave. Every time a parent bumbles around on their computer, it simply confirms for their kids that their parents are talking a completely different language, giving them little reason to be open.

The net gives boys new freedoms. Previous generations had to rely on adults for their knowledge. While this wasn't always ideal, it enabled parents to be gatekeepers, and helped them frame the information they passed on to their kids. Now boys have access to material their parents have no concept of, which is why in part this new world is so seductive. If a parent chooses not to talk to their boys about certain subjects, they simply go on the net. There are no guarantees this material is correct, appropriate or helpful. As Ray Wood, the father of a cyber whiz kid, points out, 'Cyberspace is like the Wild West, with no rules or laws.'[2] Parents are increasingly bypassed, which is cause for concern, especially if a boy is feeling suicidal or decides his only hope is to share his feelings on an online teen forum. There are times when teen forums can really

146

help, but difficult issues often need greater life experience or expert assistance. Or he may be confused about his sexuality and begin cruising porn sites for answers, ending up in questionable areas.

'Older people didn't have the internet and stuff growing up. But it's what we know. It's our generation interacting with our environment.' *Gary, 17*

THERE'S A BIG VIRTUAL WORLD OUT THERE

In part it's the immensity of cyberspace that appeals to boys. The problem is that often boys take all the information they access on the net as fact. This is a concern for many professionals, as there's little room for problem-solving or critical thinking. As neuroscientist Susan Greenfield points out, knowing a handful of facts isn't the same as building up a body of knowledge and understanding how different pieces of information relate to each other. Greenfield fears that today's kids may end up drowning in information, because they haven't sufficient life experience to know which information to take note of. She also challenges us to think about what this new generation will be like as adults, having been brought up on 'the same software with the same images' as each other.

'The huge thing about this technology is that it's passive.'
Siobhan, high-school teacher

SOCIAL NETWORKING

There are many reasons why computers appeal to boys. They love chatting online, possibly because it's 'safer' and less emotionally demanding than face-to-face encounters. However, this new world is not without its pressures. When you talk with boys about social networking, you sense their very real need to stay in touch around the clock. They are well aware that if they don't keep up-to-date with peers they risk 'social suicide'.

'I don't think parents realise how much change there's been since the way they were used to doing things,' said Aidan, 22. 'It's things like not understanding how important having the internet is, that is frustrating. It's a social thing. Kids find it hard trying to convince parents to get on the internet, because social interests are organised on Facebook. If you don't check your Facebook account, you miss out on social events.'

'I like having that access to communicating with friends over the phone and internet. Sometimes it's an anxiety if you don't have access because you've got so accustomed to being able to easily communicate.' *Mark, 15*

The internet, along with mobile phones, is now central to a boy's sense of belonging. Today's teens are as likely to hang out in their cyber community as they are face-to-face. Parents need to understand this and help them find new ways of connecting, by encouraging different friend-ship groups and interests. If parents don't tackle this issue, they're likely to face constant standoffs about time spent on the computer. Certainly the boys I spoke with who have rich and varied lives spent far less time on the computer than those who didn't. As Dr Timothy Hawkes of Kings School puts it, 'We need to teach boys the glory of the off button, that reality has more to offer than virtual reality.'

ADDICTED

The simple fact is that the more time boys spend on computers, the more addicted they can become. 'I'm addicted to the Facebook world,' says Joel, 19. 'I jumped from Bebo to MySpace to Facebook. When I was on holiday, I wasted all my credit going on Facebook on my phone, because I had no internet connection.' Ashton, 12, agrees. 'I do spend a lot of time on the computer. It might keep me up late because I'm so into it. I can't pull my mind away from it. I kind of lose track of time. It is a bit addictive.'

'People do spend hours on MSN. I'm trying to spend less time.'
Daryl, 17

This can create tensions in the home when everyone is held hostage to a boy's moods and routine. A number of parents spoke of how difficult family life had become as a result. 'We've had a real job trying to keep my son away from his Game Boy, Nintendo and things,' admits John, whose son is always on his computer. 'If we tried to limit him he'd ask if he could go over to see a friend, and we know it was just to get on to his computer. The thing I noticed was if he'd played for hours and didn't win, he'd come out of his room and he'd be so angry and cranky.'

'When I talk on MSN I have music on, I'm looking on eBay, and I have a game up in the background.' *Flynn, 16*

It's staggering to see how much time some boys spend on the net. It's estimated that the average MySpace page is visited thirty times a day.[3] Talking with boys about their computer habits gives some useful insights into their obsession with new technology. 'Yeah, we're definitely addicted to computers,' said Aidan, 22. 'I know a few people spending twelve to sixteen hours playing games.' A number of boys admitted to feeling agitated if they're away from the computer for too long. 'My internet was down for a couple of days,' admits Joel, 19. 'I was pulling my hair out. I kept thinking I could be on the internet talking to people, organising things to do. I've become very reliant on my computer.'

'My concern is to get my boy outside away from the computer, the XBox, the PlayStation. Their bodies are growing and yet they're just sitting there on their bums.' *Martin, father of Brad, 9*

LACK OF READING

The struggle to get some boys to read is nothing new, but the prolonged use of computers doesn't help. A number of teachers expressed concern at how much time on computers is eroding this vital life skill. 'Kids access information from Google and YouTube and things, but they don't do sustained reading,' explained one high-school teacher. 'Or they may be very capable at gaming, but again there's little reading there. Reading is integral to being able to do their classes in high school. Even in maths they need to understand the questions being asked of them. Boys tend to take shortcuts so they don't have to read. And if they can't read we then see a lot of discipline issues and acting out in class.' Again, reading to boys from when they are small encourages them to make books and reading part of their lives.

ADHD AND AUTISM

Other concerns are emerging about possible links between the time children spend on computers, and ADHD and autism. According to psychologist Sally-Anne McCormack, an expert in childhood and teenage depression, half the clients she sees are addicted to their computers. She is concerned that those unable to shake their addiction may be vulnerable to Asperger's syndrome, a form of autism, where kids show no interest in social interaction with others.[4] While we need more research in this area, what we do know is that more boys than girls suffer from these disorders, and that those with autism are often very comfortable with computers, so there may well be a link. There are also concerns around possible links between ADHD and the massive over-stimulation our kids face, largely from time spent on their computers and with other gizmos, which affect their behaviour and ability to concentrate.

NARROW WORLD

While many boys wouldn't want to live without their computers, they readily admit to how much time they waste online. 'It can lead to distractions if you're on the internet all the time,' explains Joel, 19. The more time boys are holed up in their bedrooms, the less time they have for real life. More than one expert has questioned whether our kids are becoming like battery hens due to time spent in their bedrooms. The immense fear of predators and concerns about keeping kids safe doesn't help, because parents naturally want to keep their boys close. Some boys were wistful about how contained their lives had become. 'I would much rather have adventures outside, rather than sitting at home talking on the internet,' Mark, 15, told me. 'We've become a bit more restricted being indoors.'

FRIENDSHIPS

In a few short years texting and the internet have transformed the nature of teen friendship. Now kids are constantly in touch, they have the opportunity to connect in ways that weren't previously possible. Yet as these encounters are short, frequent and rapid, this does not encourage the opportunity to experience the many textures of friendships in greater depth – putting yourself out for someone, being there when times get tough, negotiating differences and so on. 'The whole internet communication thing can become a disadvantage, as it's always going to result in some sort of gossip over the internet, or hatred, or something like that as a result of communicating not in person,' said Mark, 15. Teen friendships have always been intense, and are now more so, as kids immerse themselves in the minute details of each other's lives, but with the anxieties around popularity and appearance and round-the-clock networking, it can compromise more meaningful interactions.

The dynamics between friends seems to change almost as fast as their communications. Mark told me, 'Gossiping and fights are constant, and it's not a good thing. Relationships are always up and down, being broken and restored over the internet. You're thinking of other people differently all the time, because of things you've heard, and what you're talking about on the internet. That's always changing your emotions.'

'It's almost like we have to teach people again about the value of friendship,' *John Lenarcic, RMIT School of Business*[5]

There are concerns amongst professionals that popularity is being mistaken for friendship. When you talk to boys about their online friendships they will often tell you they have friends all over the world. But when you dig a little deeper, they admit these are acquaintances at best. Living in a virtual world encourages boys to avoid the messy aspects of relationships, which are often best tackled face-to-face. Whether it's sorting out differences or bringing a friendship to a close, firing off a nasty email, or dumping someone by text, it doesn't help boys learn how to get on with others. Real-life friendships are complex and demanding. But, hopefully, through real interactions we learn to genuinely be there for our friends, to handle difficult situations, be considerate and cut others some slack. There are many wonderful opportunities computers offer our boys as long as they don't overtake the rest of their lives.

Help your son balance out his computer time in the following ways:

- *Take an interest in what your son is doing on the computer.*
- *Be aware of your own computer habits.*
- *Encourage him to be the family's online tutor.*
- *Agree on time limits and stick to them.*
- *Balance out computer time with other activities.*
- *Be creative about ways to make real life as appealing as virtual life.*
- *Look at www.webwisekids.org, where there is an interactive game, It's Your Call, that addresses the consequences of choices kids may make on the net.*
- *Also investigate http://isafe.org and www.wiredsafety.org*

Not enough sleep

One of the side effects of the time boys spend on their computers is sleeplessness. Often this is made worse by the overstimulation they experience online. Most boys I spoke with had several screens open at the same time. 'I have six or seven things going on at once,' explains Joel, 19. 'But I also have my TV screen on and my laptop and my desktop going on all at once, so there's a lot of things to look at.' Jacob, 17, is also on his computer for hours with a number of screens on the go. 'While I'm online I have MSN running most of the time, even when doing some schoolwork. If I'm not on MSN, I'll have some music playing and a web-site game running, and MySpace open as well.'

> 'I have anything up to eight screens open at once. I like the conversations on MSN, Facebook and MySpace, browsing photos and stuff.' Jonathan, 16

OVERSTIMULATED

As well as less time for exercise and other activities, many boys are on their computers until late at night so there's no time to 'come down' from the constant barrage of sound, information and graphics. This in turn can make it almost impossible for boys to sleep. 'Time on my computer is leading to real issues around sleep,' admits Mark, 15. 'I've sort of developed a new body clock really over the last couple of years, just because the schoolwork piles on, and I always want to go on the computer. On school nights I get to bed at 11.30 or midnight. I wake up tired, but if I go to bed earlier I wake up even more tired.' Even those who can get off to sleep often don't get a restful sleep, as many still have their mobile phones on. Unless parents intervene, boys will take calls and texts regardless of the time, and end up with fractured sleep.

> **'A lot of people in my school get to bed late, like the earliest is around 11.30 p.m. Some stay up to 2 a.m. talking on MSN, watching TV and stuff like that.'** *Flynn, 16*

According to experts, teenagers' lack of sleep is becoming acute. 'They're building up huge, huge sleep debts, night after night,' says Mary Carskadon, professor of psychiatry and human behaviour at Brown University in the United States.[1] Many teenagers compensate for the crazy hours they keep during the week by sleeping in at the weekend. While this helps make up their sleep debt, it confuses the body about when it's meant to be sleeping, making it even harder to sleep at night.

BROKEN SLEEP

When you talk with boys about sleeplessness, you begin to see how acute the situation can be. 'Sleeping is a major issue I think I need to fix up,' says Joel, 19. 'I don't know quite what I'm going to do, I just can't get to sleep. I'll be tired and I'll lie there, everything off, and I still can't sleep. On a very bad night it's four and five, and I'm still awake. A good night will be one o'clock I'm in bed. I always find that, like, in the afternoon I need to have a nap, but I refuse to have one because

I know that it will affect my sleep later on that evening. Usually by that point I've got my second wind and I end up staying up to five or something. Getting up any later than two o'clock I feel like I've wasted the day, but about twelve o'clock I think it's like personally my perfect time to wake up.'

'Sometimes I really can't get what I've been doing on the computer out of my mind, and sometimes it's hard to sleep.' *Ashton, 12*

Even though he suffers from constant fatigue, like many of his peers, Joel isn't about to change his habits any time soon. 'I know a lot of people do have sleeping problems because they get distracted, because they've got so many things happening. But the idea of going to bed at, like, ten o'clock is early. It's like, "Why am I going to bed at ten o'clock, I could be up talking to people on the internet, playing computer games and whatnot?"' Flynn, 16, is no stranger to insomnia either. 'Yeah, all this stuff on the computer does affect my sleep. It is hard to sleep, because you're thinking about a lot of stuff. Sometimes I hop into bed and I get thinking. There's all this stuff going around in my head, and it can take one to two hours sometimes to get to sleep.'

THE FALLOUT
According to sleep expert Dr Arthur Teng, teens need nine to ten hours sleep per night to function well. Neer Korn of Heartbeat Trends also points out that it's in the hours between 10 p.m. and 1 a.m. that kids do most of their social networking,[2] creating what Dr Teng calls a 'sleep deprivation epidemic'. So a boy's bedroom isn't necessarily a restful place to be. There are some very real short- and long-term consequences for teenagers suffering prolonged sleep deprivation, from an inability to concentrate to disruptive behaviour.[3] There are also links between sleep issues and early-onset diabetes.[4] Further down the track, boys may

also end up suffering heart disease, memory problems or hypertension if they don't get into good sleep habits.

'Teenagers like to sleep in to four o'clock in the afternoon, and that's when the day begins.' *Joel, 19*

Good regimes are essential for computer and mobile phone use, because once boys get into the pattern of sleeplessness they can find it very hard to shake. 'Most people my age have problems going to bed,' said Aidan, 22. 'When I was younger I was worse. I'd stay up till 4 a.m. A lot of others would stay up till then. It didn't make that much of a difference. It wouldn't be an everyday thing. I wouldn't do it again for another couple of days.'

MAKING CHANGES

Experts stress that teens need nine to ten hours sleep a night. For a lot of kids, reversing sleeplessness is not just about switching off their computers. They also lead busy, often pressured lives, with mountains of homework. Many teens enjoy staying up late and don't want to miss out on what their friends are doing. Parents need to model and encourage good sleep patterns, and to have firm rules about the amount of time spent on computers. Placing mobile phones in a central location each night is a good habit to get into. Recent research suggests that the brightness of computer screens affects the body's melatonin levels, which regulates sleep and wakefulness, making kids wide awake when they should be feeling sleepy. One study at the Akita University School of Medicine in Japan, for example, showed a significant drop in melatonin levels in those working in front of a bright screen, as well as those playing video games or working before bed.[5] Bright Light Therapy is now used with teens unable to sleep, as it helps regulate their melatonin production. The treatment focuses on avoiding bright light exposure, such as computer screens, before bed and exposure to bright light on waking. This way the body clock is readjusted and starts shutting down in the evening in readiness for sleep. After a good night's sleep, participants feel rested on waking and ready to start the day. When used with a regular sleeping and waking regime, Bright Light Therapy appears to be quite effective at reversing sleeplessness issues.

Help your son to get into a good sleep routine:

- *Have a chill-out regime in the home before bed, when TVs and computers are off.*
- *Encourage your son to avoid using the computer for at least half an hour before bedtime.*
- *Catch-up sleep at the weekend won't reverse sleep problems; regular bedtime hours do.*
- *Help your son get into a pattern of waking at the same time each day.*
- *If problems persist, see a doctor.*

The weird world of cyberspace

As we've seen, the net is very appealing to boys because it offers them endless worlds to explore. And there's the added attraction that in cyberspace boys can be anyone they want to be. Having a second, secret identity is very attractive to teenage boys still coming to terms with who they are and where they belong. There's been a lot of coverage about adult predators posing as kids on the net, and for good reason. But boys also need to realise that it's not only adults who groom teenagers for sex and other activities; increasingly, so too do kids their own age. Cyberspace does give boys the chance to indulge their fantasies. While some of this is quite innocent, this approach can lead a boy into some very dark places. *All* strangers on the net must be treated with caution. Boys need to be wary of the gifts or other incentives cyber-friends may offer.

Boys also need to realise that it's not only adults who groom teenagers for sex and other activities; increasingly so too do kids their own age.

GROOMED TO MURDER

One of the most bizarre online scenarios in recent years involved a 14-year-old in England, 'John', who met 'Mark', 16, on the net. The schoolboys soon became friends. On the surface there was nothing out of the ordinary. However, depressed and confused, John had retreated into a fantasy world. Drawing on scenarios in the James Bond movies and *Men in Black* and *Catch Me If You Can*, John dreamt up eight different online personas, including a mysterious middle-aged female British MI6 agent. Unaware that these different online characters were all his friend John, Mark found himself drawn into an increasingly complex world.

> Cyberspace does give boys the chance to indulge their fantasies, but this can lead to some very dark places.

As their relationship grew, John pretended he had a brain tumour and only days to live, and persuaded Mark to perform a mercy killing. He gave Mark precise instructions about how and where to carry out this hit. If Mark delivered, he was to become a member of the British secret service, receive a substantial cash payment, and have sex with the alluring MI6 female agent he'd met online. He was also to meet Tony Blair, and be given a gun.

In their last internet exchange Mark asked, 'U want me 2 take him 2 trafford made plans centre and kill him in the middle of Trafford centre?' Having got the go-ahead, Mark set off to complete his mission. Following his instructions, Mark met John in an alleyway and stabbed him with a six-inch knife in the chest and stomach. Even though he'd meticulously planned his own murder, John survived.

When the authorities discovered Mark had carried out the stabbing, John said he'd no idea why Mark had done this. Fortunately for Mark, their internet exchanges were retrieved, and John's web of deceit was revealed. Summing up the case, Judge David Maddison commented that, 'Skilled writers of fiction would struggle to conjure up a plot such as that which arises here.' The conditions laid down at sentencing stated that the two boys are never to meet again. John is only allowed to access the internet or to enter chat rooms with adult supervision.[2]

ANOTHER WORLD

While it's concerning to read of such cases, it helps parents see just how different a teenager's life can be from their own. As boys have almost unlimited access to others on the net, and to material not previously available to them, parents need to be aware of the scenarios their boys may be exposed to. When you enter cyber safety sites you see some of the heart-breaking situations parents find themselves in, as this mother tells: 'My 14yr old son has been "groomed" for last 6 months by a 16yr old with whom he blogs, has "fell in Love". Just found out by reading his MSN. I am really worried. Havnt told son that I know yet. He has talked on line about running away with him, or will "Die" if he is separated . . . He is very vulnerable and dependent on this person who threatens to commit suicide if he breaks contact.'[3] As well as protecting boys, parents also need to know how to deal with the increasingly complex issues the net creates. While some parents resort to spyware, it can never take the place of respect, and relaxed and open discussion of such issues. Keeping the lines of communication open and talking about the kinds of emotional blackmail and grooming that can happen helps boys to be forewarned. Where a boy has been exploited, he is likely to be extremely fragile. In such situations professional help must be sought.

IDENTITY THEFT

As kids become ever more sophisticated users of the internet, they find new ways to test their skills and boundaries. A growing number of teens are now finding their Facebook or MySpace content altered, often with inappropriate photos and comments. Sometimes this sabotage is by peers, sometimes by cyberspace creeps. You don't have to go far on the net to come across their victims. 'Hey somebody has taken over my Bebo account by hacking into my email address,' says Kev. 'They have changed the password and changed the email address associated with the account to their own email address . . . They have started posting rude messages to my friends everyone in my school thinks this is really me doing all of this and even my parents have seen the account. I would be really grateful if anyone can help me get this account deleted.'[4]

To have something that belongs to you appropriated is upsetting, but to be represented in such misleading and graphic ways to the world can cause boys great distress, as Flash25 explains: 'Recently discover a profile that someone has make using my pics and myspace i have reported it but nothing has been done . . . this is very upsetting and honestly to god am tired of all the harassment, i feel like just ending my life to get rid of all this humilation.'[5] As teenagers' online profiles are central to their lives, parents need to be sensitive to the level of hurt their boys may feel when they have been misrepresented.

PREDATORS AND PERVERTS

The instant familiarity new technology offers can leave kids vulnerable in ways previous generations never had to deal with. Those seeking to groom boys will cruise chat rooms and infiltrate teen forums, and anywhere else they can contact boys directly. The police who work undercover on the net use the same approach as sexual predators, posing as teens so as to catch online predators, who immerse themselves in teen culture so they get the language and detail of teen life right. Those seeking to groom boys use many clever ploys, from listening and sympathising with a boy's problems to flattery and the offer of gifts. In one study six out of ten teens interviewed had received an instant message or email from a stranger. Half the kids had contacted a stranger by the same means. Less than a quarter were concerned by this.[6]

DIRTY LITTLE SECRETS

Chat rooms and virtual worlds are wonderful escapes for boys from everyday life, but they're also perfect places for predators to hang out. Many boys now test their boundaries on the net. So, while certain websites are age-restricted, a boy doesn't have to be a genius to work out the age he's meant to be to gain entry. In one survey a quarter of the boys interviewed lied about their age to access restricted websites, many of which were pornographic.[7] In this same study parents talked about limiting their teen's access to the net. Yet few of the surveyed teens felt restricted on the net, possibly because there are so many ways boys can access inappropriate material beyond the family computer.

In the fantasy and science fiction online games MUDs (multiple user dungeon virtual games) and MMORPGs (massively multiple player online role-playing games) such as Rune Scape, there are opportunities for boys to take part in virtual sex, also known as cybering or mudsex. Their avatars (their online personas) are able to move around and simulate sex with other consenting avatars. Those in the know can also hijack someone else's avatars and use them in violent or sexual ways.

In virtual worlds such as Second Life, there are thousands of 'sex workers' willing to perform virtual sex for Lindens (Second Life currency), or for real money, while other sites such as RedLightCenter offer virtual sex.[8] As well as YouTube, for those in the know there are also the endless video clips of live sex. Some videos are professional, many homemade. While the content of some sites is free, others charge per view. Then, of course, there's text-based sex, available by mobile or email. And, with the introduction of webcams, people can perform live sexual acts for each other in real time. Boys are naturally curious about sex, and where there's little outlet for them to learn more, the internet often fills in the gaps. With the breakdown of family and community, often boys spend a lot of time on their own. The net is one way they can overcome their loneliness and shyness. This isn't necessarily a bad thing; it just depends where they spend their time in cyberspace.

HACKERS AND CRACKERS

Some thrill-seeking boys prefer the excitement of hacking into other people's websites to real-life adventure. In New York a 15-year-old boy caused havoc when he found his way into his school's computer network, accessing private security details of staff.[9] Mentored by a 20-year-old hacker, another 15-year-old boy from Michigan found his way into the websites of NASA's Goddard Space Flight Center and its Jet Propulsion Laboratory.[10] Although he didn't access sensitive information, the police found 76 000 passwords on his computer.[11]

Some boys are brilliant on computers. They get into this kind of crime because they're tech-savvy and looking for adventure. Some boys are recruited by cyber gangs. Once in these gangs, kids work together and compete with each other as to what they can pull off. While most kids don't have criminal intent, they can cause real problems and end up with hefty fines, if not jail sentences. Some kids are bent on being destructive. Over a three-year-period one Massachusetts hacker, known as Dshocker, made a number of bomb threats, was involved in credit card fraud and found his way into a number of corporate networks. He was only 17.[12]

There are plenty of tech-savvy boys out there. It took 16-year-old Tom Wood only thirty minutes to crack the Australian Federal government's $84 million porn filter. Tom Wood was hired by the government to see just how effective their porn filter was. Like Tom, more boys need constructive ways to express their interest in technology and be recognised for it. There are dozens of community organisations that could benefit from their expertise. By inviting these boys to assist these groups we give them a much-needed sense of belonging and acknowledgement, which could be honoured by a write-up in the local newspaper or formal award. How many more talented kids could use their talents in constructive ways and become great spokespeople for cyber-safety?

GAMBLING

Gambling is increasingly easier to access online, meaning that more teens are becoming compulsive gamblers. Poker is of particular concern, as virtual poker is readily available on the net, including such sites as Facebook. Experts dealing with gambling addictions are concerned with the way the game is now presented as just another sport. Programs such as *The World Series of Poker* are attracting more viewers: all players' hands are shown on camera and people can now join in the game at home.

> **'[Gambling] was everywhere. If friends weren't playing it, it was on TV. If it wasn't on TV, it was on the computer. If nobody is doing it, we're talking about it.'** *Dustin, teen gambler, now 20*[13]

Many teenagers addicted to gambling often say they started at around the age of 10. American research suggests that seven out of ten kids aged 10 to 17 have gambled, and that just under one in three of high school students do so regularly.[14] A recent local study by the Central Coast Problem Gambling Service revealed that 62 per cent of under-14s and 77 per cent of under-17s had taken part in gambling for money, or items such as MP3 players or mobile phones.[15] Parents of addicted teenagers speak of their despair at the ways operators constantly contact their kids by email with offers to play. Psychologist Wayne Warburton, who counsels those with gambling addictions, told of how some gambling operators are now also sending random SMS messages, offering free vouchers for online gambling.

This is a worrying trend, as studies suggest underage gamblers are three times more likely to become addicted to gambling. They are also more vulnerable to other risky behaviours. Of all teens suffering addiction they are most likely to commit suicide as well.[16] One New Zealand study of a thousand 18-year-olds also revealed gamblers had very similar personality traits and vulnerabilities as those suffering marijuana, nicotine and alcohol addictions. It's also important to note that where a boy is exposed to compulsive gambling in his family, he is more likely to go down the same route.[17]

When talking with parents struggling with teenage addiction you begin to see the battle they face. 'It is very insidious,' one mother told me. 'They contact them all the time by email, with messages like "Happiness is playing with real money." They're invited into poker tournaments for free, or to have free spins.'

The only way to protect boys on computers is to get up to speed with what's going on, and stay up to speed. While this material can be disturbing, it's important not to panic. Show an interest in the good stuff available on the net. When you can forewarn your son about the negative material he may encounter there, and how to handle it, he's in a far better place than if he has to find his own way.

Help protect your son online in the following ways:

- *Keep computers in a central place in the home.*
- *Join a teen chat room so you know what it's about.*
- *Make computer experiences part of family discussion.*
- *Take an interest in your son's online friends, as well as the rest of his friends.*
- *Take a look at Net Alert site, www.netalert.gov.au and Net Family News, www.netfamilynews.org/letterindex4.html.*
- *Ensure your son is aware of the risks he may face, and the potential for personal fallout.*
- *Be balanced in your discussions around the internet: it's not all bad.*

The secret lives of boys

The net is the perfect place for twenty-first-century boys to hang out, as it's global and available round the clock. Blogs, Twitter, Facebook, Friendster, 12Seconds, MySpace, Digg, Xanga, Flickr, Bebo and all the other online sites they're attracted to enable boys to check out what's hot; trade possessions; date; share photos, music and videos; get sports and entertainment news; shop; make short films; find material for assignments and much more. Way beyond the influence of parents, the internet offers teens new freedoms, including the opportunity to lead secret lives.

Teen lives are speedy and technology-focused, as computers allow them to stay connected with each other all the time. So, unlike adults, they don't distinguish between being on and off the net, texting or doing all the other things they do. Their lives are about communication. As they respond to each other almost instantly, there's little time to pause or reflect about what they say and do, so there's less caution. Teenagers live in the moment. Research suggests the more teens use the net, the less worried they are about its dangers.[1] Boys prefer to use these new technologies to communicate with friends, look for love, share personal information, tease or bully, and find out what they need to know. It's an exhilarating world with endless possibilities and dangers few could have foreseen.

NEW TECHNOLOGIES TRANSFORMING TEEN LIFE

Before we examine the secret lives of boys, it's important we understand why these new technologies mean so much to them. As teenage life is pressured, it's natural for boys to look for an escape. Cyberspace offers boys an infinite number of ways to do so. As they mature, boys are also looking for new experiences of intimacy and ways to belong. They want somewhere to express their concerns and frustrations, and explore new ideas. Social networking is the perfect channel for these needs. It enables boys to immerse themselves in the world of their peers. It also removes the awkwardness of face-to-face encounters. When you're texting, emailing or in a chat room, there are no worries about how you look or what you're wearing. And if you're not feeling good about who you are, you can be somebody completely different. As boys connect in real time, lose themselves in chat rooms and teen forums, send endless tweets and write blogs, it gives them the sense they're in charge of their world, especially as they can do so with little or no supervision.

> **'Parents are very oblivious about what is going on on the net.'**
> *Daryl, 17*

NO INHIBITIONS

With these new possibilities, it's easy for teens to drift away from family and real-life friends into a virtual world where little is as it seems. As boys don't have much life experience, they are not always well equipped to deal with the complexities of this online world. The speed with which relationships can get personal on the net, coupled with a boy's desire to be popular and make his mark, can make him vulnerable. And, having grown up in a world of celebrities behaving badly, reality TV and tell-all newspapers and magazines, it doesn't seem such a big deal for teenagers to reveal more than is wise.

Parents are right to be concerned about the lack of inhibitions many teenagers display on the net. Lured by a chance to be noticed, increasing numbers of teenagers are happy to post intimate photos and details. What they need to know is that it's routine now for prospective employers to conduct net searches before they offer candidates jobs. Many universities check out potential students on the net before awarding them a place. Journalist friends tell me they find Facebook and MySpace great sources of material, as there are so few inhibitions about how much is revealed on the net. It's important parents keep an eye on their son's online presence so they know how he's representing himself to the world. They need to ensure a boy isn't giving out details that might enable strangers to find out where he lives. The more open a relationship parents have with their son, the more these issues can be discussed, and helpful advice given, so a boy is prepared for the tricky situations he may encounter.

> Lured by a chance to be noticed, increasing numbers of teenagers are happy to post intimate photos and details. They need to know it's routine now for prospective employers to conduct net searches before they offer candidates jobs.

I CAN BE ANYTHING I WANT TO BE

Kids often have two or more online personas – one for their parents to see, and others for people they wish to attract. This offers them the chance to try out different selves. Sometimes this is harmless and exciting, sometimes not. In one major study of online teens, over half of those interviewed had more than one email address and screen name. Just under a quarter had secret online names that even their peers didn't know about.[2] Twenty-four per cent of kids had pretended to be someone else when instant messaging or emailing. A little under two-thirds of boys had a selection of online names and email addresses, which they used at different times, depending on whether they wanted to hang out with friends or be anonymous. Some disguised their identity and pretended to be a friend for a joke.[3] Again it helps if parents can discuss these possibilities and likely dangers with their boys so they're more aware of when they may be vulnerable.

> 'When life is overwhelming, computers are very attractive. They allow kids to build a whole fantasy world, to escape somewhere where they can be a different person with a different life. This is happening more and more.' *Bryan Duke, a father of five, who runs a regional juvenile mentoring scheme*

CHEATING MADE EASIER

There are many ways boys can get themselves in trouble on the net. The new technologies give kids more opportunities to cheat at their school-work. With a world of information at their fingertips, it's tempting to take shortcuts by cutting and pasting material from the net, then passing it off as their own. In one study by professor Don McCabe of Rutgers University, over half the students surveyed said they copied material straight off the internet. More than one in ten admitted to handing in assignments they'd downloaded directly from the net, without modifying them in any way.[4]

There are also a burgeoning number of sites that offer kids the opportunity to download assignments for a fee, or sometimes for free. Aware of this issue, an increasing number of schools are now using internet detection programs. Sometimes teens don't fully understand that unless they credit the material they take off the net they are cheating. And, at the end of the day, learning is about a whole lot more than cutting and pasting. Again it's important parents and teachers explain this to them, as the consequences can be devastating.

Keeping on top of cheats places extra pressure on teachers, as kids are now using mobile phones to get ahead. Even though phones are banned in tests and exams, teenagers are adept at concealing them, then consulting notes they have stored on their phones during exams. Other kids photograph test papers to share with friends sitting the same test later in the day. Texting also offers boys the opportunity to contact friends outside the exam for answers. And now most phones are internet-enabled, they can also Google facts. In a Benson Strategy Group poll of 13- to 18-year-olds, one in four teenagers didn't see there was anything wrong with accessing notes from their phone.[5]

REPUTATIONS MADE AND BROKEN

New levels and forms of intimacy are developing amongst teens. Giving access to a friend's usernames and password is an expression of closeness, as is the sharing of intimate photos. Like all forms of 'real life' intimacy, these gestures have their risks, and can leave teens extremely hurt. When relationships fail, friends have plenty of ammunition for payback. When explicit photos and texts are circulated, kids are shattered. They need to realise that they have to be careful about what they show people. Teenagers need to express their feelings for close friends, and parents play a big role in helping boys best express how much a friendship means.

WIDENING GAP BETWEEN GENERATIONS

The growing distance between boys and their parents is of concern, as it can cut boys off from the essential support and nurture families can give. One of the many reasons for this gap between generations is in the rise of a new teen language which has left parents and teachers out in the cold. Teenagers have always had their secrets – it's part of stretching their boundaries. Made up of hundreds of abbreviated words, codes and acronyms, kids can now talk to each other without fear of being heard or understood by parents. A boy can be texting right in front of his parents, and they will have no idea what he's saying. This wouldn't be so concerning were it not for the fact that with few boundaries and little sense of consequences, today's teens have a level of freedom they may not be ready for.

As popular culture encourages teens to go their own way, parents now have to fight to stay relevant. With the billions spent on marketing directly to teens, and a constant diet of celebrity news, teenagers have a new sense of belonging, where parents have little or nothing to contribute. Unless parents stay close to their teens, their boys can so easily become lost in the carefully crafted, ever-changing online world, constructed purely to make money out of them.

Even if a parent sees a text, they're unlikely to understand what it means. Few would know that 'HT HRU? MorF IRL? TMI LMIRL ADDY PAW CTN WYC' means 'Hi there, how are you? Male or female in real life? Too much information. Let's meet in real life. Address? Parents are watching. Can't talk now. Will you call me?' Parents can, however, go to www.urbandictionary.com, a comprehensive dictionary of popular culture expressions, if they need a translation. On this and similar sites they will also see how teen language reflects the growing lack of inhibitions in the culture at large.

'Those 3 special words every girl longs to hear, "You know i love you, you don't need to hear it again. Now Suck my cock."' *Ze 1*[6]

KEEPING TABS

While some of this online material is concerning, it's vital parents stay calm. Freaking out will only alienate their kids. Ongoing family discussions help educate boys and keep them safe. At the same time parents can't afford to be naïve. Just because a boy phones or texts to say he's at his friend's place doesn't mean that's where he is. Often parents are more casual about a boy's whereabouts than they would be about a girl's, because they assume boys can take care of themselves. But boys need protection too. Parents need to get to know a boy's friends and his friends' parents. It's vital parents also enlist the support of a boy's older brothers and sisters, and other young family members, as they also have an important role to play. Not infrequently it is siblings or cousins who introduce boys to inappropriate friends, help acquire drugs and alcohol, or supply them with a fake ID, because they think it's funny or cool.

'You cannot parent the most vulnerable generation of teenagers in our history via the mobile phone.' *Psychologist Michael Carr-Gregg, The Princess Bitchface Syndrome*[7]

Parents also need to get to know more about computers and the net, so they can have informed conversations with their boys. They need to teach their boys about boundaries and consequences. The parents who can bridge the gap are in a much better position to talk about these issues in a way that will engage their boys.

To protect your son:

- *Ensure he knows not to give out any personal details to strangers.*
- *Help him develop a script should he be exposed to material he's uncomfortable with when out with friends.*
- *Use spam filters and an internet provider which has filters.*
- *Openly discuss computer dangers raised in news and current affairs programs.*

Addicted to gaming

Time on the computer can give boys the sense of adventure and daring they crave, but it's a poor substitute for real-life adventure and exploration. 'When Brad was five he came home to tell me he'd been playing *Grand Theft Auto*. I didn't think much about it at the time,' his father Martin explains. 'But then when you look at these games and see boys riding around LA stealing cars and killing people, you have to ask yourself what that's about. The war games are worse. Boys are meant to kill all these people. There's blood and everything. They're quite horrifying. I try to ban these games, but they sneak in.'

'Mindless violence with an awesome storyline and lots of shooting/ fighting gets my vote.' *Mr_Korean, Level 21, Rescue Ranger*[1]

The profits from successful games are huge. In 2007 alone they reaped an estimated US$62 billion.[2] When *Grand Theft Auto IV* was launched recently it achieved sales of US$500 million in its first week.[3] The challenge the game sets is for boys to progress as far as they can in the world of organised crime. To do this they need to commit a whole range of

173

crimes from assassinations and killing cops to prostitution. In one game there's even a drink-and-drive feature.[4] In the Microsoft and console versions of the *San Andreas* game there's a sex mini-game, the 'hot coffee mod', where players can have sex with their online girlfriend.[5]

'*Grand Theft Auto: San Andreas* contains a hack that allows you to have sex with willing females. Nice.' *Cmdr_Zorg*[6]

ESCAPE FROM THE REAL WORLD

When they're playing video games boys get the chance to be everything they're not in real life – powerful and in charge. These games allow them to immerse themselves in rich and exciting fantasies of power and combat. Here boys are encouraged to play to the death. These games are engrossing. Research suggests many boys play up to thirteen hours a week.[7] According to Harry, 14, 'Boredom is the big attraction. It's something to do . . . something fun to do.'

When you listen to the excitement in boys' voices when talking about gaming, it's no surprise to learn that in the United States sales of video games outstripped that of music sales in 2008.[8] 'I love gaming,' says Jacob, 17. 'It's an escape thing. It's so unrealistic, but it's fun. I like the adventure and role-playing, going on missions and stuff. There's a real feel of satisfaction winning points and medals. There's also the bragging rights with mates who have the same game. I probably spend around six hours a week on it.'

'Whatever happened to the noble art of beating the crap out of someone with your bare knuckles, eh? Or battering them with a swift succession of uppercuts to the jaw?'[9]

One of the reasons boys love the games is that they provide an adrenaline fix in a world where there are few opportunities to experience this level of excitement. As Richard Aston from the Big Buddy Project points out, 'Boys have needed heroes from time immemorial. Heroes represent something deep they want to be.' These games help boys experience what it's like to be heroic. The problem is that gaming heroes are one-dimensional figures, whose only solution to problems is to obliterate them. Boys would be better served to have heroes able to deal with the complex emotional and social challenges they will face as adults.

VIOLENT WORLD

While gaming gives boys an action-packed experience, there's no getting away from the violence. 'What concerns me about the gaming is the detail boys are subjected to,' says teacher and founder of The Rite Journey, Andrew Lines. 'It's almost an education in killing – choosing weapons – learning how to mount surprise attacks. It's frightening.' Boys do need to test their limits, be adventurous and know what they're capable of. It's just a pity they have to go online to experience this. Our growing use of violence to entertain boys is highly questionable. 'The experience of war is really attractive,' says Flynn, 16. 'Like, the thought of shooting people. It does make you feel powerful.' The physical violence in games isn't the only concern. In some games there's also a sadistic twist when dealing with foes. 'You'll have at least four opportunities in the first hour of game play to fight with knives,' explains Chris, reviewing the Red Steel Hands-On game. 'Plenty of chances to practice the noble art of beating the living crap out of a guy, then letting him live so you can earn Respect points and become a kinder, gentler yakuza murderer.'[10]

RECRUITMENT

Not all gaming is bad, but it can be used to manipulate boys. A number of armed forces from different countries, notably the United States, have got into the gaming scene, as this is an excellent way to expose boys to warfare and ultimately to recruit them. Recently the US Army announced it would be spending $50 million on video games for recruitment and soldier training. Now several years old, America's Army has won several awards and attracted several million players. When a boy logs on, he can download the game, read *America's Army* graphic novels, scan the Real Hero Blog, and more. Or he can cut to the chase and consider recruitment in 'the strongest force in the world'.

A CHANCE TO SOCIALISE

One of the attractions of these games is that boys can make new friends and team up with other boys interested in the game. 'At school we talk a lot about computers, about the shooting type games,' Flynn, 16, told me. 'They're the most popular games.' Terry, a childcare worker who supervises boys aged 7 and 8, agrees. 'There's a whole online culture for boys with games tuning into chat, creating characters, adjusting the skills of their characters, joining other teams.'

'I like playing games because they're cool,' admits Mark, 10. 'Boys like racing games and fighting games. I enjoy playing with others racing and fighting. Sometimes it makes me stay up late at night.' Tommy, 12, also finds gaming compelling. 'I'm playing World of Warcraft. You can meet up with friends, conquer things. It's quite a social game. It's an amazing game with limitless possibilities, but it is addictive.' While gaming may provide a social outlet for boys, these games are not necessarily strengthening a boy's social skills. Certainly these attitudes to girls and women are questionable at best. In Grand Theft Auto players are rewarded for having sex with prostitutes and for killing them.

A WHOLE OTHER WORLD

There's no doubt gaming provides boys with a high-action alternative to their everyday lives. In this virtual world, over time they develop new hierarchies amongst those they play with. 'It's an extreme microcosm of real life,' explains Mick, a childcare worker. 'As there's no cultural norms interfering they get to do things they'd like to do, but can't in life. They build teams, agree on a hierarchy. After a while you've leaders who take over, and newbies who play a weaker role. The leaders lead them into battle. They can be ruthless and chew them up, but they can also be friendly.'

'Welcome to the future where anything, absolutely anything goes . . . If you got the guts to do it.'[11]

PROCESSING EMOTIONS

There's no doubt that for many boys video games are a way of processing their feelings, enabling them to take out their aggression on an onscreen foe. Robin, who has a teenage son, feels that this can be valuable. 'Boys need ways to regulate their emotions. Perhaps the XBox is their way of processing.' Martin, also a father, isn't so sure. 'Video games desensitise boys, because they're too young to understand what they represent. They're taking advantage of young men at a very vulnerable time of their lives.'

'It can be a good way of letting go of all the frustration by killing someone – the pressures of school work and stuff.' *Flynn, 16*

Kath, a primary-school principal with two sons, can see the value of games. 'Gaming does have a valid appeal for boys. They can do some risky things in a safe environment.' The boys themselves do enjoy this outlet. 'On a weekday I'd spend one to two hours playing games, and about four hours a day at the weekend,' said Tommy, 12. 'I guess they're gruesome, violent and bloody. But games give you freedom to express your emotions through shooting and things. You can let go of a lot of anger by blasting things. You do get pretty immersed in it, and you do lose track of time.'

SOMETHING TO ACHIEVE

One of the things boys love about gaming is that it gives them a sense of fulfilment, as they have to work hard to get each new game under their belt. 'I spend a lot of time at home in my room doing homework and playing games,' explains Flynn, 16. 'When I get a new game I spend a lot of time trying to conquer it, to be the best at it.' For Col, 19, it's the thrill of the new challenge in a game he likes best of all. 'The games are fun. They're something to do. They do get addictive in the beginning, but after a while they get easy, then you get bored.'

Many games are designed to push the envelope to keep boys playing. 'When I've got a bit of time I get into things like Rollercoaster Tycoon,' says Tim, 17. 'You can only get to the next level if you have finished certain scenarios. Because you can't save the game part-way through, it keeps me up.'

RELAXATION AND STRESS

With the increasingly pressured lives boys lead, the games do seem to provide a chance to switch off. 'I enjoy going online and playing games like Age of Empires, Counter-Strike and Rune Scape. It's a way to wind down after school,' Luca, 15, told me. 'In a way it's quite pointless, but I enjoy talking to people and getting my character to the next level. I enjoy the whole concept. It relates to real life, but goes much faster.' Jacob, 17, agrees. 'I do play for relaxation. I walk away feeling better. It is a distraction and can take away any feelings of frustration.' But in the same breath he talks of the heightened stress he experiences during high-action games. 'It's not really effective as stress relief though. The games create high-pressure situations. So while you're not there, you get the feeling that you're there.' One recent Stockholm University study bears this out. A group of boys aged 12 to 15 had their hearts monitored while playing two different games at home. The greatest variations in their heart rate were found when these boys were playing the most violent games. Interestingly these variations in their heart rate continued even when they slept.[12]

So what, if any, are the effects of violent video games on boys? A wide range of professional bodies from the Australian College of Paediatrics and the American Psychological Association to the Ontario Office for Victims of Crime state there are clear links between boys playing these games and violent behaviour. Craig Anderson, an international expert in violent video games and professor of psychology at Iowa University points out that gaming is not a passive pursuit. To play the role of aggressor, boys must become psychologically and emotionally engaged with the game while choosing their weapons and considering how best to harm their victims. 'Active participation increases learning,' says Craig Anderson, 'Repetition increases learning.' A boy's exposure to violent subjects does affect his beliefs and attitudes, creating aggressive thoughts, an aggressive outlook and a decline in empathy towards others.[13] The consolidation of these negative patterns happens from age 8 or 9 up.[14] Professor Anderson also discovered the more a boy plays these games, the lower his grades are likely to be.[15]

Psychologist Wayne Warburton, who is deputy director of the Children and Families Research Centre at Macquarie University says that, like the rest of us, boys become what they consume. 'Basically we're talking about neural (brain) plasticity,' he explains. 'Every time you have an experience the brain sets aside some cells to recognise that experience again. Whenever experiences are activated together they become literally linked together in our brain's wiring. The more these experiences are repeated, the stronger the links become and the more easily thoughts, feelings and action plans related to those experiences are activated. So, when kids are exposed to a lot of violent media, their brains contain a lot of representations of aggression-related concepts. In addition, aggressive attitudes, thoughts, feelings and patterns of behaviour become coded together in their brains. The greater the exposure, the more entrenched are the aggressive attitudes and beliefs, and the more automatic is the tendency to behave with aggressive, hostile and demeaning behaviour, hurting people. The research shows that regardless of who you are in real life, in the short term you're more likely to be aggressive after playing violent video games. Long-term, this aggression becomes internalised, in the manner described above. There are numerous examples of long-term exposure to violent games leading to similar violent behaviour in real life. For example, BBC News reported that sales of the violent video game, Grand Theft Auto IV, had been halted in Thailand after an 18-year-old boy confessed to robbing and murdering a taxi driver while trying to recreate a scene from the game.'[16] Wayne Warburton is also concerned about the socially isolating aspect of gaming. 'Our screen obsession is almost an addiction for some,' he points out, adding, 'it's affecting the way many people relate.' As boys can struggle to connect with those around them, they need all the positive tools possible to help them achieve this.

LACK OF EXERCISE

Unless boys are also playing sports, the hours they spend gaming leaves little time out in the fresh air or for exercise. And while there may be merit in boys working through their frustrations in a virtual world, gaming allows them little chance to explore other ways of letting off steam, which is an important life skill. 'This change in their willingness to play outside starts from when they get the machine,' says Mick, a childcare worker. 'They're losing physical play time, which boys need.'

Another side effect may be that games can deaden the imagination. This can be a real challenge for parents, even those who are vigilant about what their boys get exposed to. 'I noticed a difference in imagination and play with the kids I work with at childcare whose parents are more alternative,' says Mick. 'At first they were enthusiastic and creative, but very quickly they got pulled into the video games like the other kids, even though they don't have them at home.'

There's no doubt gaming offers boys excitement, an opportunity to escape the pressures of daily life and the chance to chill out. At the end of the day electronic games can never be a substitute for real-life interactions and experiences.

As with many of the new technologies, it's not so much about banning gaming, but looking at ways to use games to provide valuable opportunities for boys to learn important life skills.

If your son gets into gaming:

- *Be aware of the content of the games your son plays.*
- *Read the material that comes with the game.*
- *Discuss the use of violence.*
- *There's no substitute for real-life adventure.*
- *Establish clear rules about how long your son can play for.*
- *Encourage him to talk about the game.*
- *Balance time on the computer with engaging real-life activities.*

The alcohol generation

Amongst the many challenges teen boys face is that posed by alcohol. Teenage boys who drink aren't exactly new, but what has changed is the number of teens drinking simply to get drunk, often very drunk. 'I know a lot of people who've had their stomach pumped from the age of 15 upwards,' said Aidan, 22, recalling his teens. Boys themselves see drinking as a concern. 'It's definitely a real issue,' Mark, 15, told me. 'I see it around me. There are so many people in my year who are getting drunk constantly. I'd say more than 60 per cent, maybe 75 per cent. It never leads to anything good.' According to Hunter, 18, the pressure to drink amongst teens is a social thing. 'It's what you do when you go out. You're frowned upon if you don't.' Like most boys, he sees alcohol as a much bigger issue than drugs.

'If you're not drunk at the weekend, you're not cool.' *Dylan, 18*

LET'S PARTY

Drinking is now seen as part of having a good time. Teenagers have had a big week, so at the weekend so they get wasted. It's time to catch up with mates, or celebrate someone's birthday, so they get wasted. In films, TV shows, and celebrity culture, life is represented as endless parties and drinking. And in the sports arena boys constantly see their heroes wasted and acting out. While alcohol isn't something many parents focus on, alcohol abuse is the biggest killer of our kids. It's the main cause of death on our roads, and ranks first in drug-related teenage deaths. Even greater numbers need regular assistance from police and emergency services because of drinking sessions that end badly.

Today's kids are also drinking more than previous generations. 'My group drinks quite a lot,' says Joel, 19. 'Usually a bottle of spirits to a person, or split a case with someone for the night. It usually takes a bit to get me drunk so I usually end up buying a bottle of spirits to myself. I don't finish it necessarily. I get to the point where I'm drunk but not too out of control, I'm fine. But you get people who drink to excess and do things.' According to one inner-city doctor I spoke with, 'Alcohol problems are more common than we're led to believe. In the late teens I see, they think an evening with ten to fifteen drinks, or more, is perfectly normal. This is the norm often for Friday and Saturday nights. Though you speak to them about the risks they've got no intention of stopping. They have to go this far to have a good time – this is how they celebrate the end of the week.' Parents play a key role in the attitude their son has to alcohol. If there's a big drinking culture in the home, or if alcohol is a major focus during social activities, then this is how their son is likely to view alcohol. Knowing where your son is, and who he hangs out with, is essential, as are regular, relaxed discussions around the dangers of alcohol.

Teenagers have also started drinking stronger alcohol. Experts are now concerned about the number of teens drinking spirits. 'Guys have stopped drinking beer for Smirnoffs and that kind of stuff,' explains Dylan, 18. 'Kids get drunk so easy off it. The attraction to being drunk is because it's funny and cool. They get it off the TV shows. When you look at photos of parties, kids all have a cocktail or a bottle of vodka in their hands.'

'When they're drinking, kids dare each other to do things. They're getting so drunk they can't remember what they've done.'
Harrison, 15

PEER PRESSURE

When talking with boys about peer pressure, the pressure to drink was top of their list. 'People start drinking to fit in. It's part of going out,' explains Joel, 19. 'There's a lot of times someone will call you and say, "Hey, do you want to go out tonight?" and you say, "No", and you get the, "Why the hell not? Why wouldn't you want to come out now? Come on, stop being such a pussy. Just come on and do it." You're like, Christ! I guess I'll go. They really want me to go. If I don't go they're not going to like me, sort of stuff. To be acceptable among all your mates is big.'

For some boys, drinking is a way to prove themselves, as Harrison, 15, explains. 'Fourteen to fifteen is when drinking really picks up, because boys' bodies are growing, they're wanting to prove themselves, to be like their older friends.' Others are reluctant but feel they have little choice. 'There is an issue around alcohol. A lot of boys don't want to take it, but they will because they don't want to seem weak,' says Luca, 15. 'They do drink to get drunk, to show their status.' It's not just younger boys, however, who feel this pressure. 'Alcohol is a major thing. You see it with mates drinking. They expect you to join in,' says Andrew, 18. This was Aidan's experience also. 'Binge-drinking is a massive, massive habit, it's almost a necessity. If you're not getting drunk off your nut every weekend, then you're on the outer.'

STRESS, MONEY AND BOREDOM

Studies also point to the roles of stress, boredom and disposable income in teen drinking habits. In one of its back-to-school surveys, American think-tank The National Center on Addiction and Substance Abuse found that the teens who felt very stressed, as well as those who had more than

US$25 a week spending money, were twice as likely to drink and get drunk. Students who were bored were 50 per cent more vulnerable to drinking and getting drunk than the kids who said they weren't bored.[1]

> **'Kids are expecting to try things at a much earlier age. It's no longer a 17-year-old trying alcohol, sex and drugs, it's a 12-year-old.'**
> *Siobhan, high-school teacher*

UNDERAGE DRINKING

Increasing numbers of boys are starting to drink at 12 and 13. 'Drinking at a young age is a big thing,' says Harrison, 15. 'The alcohol is masked by sugar and things. Kids end up getting drunk really quickly and doing stuff they later regret.' Dylan, 18, agrees. 'They see older kids doing it and want to do it. It's the alcohol generation.' It's tempting for parents to assume early drinkers are just going through a phase, but research suggests otherwise. In his long-term survey of high-school students and their drinking habits, researcher Dr Paul Rohde found that the kids showing signs of drinking issues and those with drinking problems were more vulnerable to drug use, depression and other personality difficulties than teens who didn't drink. His study also indicated that those with drinking issues who didn't get help only got worse.[2]

> **'There is a growing body of knowledge that suggests strong reasons for parents and other concerned people to try to keep alcohol out of the hands of young people as long as we can.'**
> *Susan Foster, National Center on Addiction and Substance Abuse, Columbia University*[3]

Perhaps one of the most worrying findings around alcohol abuse is the link between teen drinking patterns and alcoholism in adult life. When the results of one 2006 survey of adults in America were analysed,

47 per cent of those who started drinking alcohol under the age of 14 became alcohol-dependent further down the track. This compared with only 9 per cent of those who didn't start drinking until they were 21.[4]

THE 'BENEFITS' FOR BOYS

For a lot of boys, teen life is very pressured. The combination of study, family issues, peer pressure, concerns about their future and feelings of isolation can create considerable stress. Drinking gives boys a break from the pressure. 'Having a drink just relieved any pain or anything,' said Jarryd, 14, who has struggled with issues around alcohol. This was also John's experience at 15. He got into the habit of taking a hip flask and 'that sort of stuff' to school to help him get through the day and 'just to deal with life'. In an environment that allows boys few forms of expression, emotional or otherwise, drinking is one way boys can chill out or let things rip. Joel, 19, agrees. 'Drinking is definitely an escape – pressure from parents, trying to succeed, to make your parents happy, and I guess I'm happy they're not around then. I'm going to relax and let go.'

'I guess there is a pressure to drink, but most boys want to drink so they can get pissed, because it feels good. You can relax. You get to hang around your friends. It's a good social environment.' *Col, 19*

During teen life many boys have far less social confidence than girls, so drinking also helps bridge the gap, giving them the illusion they're more attractive, more fun to be around. 'It sort of became a social dependence I guess,' says John, 15. 'Yeah, drinking half a bottle of whisky a day, just getting through.' As Jim, a dad, points out, 'Problems around teen issues are about kids having their needs met. There's so much pain and suffering in some kids, they numb it out with alcohol and drugs. For a little while they can relax and forget about everything.'

'Vomiting and passing out is no longer embarrassing, and it's no longer the point at which you stop.' *Sara, high-school teacher*

IMPACT ON THE TEEN BODY AND BRAIN

Often boys still seem okay, even though they may have drunk a great deal. As a result boys keep drinking and end up with a blackout, an alcohol-induced memory blank. During this time they may still be walking and talking, or being dangerous or violent. Afterwards they'll have no memory of this, because their brain was unable to retain this short-term memory due to the alcohol. Studies indicate that the part of the brain which looks after memory, the hippocampus, can shrink by 10 per cent in teens who drink heavily, and that their memory recall can be 10 per cent less than that of adults.

It's also important for boys to realise that when they throw up after excessive drinking it's because the alcohol has poisoned their system. Drinking impairs people's ability to focus, so boys are less able to size up a situation or to make good decisions when drinking. Their motivation and self-control can also suffer. Drinking also inhibits the growth of new brain cells. Experts are at pains to emphasise that a teen with drinking issues isn't just acting out. He has a *medical* problem, and needs professional help.

Sometimes it's hard to understand why boys are so committed to drinking. 'We had a school trip away last year where there was no alcohol,' one young teacher told me. 'But one of the boys managed to sneak out and get drunk. He was complaining of all kinds of pains, so we got him to hospital. The doctor explained he had serious liver damage and had to stop drinking. But this boy's response was he couldn't stop because what would he do with his mates? It was like he'd rather die than not drink.'

WHAT DOES ADVERTISING HAVE TO DO WITH IT?

The relentless marketing to youth has helped create this new drinking culture. It's almost impossible for kids to avoid alcohol ads. Boys see these ads at sports and music events, at the movies, on the net and billboards, in newspapers and magazines, and on branded clothing. The message is that drinking is cool and manly, and that it takes a real man to hold his liquor. There's growing evidence that exposure to alcohol advertising does affect teen drinking habits. In one study, for each additional alcohol ad teens were exposed to, above the monthly average of 23 ads. And the teenagers in societies with more alcohol ads drank more into their late twenties, whereas teen drinking habits in societies with fewer ads stabilised by the time they were in their early twenties.[5] The promises these ads give of an instant hit, doing something risky and improving your social status are all very alluring to teenagers struggling to find their way in the world.[6]

ACCESS TO BOOZE

Often boys steal alcohol from home or local shops. Some have fake IDs. Older brothers and sisters and peers often help out, as do other kids' parents. Now more teens are working, they can afford to buy their own alcohol. And depending on what they're buying, it may not be that expensive. Boys are very aware that having ready access to alcohol helps them look cool and powerful, and can help them assert themselves over their peers. I learned recently of boys in one school demanding oral sex from girls as young as 13 in return for alcohol.

THE FALLOUT

While it may be more comfortable for parents to assume teen drinking habits remain pretty much the same as they've always been, kids are getting hurt. When you combine young people's sense of invulnerability with their total confidence in their peers, it can create lethal situations. 'If you've got people you trust around you, then you're safe, really,' says, Liam, 16. It was interesting to hear a number of older boys like Dylan, 18, express their concerns about younger boys drinking. 'Young kids who drink have never seen the reality of what can happen with a person drinking one minute and across the table at you with a glass the next,' he told me. Joel, 19, agrees. 'They think they're invincible. It's getting younger and younger. Kids lose their sense of risk, lose all sense of risk.'

'Some pretty scary things can happen when boys are drinking. They're prone to getting violent after a few drinks.' *Tim, 17*

Drunkenness also makes boys far more vulnerable to attack, accidents and abuse. With impaired judgement they're more likely to be involved in vandalism, drink driving, violence and sexual assault. Every weekend police and emergency services end up in dealing with teens in car smashes and other accidents, and hurt in fights and attacks. If drunken teens are left alone on their backs, vomit, then inhale their vomit, they can die. 'I had one guy so drunk his legs were sticking out over the platform when a train was approaching,' one doctor told me. 'Another had been sitting in broken glass. Often significant injuries aren't dealt with because boys are so out of it, so they don't present until days later.'

One study of 12- to 17-year-olds indicated that the heavy drinkers were three times more likely to harm themselves or commit suicide.[7] When kids drink, especially to excess, it alters their body chemistry, making them more vulnerable to emotional and behavioural problems. This may mean boys running away or not turning up at school, becoming depressed or suicidal, or self-harming.

THE WAY FORWARD

Many parents feel helpless in tackling teen drinking because of the number of other parents who don't see alcohol as a problem, and because of the pressure their kids are under to drink. Some support their son's early drinking, because they see it as a macho thing to do. There's also a widespread belief that allowing kids to drink early at home promotes responsible drinking, but studies suggest otherwise. Across the western world governments are trying hard to tackle the problem with scare campaigns, but for teens the allure and pressure to socialise, to be part of the action, is far more compelling. Dylan, 18, sums it up when he says, 'Binge-drinking is definitely a problem. The government has tried to solve it, but quite frankly I don't think it's going to work. Drinking has become cool.'

Parents need to be prepared for the fact that these problems might be happening closer to home than they think. Joel 19, agrees. 'Not all parents know what their kids drink. It's kept secret. My younger brother's been driven home by the police a couple of times. My parents don't know. He's a master of deception.' It's important parents discuss these issues in detail with their son. Whenever a celebrity or sporting hero has landed in trouble with their drinking, this presents an ideal opportunity to chat about these issues. The best discussions are those where boys are carefully guided to come to the appropriate conclusion. Cover the facts and likely consequences in a relaxed, open manner, rather than lecturing your son. As you discuss the issues, empathise with the pressures teenagers are under. Then set some clear rules as to what is acceptable and why.

You support your son when you:

- *Are aware of your own drinking habits.*
- *Know your son's friends and their parents.*
- *Are in touch by phone with your son when he is out.*
- *Are sensitive to the stress in his life and how hard it is to be a teen.*
- *Are aware of when your son is bored, and help him deal with his boredom.*
- *Teach your son how to regulate his behaviour and why.*
- *Praise him for doing things right, and be reasonable about minor mistakes.*
- *Let your son know you want to be the first person he goes to if something goes wrong.*

The drug scene

Parents cannot afford to ignore drugs, but when I talked to boys, they stressed that alcohol is a much bigger issue for their generation. In spite of alarming media reports, it's important to realise most boys *don't* do drugs. That said, drugs do have a certain mystique for teenagers. 'Drugs aren't as big as alcohol in my year, but there are still obvious signs,' explained Mark, 15. 'More people talk about it. The way they talk about it, it's, like, so good, like they're having so much fun.'

Most boys don't see themselves as vulnerable with drugs. 'It does come back to that thing of feeling invincible,' admitted Dylan, 18. There's also the sense when talking to teenagers that the moment is what matters. As Daryl, 17, explained, 'A guy at school says he doesn't care he's using, because he doesn't want to live past 30 anyway.' What we do know is that the earlier boys start using, the more likely they are to use more drugs and experiment with different drugs.

GETTING THE MESSAGE THROUGH

Kids expect adults to disapprove of drugs, so in trying to keep our boys safe, we have to be smart about how we tackle the topic. 'Drinking,

191

drugs and sex have always been there, but more so now,' said Dylan, 18. 'It's one of the few ways kids can rebel, because they now have so much, and more freedom. There's so little they can rebel against.' Ideally talk about drugs will begin before a boy gets to high school. Early informed family discussions will have a far greater impact than waiting to talk to a boy about drugs when he's 16. Before parents do talk to their son about drugs, they need to understand where his generation is coming from.

While governments work hard to do their bit with multi-million-dollar campaigns, according to many teens, scary drug ads only frighten parents. The thing is today's kids want to find things out for *themselves*. They also feel lied to when adults say drugs are bad, when in fact drugs make them feel unbelievably good at the start. That's why kids go back for more. What we need to tackle are the aspects of their lives that *don't* feel so good.

MARIJUANA

Without doubt the most popular drug is marijuana, especially for boys. A number of boys I interviewed began smoking marijuana because their parents or friends' parents were happy to share their stash. Marijuana use is not without risk. It is stronger these days because the buds of the plant now contain higher concentrations of the mood-altering tetra-hydrocannabinol or THC. This means some users can encounter harmful levels of THC without realising it.[1] Like all illicit drugs, concentration varies, making cannabis use a little like Russian roulette.

> **'Cannabis really does look like the drug of choice for life's future losers.'** *Professor George Patton, Centre for Adolescent Health, Melbourne University*[2]

A ten-year study which looked at school-aged children through to age 25 and compared kids who drank with those who smoked marijuana, found that heavy marijuana users were more likely to be in an unstable relationship, unemployed and to have dropped out of study. They were also more likely to use other drugs as well. Professor George Patton of Melbourne University, who headed up this research, also emphasised that the drug is far more readily available than it was two or three decades ago.[3]

'Experts estimate about one in ten people who use cannabis will go on to experience some sort of problem with the drug.' *Paul Dillon, Teenagers, Alcohol and Drugs*[4]

The boys I spoke with were very aware of the negative effects of marijuana on their peers. 'You do see a change in appearances,' said Daryl, 17. 'Red eyes, no direction. They smell of cigarettes and stuff. The chronic cases are bottom of the class.' Aidan, 22, agreed. 'A couple of my friends have drifted out of my existence with weed. They've lost their motivation to do anything. They don't turn up to school or anything.' While Mark, 15, noticed that 'It's mainly marijuana people are raving about. With regular users, their appearance is depressing. They look like they're wrecked all the time. They're the people who take school and work for granted a lot more.'

'I'm in a band. Some of the guys have been smoking dope since they were eleven. You can tell. It's like they've only got four brain cells between them.' *Dylan, 18*

GETTING WASTED

Weekends are the times when teenagers are often most at risk, as it's their chill-out time. There's also an expectation amongst boys it's the time to get wasted and/or high. As boys mature and enjoy more freedom, they're more likely to be exposed to different drugs when mixing with older friends. 'You get people who sell a lot of weed and whatnot,' explained Joel, 19. 'There's not a lot of hard stuff until you're about 16, then other things start to get introduced like speed and ecstasy. Then you get acid, which came around [when I was] 17 with a specific group who do a lot of drugs.'

It's helpful for parents to be aware of the increased exposure their sons will have to drugs as they gain more independence, so they can discuss the situations their boys may find themselves in. Risks come in many guises. Impromptu raves held at weekends in deserted buildings and warehouses are cause for concern because of drugs. And as these venues rarely have proper exits they can easily become fire traps. These gigs appeal to the teenage ache for adventure, and are generally organised at short notice. Without supervision, there's also the worry of what happens should there be a brawl or someone overdoses. Again, canvassing this risk makes boys more aware. Teenagers are also using caffeine-laden energy drinks so they can drink more, take more drugs, and 'club' harder. As a result some clubs are now banning energy drinks as they help fuel violent, anti-social behaviour. So be conscious of your son's use of these drinks, as they may not be as innocent as they seem.

THE THING ABOUT ECSTASY

We now know that ecstasy use is on the rise. Some studies suggest it's the fastest growing illicit drug. According to drug and alcohol expert Paul Dillon, ecstasy is the drug of choice for many inner-city kids, and for kids into clubbing. Ecstasy is closely linked to music culture, and is readily available at festivals and raves. 'Ecstasy came along with a certain group who tended to do clubbing, so there's ecstasy there,' Joel, 19, told me. 'In my group people do ecstasy. They're going to a party, so it's like, "This'll give me a really good night instead of an average night", but they don't listen to dance music and jump around with sticks.' Compared to drugs such as ice, ecstasy is often seen as relatively harmless. However, like all drugs, it depends on the batch. While it may seem like an attractive addition to a night out, it too can be lethal.

LOOKING COOL

As we examine the issues around the drugs, we see yet again how vulnerable the cool kids are, because there's an expectation they're willing to take more risks. 'One guy in my class is hooked on drugs,' Daryl, 17, told me. 'He seems to think it's good, and he's proud of it, always saying it's awesome. The negative side effects don't worry him.' This is 15-year-old Mark's experience also. 'It's, like, very cool if you've done it sort of thing, and, like, for those who look up to the cool kids. I guess the argument is that if you just do it occasionally or once then it's okay. I sort of see where they're coming from and everything, but there's always a chance you'll go back to it.'

It's helpful to see the drug scene through a boy's eyes, and just how exciting it may seem. 'Like, we had kids dealing acid in maths,' explains Joel, 19. 'Like you know them. They're good friends, funny guys. But it's like, "Wow." They sit there and get a phone call in maths, grab their ice box, and say, "Yeah I'll meet you." Then it's like, "Sir, I need to go to the bathroom." So it's, "Okay," like more money for him.' However, not all boys see the drug culture this way. 'At school the cool guys get stoned, sleep with girls, do graffiti and stuff. They're just idiots,' Dylan, 18, told me. He went on to explain just how vulnerable the cool kids can be, when they become locked into a certain image. 'It's not that hard to say no, but for those who want to be cool it's very hard.'

It's not only parents who are battling the drug issue. So too are schools. 'Drugs are definitely more prominent with boys,' explained Sasha, a young high-school teacher. 'Boys are more willing to take chances. They like the high from it. We're seeing drugs creeping in from boys aged 15 and up, because they're now mixing with older friends. Marijuana and speed are the main drugs we're tackling.' If we are to keep boys safe, it's essential parents and teachers are on the same page.

ICE

While there have been a number of articles in the media about ice (meth-amphetamines), there are relatively few teenagers using the drug. In our 2007 National Drug Strategy Household Survey of teenagers aged 14 to 17, only 2 per cent of participants had been exposed to non-prescribed amphetamines. Studies suggest that ice use begins for most male users at around the age of 18. Certainly the effects are highly detrimental to those who do use. It's estimated that four out of every ten people taking ice become addicted. A recent University of Western Australia study revealed that the brains of many young users had shrunk to such an extent they looked like the brains of 70-year-olds. Even though these kids may kick their habit, they are unable to reverse the brain damage. According to Dr Daniel Fatovich who headed up this research, 'Not only does crystal amphetamine take a lot of time and resources in our emergency departments, it also causes structural abnormalities of the brain.' The effects can include memory loss, psychosis and a greater vulnerability to Alzheimer's further down the track. Of those being admitted to emergency wards, just over seven out of ten were male. A third needed to be sedated, and just over one in three needed to be evaluated by a psychiatrist.[5]

> 'I do know of people dealing outside school. People are aware of drugs now, so they're more likely to try it. They're told take this, but as long as it's at this level you're okay.' *Daryl, 17*

GETTING OUT THE DEXIES

Recent figures indicate that almost 4000 children under 10 in Australia have been prescribed anti-depressants. Over 500 of these kids were under 5.[6] With the number of prescription drugs now taken during the childhood years, it's less of a leap for teenagers to take prescription drugs for recreational purposes. While it's hard to gauge the extent of this, the use of pharmaceutical drugs for recreation is clearly on the rise. Some kids who take drugs for their ADHD are now selling their pills to peers. Also known as kiddie speed, 'dexies' help teenage users to party on without running out of energy, as well as giving them more confidence. With these pills so cheap to buy from friends compared to other drugs, it's not hard to see their attraction.

It's not only 'dexies' teenagers are getting into. They're also gaining access to cold-and-flu tablets, cough medicine, their parents' anti-depressants, sedatives and painkillers, and other medications to be found around the house. This is an attractive route for teenagers wanting to try different drugs, as it's a whole lot easier than trying to find drugs through dealers. Many teens also mistakenly see prescription drugs as relatively safe. But as Steve Allsop, the director of the National Drug Research Institute at Curtin University, points out, 'If you're combining depressant drugs such as narcotic analgesics, painkillers or tranquilisers with alcohol, you substantially increase the risk of overdose.'[7]

'Parents are passive pushers by not taking care of their drugs.'
Joseph Califano, National Center on Addiction and Substance Abuse, Columbia University[8]

Kids can now illegally source pharmaceutical drugs online and find pill mixes for getting high. This new twist in the drug culture has its own language. A collection of random pills is known by some as 'trail mix', and raiding the family medicine chest as 'pharming'. Teens are now getting together for 'pharm' parties. Here meds are placed in a central bowl, then everyone takes a few and sees where it takes them. So emergency departments now have the challenge of treating teenagers who have overdosed on a complicated combination of pills. While local figures are hard to come by, one American survey revealed that just under two in ten teenagers had used painkillers or stimulants as recreational drugs.

THE FEEL-GOOD FACTOR

What we cannot deny is that drugs make kids feel great initially. Then life can become a journey destined for disappointment as kids try to recapture their first high. One of the many reasons boys do drugs is it helps them be more expressive. What a pity we don't offer them less harmful, more appealing ways to do this. 'By 13 or 14 I was smoking marijuana,' admits Tony, now 26. 'I took a lot of LSD at school. The drugs allowed things. They made you feel closer to other people, and it gave you the chance to be emotional, because you could always blame it on the drugs.'[9]

Without more constructive support to help them open up, boys resort to self-medication to cope with issues they're struggling with. A recent University of British Columbia study into teen marijuana users found that just under a third of their sample smoked it to help them deal with anxiety and depression, sleep and concentration issues, and physical pain. Those who had been taking Prozac, Ritalin or sleeping pills also said they didn't like how the drugs made them feel, or found they simply didn't work, so they moved on to other drugs.[10]

OPENING UP TO PARENTS

One of the themes that emerged during my discussions with boys is their unwillingness to talk to parents about these kinds of issues, and how they feel more comfortable about turning to peers or the media instead. While peers and the media can be a source of comfort and information, boys don't necessarily form an accurate or complete sense of an issue in this way. It's tragic so many boys don't feel they can open up at home. Brad, 20, who experienced drug issues as a teenager, never even thought of sharing his struggles with his parents. While Robert, now in his late 20s, also felt unable to do so. 'I drank and smoked,' he admitted, 'but when my friends got into drugs I walked away. I never discussed it with my parents. I was too afraid to discuss these things with them, in case they rubbished me.'[11] The critical issue is that these boys *didn't* feel able to approach their parents. Like so many boys, they found their own way through and, luckily, managed to come out the other end relatively unscathed.

OPENING UP THE LINES OF COMMUNICATION

We need to stay close to our boys and give them good advice. As often they don't think rationally, vague statements such as 'drugs are danger-ous' don't really help. Boys need good information shared in an engaging, *collaborative* way. Therapist Laurie Wilmot, who runs a program for at-risk kids, encourages parents to have regular family conversations where their sons do most of the talking about difficult issues such as drugs. He suggests asking if they have any friends they're worried about first up, then inviting boys to share their concerns for their friend, what they would do in that situation, and how they might help this friend.[12] This approach allows for a more general discussion, where parents can give their boys good advice and information.

As with all challenging teen situations, boys need their parents' help to develop a script that will assist them to say no to drugs. The script needs to be convincing and in a language that doesn't sound uncool. Such phrases as, 'It's great being with you, but I'm just not interested in drugs', 'Dad is keeping a really close eye on me at present, which could be a problem for everyone, so I'll pass', or 'I have health issues so I can't', give boys a *credible* way out, and takes the pressure off them.

199

WHAT PARENTS CAN DO WHEN FACED WITH DRUG ISSUES

There's no point talking with your son when he's angry or high. Find the right time. Begin by telling him how much he means to you, then how you want to help him with teen life. Find out what he's up to and why. Don't interrupt. It's important he feels heard. It's a good idea to get him talking about how *he'd* like life to be at home and school, and with family and friends. Listen closely. Then discuss his use of drugs in relation to his aspirations. Out of this you can help him plot a way forward.

This is an important step, but only a first step forward. It's important you continue to stay close to your son. Remain interested in what interests him. If you feel it's time to seek professional help, don't hesitate. Talk with your family doctor, who will be able to make a referral. Either way, keep the lines of communication open – not just about where your son is going and what he is doing with friends, but about how he's tracking.

You can help educate your son about drugs when you:

- *Talk openly about the temptation of drugs for teenagers.*
- *Acknowledge how hard but important it is to say no.*
- *Invite difficult questions and conversations.*
- *Use media coverage to introduce these complex topics.*
- *Keep your prescription drugs under lock and key.*
- *Be sure your son knows prescription drugs aren't safer than illegal drugs.*
- *Respect his need to be with peers.*
- *Praise your son for what he does well.*
- *Are frank about the ups and downs of teen life, and how normal these are.*

Boys and cars

Another concern for parents is boys and cars, and understandably so as more teenagers are killed on the road than any other way. A recent Murdoch Children's Institute Report revealed that our teen boys were twice as likely to die as teen girls and that the main cause (just under a third) was road accidents.[1] In spite of increased education, boys are still vulnerable on our roads. The combination of less experience, driving older and smaller vehicles, and being prone to distraction from friends, mobile phones, and eating and drinking while driving makes teen drivers more accident-prone.

Boys like to show their mates what they're made of, and are more likely to speed, race and take risks while driving. Many of the boys I interviewed had had their own nightmare moments as a passenger in a friend's car. 'There's definitely some issues around driving and cars, because of the coolness factor,' Zac, 15, told me. 'There is a problem with boys showing off. They really feel the need to show off, and I guess it's how to get noticed with the flashiest way you can, so you can belong.'

PUSHING THE BOUNDARIES

As today's boys lead much more contained lives than boys in previous generations, there are fewer ways in which they can test their limits. Access to a car gives them the chance to take a few risks. When asked whether the media exaggerated reports of boys driving dangerously, all the boys I spoke with said it did not. Some did feel, however, that the media spotlight did encourage boys to be true to form. 'There's always the focus on boys speeding and doing drunken stuff,' said Jacob, 17. 'By publicising it, it gives boys something to rebel against.' As well as wanting to show off to their mates, boys talked about the influence of older brothers who encourage them to test their limits.

For Kayt, a high-school teacher of over two decades, boys and cars in her coastal town is not a happy mix. 'You see the impact on boys' study when they get their licence,' she told me. 'They leave school in free lessons. They go down to McDonald's. They frequently have a crash within a month of getting their licence. They go out to a point near here, where they drink and drive.' While this isn't good news, boys aren't totally to blame for their reckless driving. Every action film they see has a car chase in it. So why wouldn't they want to see what they're capable of?

Professionals agree that it's no easy task to get boys to understand how vulnerable they are when driving. Or perhaps their need to prove themselves is stronger than their fear of getting hurt. 'We had one boy at school who almost died because he was driving so fast,' said Sara, also a high-school teacher, 'He had his licence suspended. But two weeks later he was caught speeding again. It's expected. It's what boys do. It's a kind of heroism. The guy who has a car is a hero. Once he has a car and a licence the car will be full and he'll be away.' Scary ads on TV and at the movies don't seem to make that much of a difference. Boys have had years of watching wall-to-wall carnage in action movies, so why would a fifteen-second ad tip the balance?

'Even though they hear about the dangers, and we've had boys killed, they don't stop. It's like a rite of passage.' *Kayt, high-school teacher*

Not all boys are immune to what is happening around them. Sometimes a car accident does make them reassess. 'One of my rugby team mates had a bad crash,' Toby, 16, told me. 'Everyone was affected. He had quite bad brain trauma. It was quite sad for him. He talks very slowly now. I can see why things like that happen, it's too easy for it to happen.' This was Jacob's experience also. 'A month ago a boy crashed his mum's car into a tree. It was a write-off, but he and his friend were okay. They were really shocked afterwards. It's had a good impact, because it really shook everybody up to see that you're not invincible.'

'Cars are a very big thing for boys. They have expensive mobile phones, expensive shoes, and when they get older they want to get a car.' *Sara, high-school teacher*

RISK FACTORS

When we look at the causes of boys getting killed in cars, we discover excessive speed is the main factor. Not surprisingly, alcohol has often been consumed. Teen boys don't necessarily drink and drive more than adults. They're just more at risk when they do. Research also shows that nights and weekends are the most treacherous times for teen drivers.[2] Many crashes take place during the early morning, so fatigue is thought to play an important role. Night is a risky time for boys to be on the roads, particularly after parties or if they are with friends. With every additional passenger, the risks are elevated. One American study showed that the risk of a 16-year-old driver having a fatal accident was 1.8 times higher with one passenger. They were more than twice as likely to suffer a fatality with two passengers, and three times as likely to do so when they had three passengers.[3]

'A lot of my friends now drive. We don't push them into doing anything, but a couple of them do like to show off by driving too fast. I guess the motivation is to show off to your mates.' *Jacob, 17*

WHY TEENAGE BOYS ARE VULNERABLE

New drivers are more vulnerable to serious, if not fatal, injury than older drivers, and boys are particularly so, as they are drawn to risk-taking. Young drivers aren't as good at spotting road hazards, or anticipating what other drivers may do. They are also less able than seasoned drivers to do the various tasks needed to drive a car safely, and are less aware of pedestrians. New drivers are more likely to tailgate, leave insufficient room and time to overtake, and change lanes in a way that makes it hard for other drivers to anticipate their actions.

Studies also show that just over a third of younger drivers are likely not to take a break if driving a long distance. If they're off on holiday, they're most likely to push themselves harder to get to their destination. Because they're younger they assume they're less prone to fatigue.[4] The number of hours a boy has driven while learning to drive also affects his safety. In Sweden provisional drivers who had around 120 hours of supervised driving, now compulsory here, had 40 per cent fewer accidents than those who had only forty hours.[5]

PARENTS HAVE A ROLE TO PLAY

Experts believe that parents have a pivotal role in keeping their boys safe. Monitoring when they drive and with whom, and ensuring they're well aware of the dangers, are essential. The boys who have greater supervision are less likely to speed or to neglect wearing their seatbelts.[6] New evidence also suggests that one of the best ways of keeping boys alive is to get them a new or recent model of car with airbags and greater stability control. One scheme working well in the United States is a written agreement between teenagers and their parents which covers all the major eventualities, from alcohol and speeding to drinking and driving, and using a mobile phone. Available through the *Roads 2 Survival* organisation, this agreement can be downloaded free of charge from www.roads2survival.com.au/download.htm

You can help your son stay safe on the road by:

- *Taking an interest in when he is driving and where.*
- *Being aware of his strengths and weaknesses on the road, and counselling him accordingly.*
- *Spending time with him in the car, even when he's got his licence.*
- *Being very clear about your expectations of him.*
- *Talking through the peer pressure to speed, take risks, drink and drive.*
- *Helping him form a script to talk to friends about cars and safety.*
- *Celebrating when he gets his licence.*

The sex lives of teen boys

While no-one would question the fact that rapid changes have taken place in recent years, often we don't realise just how much things have changed. We are now seeing a great rise in underage, often risky sex. What your 18-year-old was doing at 13 is not what a 13-year-old is now into. Older teenagers are very aware of this. 'You're now seeing guys and girls together at twelve and thirteen with serious commitments and doing crazy [sex] stuff,' Daryl, 17, told me. 'They're just kids, but it doesn't surprise me, because we're made to grow up faster.' Some boys see these changes as inevitable, others are concerned by them. 'I see younger kids doing stuff at thirteen and fourteen, like sex, alcohol and drugs, and I am appalled,' said Gary, 17.

'At twelve to fourteen relationships aren't serious. They might be sexually, but not emotionally, 'cos there's no responsibility. But older teens pay more attention to feelings.' *Dylan, 18*

Unlike most adults, teens understand why these changes have occurred because they face the same pressures and influences. 'Young teens have sex, because that's what you do. You've got young girls reading things like how to give the perfect blow job at thirteen,' Dylan, 18, told me. 'That stuff's everywhere. You can't escape it. There's not many TV shows that don't have sex. A lot of the stars are now in their teens.'

WHEN GIRLS BECOME OBJECTS

The way popular culture often depicts young girls as objects doesn't encourage boys to treat girls as much more than accessories. 'Yeah, kids my age have a girlfriend. It's more a status thing,' explained Lyall, 12. As adults we too have become desensitised to the 'Barbie doll' way girls are being represented, which in turn makes our boys and girls more vulnerable. 'When we encourage girls to see themselves without depth or difference, they take massive risks,' warns one clinical psychologist, who runs the sexual assault unit at a leading hospital. She went on to point out that this is doubly concerning as sexual predators see their victims purely as objects. She also sees the sexualised culture as abusive towards boys as well as girls, as it sets up behaviour and expectations that can be harmful. She and other professionals in this area have no doubt that the hyper-sexualised climate boys are growing up in contributes to new kinds of sexual assault girls are now experiencing, where for example, girls aged 12 to 14 are filmed being gang-raped anally.

A number of fathers I spoke with expressed similar concerns. 'Boys do have a certain disrespect towards girls now,' said Dave Mallard, father, senior executive and men's group facilitator. 'They see girls gyrating and being overtly sexual, and so boys assume that's what girls want. They get caught up in the moment and with peer group pressure, seeing girls as a commodity. They don't have the life experience to handle what they see.' Sara, a high-school teacher, agrees. 'It all starts with the language – how sex is referred to. Young boys talking about "f**king a girl", "having a f**k". They wander around the school grounds saying, "I'd tap that", or "I wouldn't tap that". Or they talk openly about "fingering her". It's this grotesque, yet casual, demeaning way to talk about girls as sex objects.'

'Your first sexual experience lays the ground for future experiences. Whether or not it's done with dignity, respect and celebration makes a huge difference.' *Michael Waring, men's group facilitator, father and grandfather*

As today's boys often have less maturity and a narrower life experience, they have fewer resources to draw on to help them make good decisions. 'This generation is going to a new level of intimacy in sexual behaviour not previously seen,' says Rowan, who works with at-risk teens. 'In past generations there was a fear and sense of the unknown around sex that isn't there any more with TV programs and the internet. It's all about fun and daring to do things. A young teen's body is willing. Their mind is willing, but emotionally they're not prepared.'

LIVING UP TO EXPECTATIONS

When talking with boys about the teen scene you begin to sense how pressured life is for them. Now boys are more anxious than ever about looking right, acting sophisticated and being seen as up for whatever's on offer. There is a desperation in the way they talk about trying to meet peer expectations. 'At times girls do put pressure on guys to take notice,' Luca, 15, explains. 'A lot of girls do then get pressure from boys, who want to take advantage. It's just like one big circle that's always going round. Everybody feels embarrassed. No-one wins really, but their status is upheld.' For the boys willing to come to the party there can be lots of kudos. 'There was a big scandal at school,' explained Wendy, a court co-ordinator. 'Footage of a girl giving a boy a blow job was doing the rounds. These things can be very empowering for boys in a negative way.' Again, as much of the emphasis is on appearance and performance, and not on what kids really want or how they feel, it's harder to make good, individual choices.

WHAT'S THE POINT OF VIRGINITY ANYWAY?

What we do know is that in some social groups it's definitely not cool for a teen, even a young teen to be a virgin. In one coastal town I visited recently, professionals were dealing with the fallout of girls as young as 13 who were going out and getting drunk, then finding someone to have sex with, so they could say they were no longer virgins. Boys were picked at random. These are not isolated incidents. It's hard for today's boys and girls to have relationships without sex, because it's now seen as part of the deal. A number of teens have told me that they like someone, but don't even consider going out with them, because of these expectations. 'Yeah, sex is now expected as part of relationships,' Dylan, 18, told me. 'Young males are starting to expect it, because that's what's shown on films and stuff.' These expectations can leaves girls vulnerable to assault, and boys to assault charges.

'There is a stage developmentally when kids become comfortable with their own sexuality. If this process isn't nurtured, that's when we see promiscuous behaviour, underage sex and risky sex. Part of nurture is about boundaries. Kids also need physical touch. If they don't get it, they go looking for it.' *Jim, father*

DISPOSABLE RELATIONSHIPS

Few would dispute that boys are wired differently from girls, and during teen life the raging hormones can be hard to handle. Living in a sex-saturated world doesn't help boys. Having to deal constantly with the fallout, one psychologist who supports sexual assault victims sees an urgent need to give children a language around saying no. While previous generations had their own issues, at least they had a greater understanding and respect for other people's feelings and comfort zones, of boundaries and consequences.

Now, it's about being the coolest dude. 'The quick relationship or the one-night stand is becoming a lot more popular,' says Dylan, 18. 'It's the soaps and stuff.' Hunter, 18, agrees. 'During fifteen to eighteen relationships are seen more as a lust thing. It's not seen as a relationship, but as something to add to the ego, to get the best-looking girl. You're sexually driven.' Psychologist and father Bill O'Hehir believes that this is cause for concern, as boys and girls are missing out on important elements of what it means to be human. 'When I saw a girl I liked I respected her,' he explains. 'I delivered papers just so I could see one girl. Now boys have seen vaginas, gang bangs, bestiality so young, so when they see a girl, they don't see an innocent girl. They see an object, a piece of meat. Then you add alcohol into the equation, and what do you expect to happen?'

ORAL AND ANAL SEX

With ready access to the internet and popular culture, boys and girls are more public about sex, as well as more adventurous about what they wear and what they're prepared to do. Once oral and anal sex were far less common. Now some kids don't even consider them to be sexual acts, and so we're seeing a rapid rise in sexually transmitted diseases, because kids often don't think to take precautions. 'For young people it's an almost universal practice now,' says Basil Donovan, professor of sexual health at the University of New South Wales. 'Among teenagers it's the new abstinence in the Clintonesque sense, because it's a way of having sex without having sex, and there are obvious contraceptive advantages too.'[1]

To some teens oral and anal sex are not really sex.

It can be hard for teen boys to know what they're meant to do in situations with girls who have few inhibitions. 'There's no doubt the sexual behaviour of teens is getting more extreme,' explains Rowan, who works with troubled youth. 'It's okay to have oral sex with anybody, because it's not seen as sex, and now we're seeing thirteen- to sixteen-year-old girls getting into anal sex.'

'I don't think boys see girls as I saw them – beautiful, unattainable, desirable, captivating. They're seeing girls as an object, a thing. If we think we've had struggles with domestic violence and the like, it's going to get a lot worse. We're raising kids who don't know what a relationship is.' Bill O'Hehir, father and psychologist

Research suggests there may be a link between oral sex and oral cancers. Health professionals were puzzled by the rise in oral cancer amongst young people, especially as many of those suffering cancer didn't smoke and weren't necessarily heavy drinkers. A study by Johns Hopkins Medical Institute found that those infected by the human papillomavirus (HPV), which can be transmitted by oral sex, are 32 times more likely to contract oral cancer than those not affected by HPV. The study also indicated that regardless of whether someone is infected by HPV, if they have had up to five oral sex partners, they are 3.8 times more vulnerable to oral cancer, and 8.6 times more likely to contract oral cancer if they have had six or more oral sex partners.[2]

SO WHAT SHOULD BOYS DO?

Today boys and girls are caught between what their peers and popular culture regard as cool, what their parents expect, and what they would like to do in the heat of the moment. Rarely are many of the scenarios they now face discussed with parents or other adults, so they're left to reach their own solutions. 'When a girl's relationship with a boy begins at this level [with oral and anal sex], then the expectation is that they'll be up for a whole lot more,' explains one clinical psychologist who runs a sexual assault unit at a leading hospital.

As teens are relentlessly marketed to and encouraged to act older than they are, increasing numbers of young girls are looking for older boyfriends, who have high expectations about what their girlfriend will deliver sexually. Apart from breaking the law, these guys often fail to realise how vulnerable young girls can be. 'It's also cool for a young girl to be going out with a 17-year-old,' explains Rowan, whose work centres around troubled teens. 'These guys have expectations. There's also a power play, because of the age difference. Girls do whatever it takes to keep the cool boyfriend.'

'There's no true understanding often of the full implications of what they're sending on their mobile phones, or of what they're seeing.' *Austin, assistant principal*

MOBILE PHONES

In previous generations kids had more boundaries and a clearer sense of likely consequences. This gave them pause to consider whether they did want to do something. If they then stepped across the line, they did so with their eyes half open. They also tended to keep what they'd done to themselves. Living in a performance culture, however, kids can't wait to tell the world what they've been up to, hoping their latest exploit will deliver them the popularity they crave. Often they have no idea how vulnerable they may be to sexually transmitted diseases, date rape, stalking or blackmail. This lack of caution is evident in the explosion of sexually explicit material recorded and circulated on mobile phones.

SEXTING

Some girls are now sending boys explicit photos to get them interested. At one school I was at recently, older teenagers expressed concern at the number of 13-year-old girls who had taken photos of themselves with different objects inserted into various orifices, then sent them to boys to be noticed. 'Yeah, teens are exposed to a whole lot of images on their mobiles and the internet. Images can be sent around so easily within groups,' Hunter, 18, told me. 'It's a regular thing, kind of bragging rights. There's a strong performance element I guess.'

> **'We're definitely seeing more sexual activity and definitely at a younger age. Inappropriate sexual activity is often being videotaped now, so it comes out more.'** *Siobhan, high-school teacher*

With girls behaving like sexed-up Bratz dolls, it can make relationships that much more full-on. A number of boys talked about how uncomfortable they were in some situations as a result. 'You've got the "out there" girls who just talk about stuff to the point that it's quite gross, and it's like, "Why bring up that stuff in normal everyday situations?" Joel, 19, told me. 'Sometimes I get intimidated by that. It's like, "Who are you trying to impress?" You don't want to hear about stuff like that. Or they talk about sex all the time in conversations, and it's like, "That's not cool, it's just weird."'

WHEN BOYS ARE VULNERABLE

With this level of attention, it is doubly hard for boys not to take advantage of what is on offer. Those who do may well wear the consequences for years. 'It's a concerning scenario,' explains Rowan, who works with at-risk kids. 'Boy meets girl. Girl likes him, so takes explicit photos and sends it to the boy. They get together. The relationship splits up. The boy is hurt and angry, so he circulates the photos. Then he's in trouble. If she is under sixteen and, depending on where he lives, he can be up for a whole range of charges from indecent treatment of a child under sixteen, to circulation of child exploitation material. Just to hang on to the explicit photos means he can be charged with child exploitation.'

PARENTS OUT ON A LIMB

Teens know their parents' take on how they should behave. The problem is that growing numbers just don't see this as relevant. While they love their parents, often the cool world of celebrities, reality TV and pop culture take first place. And living in an information age, they no longer have to rely on adults for information about the sexual landscape. They much prefer to talk to peers who are going through the same experiences and issues.

'I talk to friends, cousins who can give you advice. It's sort of learning by mistakes as much as anything, or by an adult who's cool and in. Talking about it with them is much better than parents, it's not embarrassing.' *Harrison, 15*

HOS AND SLUTS

There is still a lot of kudos for boys in sleeping around, and with the highly sexualised climate they're now growing up in, it's doubly important that boys have good discussions about how to treat girls. 'It is a bit of a double standard. Girls sleeping around are seen as skanks. For guys there's the bragging rights. It comes into the dominance and ego stuff,' says Hunter, 18. Joel, 19, agrees. 'Like, a girl's skirt is so short, it's like, "Wow you can see everything. That's hot!" But then you turn around and think, "What a slut." There's some girls who are really out there. They cut their skirt so it looks like a belt. You look at their arse and think, "Oh yeah, what a slut." There's classy, then there's those that look like a hooker.'

So what can be done? Recently, a local all-boys high school decided to stage 'Dignity Week'. Headmaster Tony Duncan wanted to help boys recognise the importance of respecting women in the hope they won't abuse the women in their lives. School guests included leading women in the community. At one school assembly the boys' mothers were invited to attend. During the gathering the mothers linked arms with their sons as a symbolic gesture of support for this pledge, creating a very powerful moment for the boys and their mums. The week-long events included raising money for a local women's refuge.[3] These kinds of positive experiences give boys a much bigger vision of what they are capable of.

To help boys handle this sexualised climate:

- *Understand that boys need to have good information about sex, not just the mechanics, but the intricacies of relating to someone – respect, intimacy, sensuality and desire.*
- *Be clear about your own values.*
- *Stay abreast of current issues.*
- *Ensure your son knows he can come and talk to you at any time.*
- *Help him work out a way to say no to unwanted sex.*
- *Be open about how complex issues around sex are.*
- *Encourage friendships across the generations, so your son has other trusted adult friends or favourite aunts or uncles he can also talk to.*

Boys into porn

Perhaps one of the most concerning issues we face is a boy's ready, albeit illegal, access to porn, and how quickly watching porn has become part of youth culture and that porn is far more graphic than the girlie magazines of previous generations. Porn is a lucrative, highly organised business generating billions. The ready availability of porn came with the introduction of videos. Instead of having to attend seedy cinemas, suddenly people could view porn in the privacy of their own homes. With the much wider availability of sexually explicit material, demand grew and now porn is available in hotel rooms, on the net, DVDs, mobiles and pay TV.

CHILD PORNOGRAPHY

What many parents may not realise is that when kids start to access porn on the net, often they gravitate towards highly illegal child porn, as that's what they can relate to. With repeated access to this material, they may well come to view this as 'normal' sex. Concerns are growing amongst experts that we may be nurturing a new generation of child sex offenders, via their internet experiences. One New Zealand Internal Affairs survey revealed that teens aged 15 to 19 were the leading age group viewing child pornography.[1]

'By and large the images we're working on depict the horrible and brutal rape of children under the age of eight.' *Agent Flint Waters, Internet Crimes Against Children*[2]

Professor Max Taylor, who knows this area well, warns, 'More babies and toddlers are appearing on the net and the abuse is getting worse. It is more torturous and sadistic than it was before. The typical age of children [involved in illegal child porn] is between 6 and 12, but the profile is getting younger.'[3] With literally thousands of sites to choose from, there is no shortage of material for boys to access. Though illegal, boys who know their way around cyberspace can watch everything from women being choked with penises to the detailed, graphic deflowering of young girls. One site encourages boys who find themselves with a drunk girl to grab a video camera and call up their mates so they can all have a good time with her, then post their exploits on the site. In porn, girls are often further dehumanised by being referred to as sluts, whores, c*nts or cum dumpsters.

According to Dr Gail Dines, who has studied this area in detail, one of the big challenges for porn manufacturers is that as viewers watch more porn, their appetite for immediate arousal grows.[4] So the demand for increasingly violent and sexually confronting experiences is fuelling the production of even more graphic material. Porn director Mitchel Spinelli believes the secret is to 'Make it more hard, more nasty, more relentless.'[5] While illegal, one approach some producers are taking is to involve younger and younger participants. These kids are frequently penetrated orally, anally and vaginally. In the closing shots they are left covered in semen. The growing eroticisation of young people has created a burgeoning number of sites specialising in themes such as incest and the seduction of a young babysitter. Child pornography is illegal, and pornography in general is meant for an adult market, but we're very naïve if we think some boys aren't viewing this material.

SOPHISTICATED OPERATORS

Internet child porn is a lucrative, sophisticated, albeit illegal business with clever operators who keep on the move, frequently crossing borders and changing service providers. As stored images can be detected by internet sweeps, some now have remote stores where each image is archived in thousands of pieces. When a customer clicks on the main website to download one of the images, the site instantaneously assembles the many pieces of that image from the separate image store. This way, the images stored remotely cannot be detected.[6]

Kids no longer have to sneak down to the newsagent or wait till they get home to access this material. They can download it at the click of a mouse or from their mobile phone pad. They can also produce their own shots and movies. The inappropriate material boys can access is no longer just images. Video-enabled phones and a whole range of technologies can deliver this material live to boys within minutes. Some scenarios offer real-time experiences. There's nothing glamorous or just a little bit naughty about this world. It's sordid, often violent, dehumanising and addictive. Writer and campaigner Melida Tankard-Reist was at a London conference on this subject recently and, in talking with one of the professionals there, learned there is an entire police department in Washington whose sole job it is to match the photos of missing children with the thousands of kids featured in porn photos and movies.

'In 2005, worldwide revenue from mobile phone pornography is expected to rise to $1 billion and could grow to three times that number or more within a few years.' *Cassell Bryan-Low and David Pringle, The Wall Street Journal*[7]

PORN IS PART OF POP CULTURE

With porn so visible, it's now part of everyday life. It's now seen by some kids as cool to dance and dress like a porn star and to be called a ho or slut. Boys now grow up watching highly erotic MTV clips and increasingly edgy reality TV shows. And teen idols now include pimp and rapster Snoop Dogg and porn star Jenna Jameson, praised by some for the huge influence she has had in taking porn mainstream.

'I'm entertaining the masses. So it's just like being Julia Roberts, but I'm a bit further.' *Jenna Jameson*[8]

While the world of porn may seem glamorous, this is hardly the reality for those working in the industry. Adult entertainment columnist Luke Ford, who knows the scene well, describes a world of renegades and outcasts, where 'most of the girls who enter the industry do one video and quit' because their experiences are 'so painful, horrifying, embarrassing and humiliating'.[9]

'Porn kind of stays in a boy's head.' *Jacob, 17*

CORPORATIONS NOW INTO PORN

The production and distribution of porn is no longer a cottage industry. A number of leading corporations now invest in the area. And, with a taste for big profits, the porn industry employs full-time lobbyists to represent their interests to governments. They have done a good job. In the United States alone it's estimated that people are spending around $10 billion a year on 'adult' entertainment. This equals the money spent on mainstream movies, music and sporting events.[10] Though cable TV companies rarely mention the profits gleaned from their adult entertainment channels, porn is a big earner for them. The Hilton, Marriott, Hyatt, Sheraton and Holiday Inn all offer pay-per-view 'adult' films because, according to them, every second guest expects this service.

This is an extremely large business and there's a great opportunity for profits.' *Bill Lyon, lobbyist*[11]

As well as adults, a growing number of teens, and considerably younger children, are also accessing pornographic material. In 2004 one *Washington Post* article estimated that more than 11 million American teens were also regularly viewing porn online.[12] The availability of pornographic material has escalated considerably since then. It can be now downloaded onto mobile phones, and it too generates millions of dollars.

'At first it's curiosity, then probably enjoyment, which is what it's designed for – sexual gratification, because it's easy to access, so why not?' *Gary, 17*

Michael Flood, who heads up the Violence Against Women Program, points out that the internet is an ideal medium for boys wanting to access porn, as there's an almost endless amount of material they can view anonymously, customise and store for ongoing access.[13] This is largely material that boys would not otherwise have access to. Many porn sites are set up to keep browsers open as long as possible. The new technologies can also make it difficult for boys to leave porn sites, or they may forward them automatically to other porn sites.[14] These new technologies now make it possible to continue to heighten the experience while viewing porn. Already the refinements in 3D technology used in the film *Avatar* are being replicated in porn films for this reason.

THE CURIOSITY FACTOR

Kids are naturally curious about sex. Some are drawn to porn because they want to expand their sexual repertoire, or as an act of rebellion. Others use it because it's seen as cool, or to take the edge off their loneliness and isolation. Parents can be very naïve about their children's access to sexually explicit material, and kids know it. 'Parents have no idea of pornography on the net, also what happens with instant messages,' said Daryl, 17. 'There's entire romances on the net that no-one would know about. There's weird stuff as well.'

Watching porn, or taking part in risky sexual behaviour, gives boys an edge with their peers. 'Yeah, teens are exposed to a whole lot of images on their mobiles and the internet,' explains Hunter, 18. 'Images can be sent around so easily within groups. It's a regular thing.' Mark, 15, agrees. 'With your close friends it might come up in conversation, or if it's a show-off it would be because it might boost their respect.' Or as Gary, 17, puts it, 'There's a bravado thing watching porn together. It's like, "This is what I look at. I'm tough." It's more like a contest to prove yourself in the alpha male chain.'

BOYS WATCHING PORN TOGETHER

As there are so many ways kids can access porn, it's hard to get a sense of who is watching what, and how much pornographic material is consumed. Boys are watching porn films together, and sharing this material. In one Canadian study of boys aged 13 to 14 in urban and rural areas, more than a third of the boys said they had viewed pornographic movies and DVDs 'too many times to count'. Just over seven out of ten of these boys accessed pornography on the net. More than half saw it on a specialty TV channel.[15] In this same study two out of ten boys aged 13 to 14 viewed porn at the home of a friend.

'Porno is so easy to access now with technology, to access and to buy.' *Hunter, 18*

'There's the porno aspect of the internet now,' explains Harrison, 15. 'Kids don't have to buy it off older boys like they used to do. It's readily accessible. Some boys use it quite regularly. There's quite a culture of it. Inside jokes and words. A lot of boys talk about it in an open and relaxed manner. Most of my peer group admit to doing it. What they know about sex becomes quite sensationalised. They realise sex isn't exactly like that, but it's quite pleasurable. It can change the way boys talk in groups.'

PARENTS IN THE DARK

One of the reasons parents have no idea of what's going on is because their kids are far ahead in covering their tracks. One study of children aged 13 to 17 revealed that just over two-thirds of the kids knew how to hide what they do online. A further third cleared their browser history to cover their tracks. Over 40 per cent had shut down or minimised the browser when their parents were around. Sixteen per cent had private networking email addresses and profiles their parents knew nothing about.[16]

While viewing porn is one of many ways boys can push the boundaries, it's not without consequences. 'Pornography of any description hurts boys, because it limits their capacity for compassion and intimacy, and puts boys at risk. They're like little time bombs, waiting to go off,' one clinical psychologist told me.

'Sometimes you hear about a girl trying to manipulate someone by sending them weird photos. There's a handful of girls in my year who would feel that's the way to seduce some boys.' *Mark, 15*

STARRING IN YOUR OWN SHOW

Experts believe that one of the reasons today's teens are less inhibited is because many have been captured on video and photographed by doting parents and family from birth. Living in a performance culture, it's no surprise teenagers are generating their own explicit material, especially as they have little sense of the emotional, social and legal consequences. Assistant principal Austin agrees. 'Access to pornography is greater now than it's ever been. It's hard to avoid. I'm surprised at what photos girls will have taken.'

Again this risky behaviour leaves boys vulnerable. Too few boys know that if they take an explicit photo or make an explicit video of their under-age girlfriend, they have committed the offences of creating and possessing child pornography. Should they circulate this material, they then commit additional offences. This is not the first generation to take dumb photos. The problem is that rarely do these images remain on someone's phone. They can be downloaded on to the net in seconds, where they can be shared by millions. A moment's lack of thought can have huge consequences as family and friendships are torn apart, and charges laid. There are long-term consequences as well: what goes into cyberspace may well stay there.

'Each time someone looks at pictures of me, it's like abusing me again.' *Sandra,16, a victim of child sexual abuse*[17]

BOYS JUST BEING BOYS?

Some parents mistakenly regard access to porn as a welcome sign their boys are growing up. There's also the view that if porn is accessed in the privacy of the home, it doesn't affect anyone else, but this is not the case. 'When we go into a boy's background after a sexual offence it's clear the majority have been accessing porn,' explains Rowan, who works with troubled youth. 'You can see this also from the kinds of acts they have performed, it's an obvious imitation of something they've seen.'

According to noted psychologist Michael Carr-Gregg, 'One of the greatest problems we face is that many adults lack the skills, knowledge or strategies to critically analyse and understand the longer term impacts that sexualisation/pornification have on the behaviour of boys towards girls and eventually men towards women. The evidence is potentially one of the most toxic elements in society and it is time that those responsible for propagating this material be held accountable. When the history of public health is written, I am sure that this battle will sit alongside the struggle against the tobacco industry, infant food formula manufacturers and elements of the alcohol industry in significance.'

Like many professionals, Michael Flood of the Preventing Violence Against Women Program is at pains to emphasise that pornography is a poor sex educator.[18] Concerns include the de-sensitising of boys, as little value is placed on intimacy, empathy or respect of partners in pornographic material. Here girls are seen as little more than sex objects. The pornification of our culture also makes it harder for boys to understand where the lines are in terms of appropriate behaviour. A growing body of research shows that viewing porn is likely to make boys more sexually aggressive, to do whatever they feel they can get away with, and to want to act out what they have seen.[19] In one Canadian study of boys around the age of 14 revealed that those who regularly accessed porn tended to think it was okay to hold a girl down and force her to have sex.[20]

The concern of many adolescent health advocates is the whole way boys relate to girls is being influenced by this graphic, often violent material. In Sydney recently a 13-year-old girl met a schoolboy she liked. Trusting him, she agreed to join him a few days later in a nearby park. To her surprise they were joined by several of his friends. Over a number of hours she was sexually assaulted and repeatedly raped. Forced to perform oral sex on a number of the boys, she was told repeatedly to 'just smile like you're enjoying it'. The incident was filmed and circulated.

Those reporting on the court case remarked on the complete lack of remorse shown by the boys.

'Some boys will definitely see girls differently after looking at pornography. It doesn't have a good impact at all.' *Mark, 15*

THE BRAIN SCIENCE

In *The Brain That Changes Itself*, Norman Doidge shows how porn rewires the male brain, leaving viewers wanting more. Continued access to porn can lead to addiction, with people obsessively seeking out certain sexual experiences, needing increasingly heightened levels of stimulation, and experiencing withdrawal symptoms when porn isn't available. In his male patients Doidge noticed interest in making love was replaced by simply needing a f**k, and that the 'sexual creativity' of these men was dying as increasingly they needed to experience the scenarios they'd 'downloaded'. The result was a decrease in interest in their regular partners, potency issues and handling their increasingly hardcore tastes.[21]

'Softcore pornography's influence is now most profound because, now that it is no longer hidden, it influences young people with little sexual experience and especially plastic minds, in the process of forming their sexual tastes and desires.' *Norman Doidge,* The Brain That Changes Itself[22]

PORN IS HARMFUL TO BOYS

Increasingly experts are realising just how harmful early access to porn can be for boys, as it shuts down their emotions and distorts their views on sex. 'Pornography has given boys a shared language, a sense of entitlement around sex, and a belief that the sexually explicit material seen in pornographic material is what girls want to do,' explains one psychologist who works with sexual assault victims at a major

Sydney hospital. 'Seeing it in their living room normalises pornography. It gives young guys a way of relating to each other, which in turn reinforces abuse.'

'Research on the effects of repeated exposure to pornography during adolescence is compelling,' according to clinical psychologist Robi Sondregger, whose work focuses on the family and on rehabilitating young people affected by war, sexual exploitation, and natural disaster. 'In addition to interference of sexual development and the encouragement of early sexual activity, pornography exposure can undermine relationships, disrupt psychological wellbeing, and promote sexually violent attitudes and behaviours,' he explains.

Robi Sondregger also talks of the links between a boy's ongoing exposure to porn and predatory sexual behaviour. 'Investigations have shown concern over the role pornography plays in grooming next-generation sex offenders. Boys regularly exposed to pornography run the risk of developing pro-sexual-offending attitudes. Some researchers now report a direct link between pornography and sexual assault. Images of sexually explicit activity are (also) luring younger participants. Not only are more young people consuming pornography online, police data reveals more children and adolescents are starting to produce and file-share paedophilic content.'

FATHERS WORRIED

Many fathers I spoke with were extremely concerned about what porn is doing to boys, and to the chances these young boys then have of creating happy, long-term relationships. 'I personally think porn is very damaging for boys, but because this stuff is happening in the playground they think it's okay,' said Peter, father of two boys. 'Porn is the biggest business on the net. When I was around ten I found some pornographic magazines in the park and was really curious. I showed them to my mother and she subtly got rid of them. What a boy sees when he sees porn is just thrashing about. There's no love, no caring. It's like sex is worth nothing. Making love is tender, sensual, it's taking your time, it's respectful.'

'Boys are placing pressure on girls to have sex. The girlie magazines of previous generations are nothing compared to what kids can now access. Porn is a booming industry. At the tap of a finger kids can access porn worldwide.' *Siobhan, high-school teacher*

WHAT PARENTS CAN DO

Most parents express concern about their boys accessing porn, but fail to have conversations with them about pornography, or to supervise what their sons are doing on the net. It's vital kids have clear rules about computer and internet use at home, on the phone and at internet cafes. They need to know that websites with crude names are best left alone. Teach them to recognise explicit spam and email addresses. Filters are important and should be used, but they aren't failsafe.

When parents have little knowledge of computers they leave their kids vulnerable. In a study of children aged 13 to 17, just over one in ten admitted to unlocking or disabling computer filters.[23] As most parents of teenage boys are busy and not tech savvy, it helps to enlist older brothers and sisters to help monitor a boy's online usage by checking his files and folders, looking for cookies, and reviewing the images stored on his hard drive. It also helps to watch for any noticeable changes in a boy's behaviour. Perhaps a teen is seriously addicted to his computer. Has he become secretive, withdrawn? If so, you need to see what he might be up to and establish why.

Often boys feel relieved at this level of protection. Theo handled the situation well when he discovered his 13-year-old son had been accessing sexually explicit sites. 'At the time I didn't have the right filters on the computer,' he explained. 'Andy googled sex and found all these pornographic sites. I talked to him about it. My whole focus was that he didn't carry the shame of this. I told him that curiosity and attraction to girls was perfectly normal, and that when I was a boy it was looking at girls in bikinis which was harmless, but that there's a whole world on the internet that's very ugly, and that it's my job to protect him from it. After that he actually called me his protector for a while. I also stressed that sex is beautiful, but some people make it sick, or use people just to make money out of it.' Now when Andy discovers something on the computer he's uncomfortable with, he talks with his dad about it. Technology offers kids wonderful opportunities, but they also need to know when material can be harmful and illegal.

What to do if your son has been accessing porn:

- *Begin by acknowledging your son's natural curiosity about sex, and likely peer pressure.*
- *Don't freak out or shame your son.*
- *Recognise that this is an invaluable opportunity to get across the points you need to make.*
- *Encourage future conversations and openness.*
- *Listen to what he has to say.*
- *Don't rush the conversation.*
- *Steer the conversation around to boundaries.*
- *Cover the abusive and addictive aspects of porn.*
- *Describe the difference between being a great guy and being a creep.*
- *Be clear about your expectations.*
- *Encourage him to continue to talk to you and ask questions.*

Camboy

In this new sexualised climate boys are vulnerable in ways we could not have foreseen, and yet again it is our ignorance that makes them so vulnerable. Perhaps one of the saddest stories is that of 13-year-old Californian Justin Berry, who bought himself a webcam in the hope of meeting new friends on the net. In no time Justin had friendly responses from a whole range of men offering gifts and flattering him. As a boy estranged from his father, this attention was very appealing. When one guy offered Justin $50 to bare his chest to camera, it didn't seem such a big deal. As Justin took off his T-shirt, the compliments flowed. Over time Justin went on to become one of a number of boys who stripped, masturbated and performed sexual acts on camera for money.

With instant messaging, fast internet connections and webcams, it has become much easier for predators to contact kids in their own homes. Net-savvy kids like Justin often prove to be commercially astute, getting men to subscribe to their services or pay a premium for live shows staged in their bedrooms. The first image Justin placed on the net was totally innocent. He posted a picture and contact details on spotlife.com, a directory for webcam users, in the hope other kids would get in touch.

Justin attracted predators instead. Some pretended to be other boys. They groomed him over a period of time with presents and money. One of Justin's new 'friends' showed him how to set up his own wish list on Amazon.com, using the name of Justin Camboy. His admirers were then able to purchase him gifts. It all seemed good fun and quite safe, as none of them knew where he lived.

Over time the requests were ramped up, as was the money his admirers were willing to pay. Each new request didn't seem dramatically different, so Justin willingly obliged. As he became more daring, Justin's popularity grew, until he had 1500 subscribers, many of whom were professional men – doctors, lawyers, teachers and the like. When there were complaints about the quality of his webcam, Justin simply put state-of the-art gear on his wish list and his fans obliged. Careful to hide most of his new gear, Justin explained away his additional purchases and money on his fledgling web development business. Unbeknown to his mother, Justin now had his own porn site justinscam.com, which another fan helped him establish.

As he got deeper into the world of cyber porn, Justin became aware of other teens competing for attention. While Justin was still only 13 one of his fans invited him to attend a computer camp. Unaware of what was going on, his mother readily agreed. During the visit, Justin was molested by this man. Later on the guy lured Justin back, offering him the chance to sleep with a girl. Again Justin was molested.

The further Justin ventured into this dark world, the tougher he became, pushing up his prices and keeping his subscribers on tenterhooks. By now Justin was being offered cash for face-to-face meetings. A 'Mr Tunno' offered him thousands to meet in a Las Vegas hotel, where Justin ended up meeting him on a number of occasions.

By the time Justin was 15, business was thriving. Concerned his mother might find out what he was doing, he persuaded Mr Tunno to rent him a nearby apartment. Here Justin set up all his gear, and it was business as usual. This was an ideal arrangement as Justin would simply pretend he was out visiting friends. But then when someone close to him discovered his site, peers distributed Justin's pictures and beat him up. Justin was desperate now to be home schooled. Upset at the bullying, without knowing why, his mother agreed.

From here on in, Justin's life became even darker. By now he was performing sex on camera with prostitutes, and featuring other underage boys on his website. He was also using marijuana and cocaine. Where this would have ended was anyone's guess, but after he turned 18, Justin was invited to meet a man he hadn't heard from before. It turned out to be a reporter, Kurt Eichenwald, wanting to know more about the world of web porn. Justin agreed to help, and proceeded to show the journalist how he operated. Within days Justin agreed to leave that world behind, and to tell the police all he knew, which he did.[1]

While most kids won't end up in Justin's situation, it's interesting to look at some of the themes that help us understand his generation. Justin set out simply wanting to meet new friends on the net. At only 13 he was vulnerable and impressionable. The lure of praise, presents and cash was too hard to resist. Justin was a bright boy with good grades. In a world that has a price for everything, Justin milked his popularity for all it was worth. Ultimately he had a lucky escape. It raises the question as to what happens to all the other camboys and girls out there.

You can help safeguard your son from falling prey to sexual predators on the net by:

- *Discussing with him the risky ways in which the new technology can be used.*
- *Making him aware of grooming techniques.*
- *Talking about loneliness and the desire to be acknowledged.*
- *Discussing the possible consequences of meeting predatory strangers.*
- *Encouraging healthy, relaxed discussions about sex.*

When sex becomes sexual assault

Living in a sex-saturated world is very confusing for boys. If you take your cues from video clips and music lyrics, then as Boston paediatrician and director of the Center on Media and Child Health Dr Michael Rich suggests, you may well think dating violence and sexual coercion is the way to go.[1] With these constant messages, boys may be forgiven for thinking that you're meant to be constantly ready and willing whenever and wherever sex is offered. Significant discussions with boys about boundaries and consequences don't happen early enough, if at all. Now, more than ever, boys need this input.

At one school I visited, a 12-year-old girl told me how her best friend, also 12, did 'all kinds of sex stuff' with boys. 'You don't have to love them or anything,' her friend informed her. 'You just do it.' The young girl I spoke with didn't feel good about this, but wasn't sure if this was how it was meant to be. This is not a rare occurrence. Growing numbers of underage boys and girls are participating in a whole range of sexual activities because they're curious, or want to be popular, please peers and appear grown-up. These kids may be aware of the basic mechanics of sex, but have little idea of how to navigate the physical, emotional and legal complexities they're being drawn into. Then it's often the schools and parents who are left to pick up the pieces.

'There are more sexual violence issues to deal with,' one assistant principal told me. He put this down in part to the explicit material kids are now exposed to. 'Access to inappropriate images is much easier, even if you don't want to see them. This leaves boys with a mixed perception of how they should relate to women,' he explained, and went on to tell me that one of the challenges of the first week of each semester is in dealing with the fallout from sexual encounters over the holidays.

What we do know is that younger and younger girls are becoming victims of assault, partly because there are predatory guys out there, but partly because young teen boys and girls are now leading very complex social lives at a time when they're less mature and have fewer life experiences than previous generations. Being allowed into the party scene so young makes boys and girls vulnerable, and binge-drinking doesn't help. When I spoke with one emergency department nurse, she was seeing kids as young as 12 admitted to her ward so drunk they couldn't breathe and often with concerning physical injuries. Frequently these girls had had sex, but couldn't remember who with.

WHEN BOYS DON'T READ THE SIGNALS

While girls are often better at picking up on what is going on in a situation, often they're not sure what they want from a boy. They want to look and act sexy, because that's what's appealing and cool, but they haven't necessarily thought through where they may end up. Boys tend to take girls at face value, which can be disastrous for everyone. Daryl, 17, agrees. 'Girls get drunk and guys get drunk, then things happen. The girls do something they're not proud of, and then it's the guy's fault. Guys don't have the luxury of changing their mind about how the situation happened.' Dylan, 18, felt the same way. 'Young guys are so hormonal. They don't understand no. They can't read body language.

233

A girl might not want to say no, but her body language will say no. But young boys are so immature. They think because they want it, girls must want it as well.'

GOTTA BE A STUD

Popular culture encourages boys to be macho men. Men's magazines are full of sexy images and editorial about different techniques to light up the bedroom. However, there's little discussion about feelings, sensitivity or restraint. Performance is the name of the game. Add to this a boy's often easy access to pornography, and it's not a happy mix. According to Gary, 17, boys are often 'trying to live up to the images they've seen, or to copy the images they've seen.' Hunter, 18, agrees. 'Porno exposure does mean boys end up doing things that aren't seen as pleasant.' Aware of how much more attractive older boys are to girls, younger boys feel the need to be more mature. 'There's also that thing of young girls dating older guys, so young guys have to catch up,' says Dylan, 18.

WRONG PLACE, WRONG TIME

When talking with professionals who run sexual assault units in major hospitals, without excusing boys, they talk about how 'ordinary' many of the offending boys now seem. Brent Sanders, who has a background in profiling sexual offenders and serial rapists and now educates teenagers on sexual issues and behaviour, agrees. 'In a date rape situation you'll often find the decision to participate was a mix of a lack of awareness of consequences, being in the wrong place at the wrong time, having a few too many beers, and pressure from peers.'

'What's happening to our kids is of real concern. There are so many mixed messages. Everything they see says it's cool to be sexy, yet the law says you're not to,' says Rowan, who works with troubled youth. Siobhan, an experienced teacher who has worked in city and rural areas, agrees. 'Kids are keen to have certain experiences without understanding the ramifications. I suspect boys often haven't understood that emulating things they've seen is just not appropriate, or that someone genuinely might not want to do something.'

UNDERSTANDING CONSEQUENCES

Boys have real responsibilities around sexual issues, but unless parents discuss these, how can boys know when they're stepping over the line? Part of the problem is that often boys genuinely don't realise where their desire to have sex with a girl might lead. Brent Sanders agrees. 'There's a misplaced view in society that by the time a boy gets to a certain age he magically knows a whole lot of things, and it's just not true.' He believes that one of the things boys now lack is a 'good old-fashioned healthy fear of consequences', because if nothing else it gives them a reason to pause in difficult situations. Boys need to know that if they end up with a criminal conviction, they have it for life, and that workplaces often do their own searches before employing someone. A boy with a conviction may never achieve his career and other goals, regardless of how competent he is.

> We need all the good men out there to help us reclaim boys from the dysfunctional, destructive role models churned out by the media and marketers.

Some boys end up in regrettable situations trying to prove themselves, or because they fear they'll lose face, but this is no excuse for sexual assault. Boys need to know there's more at stake than appearing super-cool. I believe that one of the reasons our society is in this quandary is because we place little importance on the role men have to play in teaching boys what it means to be a responsible adult. We need all the good men out there to help us reclaim boys from the dysfunctional, destructive role models churned out by the media and marketers.

KIDS ARE GETTING HURT

Whether we like to admit to it or not, this increasingly risky sexual climate is having very real consequences. 'Personally I have huge concerns,' admits one senior clinical psychologist, who heads a sexual assault support team at a major hospital. 'We're now seeing girls vulnerable to the same range of risks adult women face. Being harmed on their way home by taxi drivers, by boyfriends.' One of the issues sexual assault support units struggle with is the fact that it's no longer cool for young girls to go out with boys at high school, so they're homing in on older boys at parties, and getting hurt. 'We see a lot of 12- to 14-year-olds, targeted by boys 17 to 18 years,' this professional told me. 'These are young girls wanting to be grown-up, who're still very young and trusting, who fall prey to pre-planned situations. They're plied with alcohol and possibly drugs, and often raped anally. In the past it was rape by one boy, but now it's two or three boys, and often filmed.'

FACING THE FALLOUT

Very little is said about the emotional fallout for boys in sexual encounters that go wrong. This needs to be taken into account. It's assumed that boys can shrug off inappropriate or unhappy sexual encounters, but this may not be the case. 'When boys get drawn into certain sexual scenarios they too may be facing trauma from that,' says Rowan, who works with at-risk teenagers. 'The teen culture sees him as a lucky guy, when he may be regretful, confused and ashamed. You then see the classic symptoms of trauma develop, like a sudden lack of confidence. A boy may have been doing well at school, and his grades suddenly drop away. Or he may drop out of school altogether. He may start to be physically aggressive towards peers.'

Brent Sanders, who now spends his days talking to high school and university students, is impressed by how hungry boys are for information, and how much they appreciate someone being straight with them.

If parents are to help their boys navigate the complexities of the teen dating scene, they need to leave their boys in no doubt about what it means to be a real man, and what will bring them down.

Parents often find these kinds of discussions hard, but what's a little discomfort compared to leaving a boy to find his own way through the increasingly complex sexual world he lives in? As we've seen earlier, you'll get a whole lot further if you discuss the issues, rather than lecture a boy. How much better for him to have a clear understanding of the sexual landscape, including its pitfalls, before he gets into regrettable situations.

Ways to help your son avoid sexual minefields:

- *Use news stories to open up informed discussions with your son.*
- *Ensure he knows unwanted vaginal, oral and anal sex all constitute rape.*
- *Ensure he knows that alcohol and drugs will impair his ability to read what is really going on.*
- *Ensure he knows that he too can be a victim of sexual assault.*
- *Make sure he understands that any unwelcome sexual overture, even without intercourse, can attract a conviction.*
- *Make sure he understands that although a girl may agree to a level of sexual intimacy, it does not mean she's up for anything and everything.*
- *Make sure he understands that while a guy and girl may both be drunk, that's no protection from a conviction.*

Mental health issues

One of the positive steps forward in recent years has been an increasing awareness of such issues as male depression and suicide. Once we understand more about them, it's easier to be more open about these issues, and get help for them. Sometimes the challenges boys face become too much, and they require professional help. However, it's estimated that only half the young people with mental health issues in need of assistance get help, partly because parents don't realise what's happening or don't know where to go. Whatever the reason, it's important to know that mental health issues don't go away on their own.

> **'Social and cultural changes have made it hard for them [young people] to develop a strong sense of identity, purpose, belonging and security: in short, to feel life is deeply meaningful and worthwhile.'**
> Social analyst Richard Eckersley, Never Better – Or Getting Worse?[1]

PLENTY OF KIDS HAVE ISSUES THEY NEED HELP WITH

One in five children will develop a mental health problem by the time they reach adulthood. Around half these issues will emerge during teen life, and in some cases during the tween years. Teenage mental health issues are on the rise. Social analyst Richard Eckersley suggests that at any one time between 20 to 30 per cent of young people are facing 'significant psychological distress', while up to half of them experience regular symptoms of stress – headaches, sleeplessness and stomach pains. This can be sparked by anything from study and work pressures, family upsets and breakdowns to changes in diet and the impact of technology and the media. There's also a growing concern about the consumerism of childhood, which leaves kids constantly worried about their looks and their possessions, and distances them from a genuine sense of support and belonging.

ATTENTION DEFICIT HYPERACTIVITY DISORDER

Of all the mental health issues boys face, Attention Deficit Hyperactivity Disorder (ADHD) is the most common. Boys are more vulnerable to ADHD than girls. Often these symptoms appear before boys get to school, and may include difficulty concentrating, constantly losing or forgetting things, talking all the time, creating chaos, and/or being constantly on the go. That said, it's important parents don't mistake boyish exuberance for ADHD. A child psychiatrist or psychologist can help with the diagnosis. Medication can be effective, but it's important to know that while it manages the condition, it isn't a cure. With professional help, boys can better manage their day-to-day lives. A daily to-do list and a regular routine help, as does plenty of sleep and exercise, dividing up assignments or jobs into manageable pieces, and concentrating on one task at a time. New research from the Institute of Psychiatry, Kings College London suggests ADHD sufferers have a different perception of time. So what to the rest of us seems like a short time span can be unbearably long for those with the disorder. As hyperactive behaviour creates a surge of dopamine, the body's feel-good chemical, scientists now think this may be a boy's way of compensating for his boredom with a natural high. Whatever the reasons for ADHD, there are now plenty of resources for parents.

DEPRESSION

One of the most significant mental health issues our boys face is depression when they are engulfed by anger, sadness or despair. Often sadness comes out in boys as angry, aggressive behaviour, but true depression is debilitating. It's not something a boy can snap out of. When a boy is depressed he loses interest in life. Eating and sleeping patterns often change. He may have little energy or motivation, and be extremely sensitive to criticism. He may even complain frequently of aches and pains. Depression may also be expressed through risky behaviour, plummeting self-esteem, a lack of interest in school and declining grades. Boys may even run away or get into substance abuse.

> True depression is debilitating. It's not something a boy can snap out of. When a boy is depressed he loses interest in life.

Current theories suggest depression is often due to a chemical imbalance, and that stress is usually the trigger. Very often depression creeps up on boys. Left untreated, it can lead to risk-taking behaviour, or to boys 'self-medicating' on alcohol or drugs. Scientists have found a variant in the serotonin transporter gene which places certain kids at more risk of depression. The interesting thing is, however, that if these boys don't fall victim to stressful situations such as family strife, relationship break-ups or peer problems, depression doesn't develop. Again this underlines the importance of a stable and supportive family life.

Sleep expert Professor Mary Carskadon also suggests there may be links between sleeplessness and depression in teenagers, as lack of sleep also causes mood swings. For vulnerable teenagers, sleep problems may make their depression worse.[2] Those with long-term depression can become so used to feeling this way that moving out of the pattern may be difficult, even uncomfortable, because they've forgotten what it's like to be happy. The important thing for parents is to be supportive,

240

to stay close to their son and affirm all he means to them, and to seek professional help.

WHEN BOYS COMMIT SUICIDE

Left untreated, depression can trigger suicide. Boys are more likely to commit suicide successfully than girls. While it's often said that people who talk about suicide don't do it, studies suggest that around 75 per cent of those who do commit suicide had given some indication of how they were feeling before their death. What might seem a relatively minor issue to parents can be heart-breaking to a teenager. One of the areas where boys, like girls, are most fragile is around relationship break-ups, so it's important parents realise how wounding these can be. Just because a boy isn't acting strangely doesn't mean he doesn't have a problem. If you are in any doubt as to your son's mental state, don't hesitate to get immediate professional help.

Many of the signs of depression hold true for suicide. As well as possibly being in the depths of despair, it's also important to watch out for sudden elated behaviour, references to suicide or making jokes about it, or giving away possessions, as these situations may suggest suicide is on a boy's mind. Those who have already attempted suicide remain vulnerable, as they are likely to repeat their attempt and to succeed, so they need ongoing support and care. As with a number of mental health issues, the path to suicide isn't found overnight. A new Finnish study found that over seven out of ten of the boys who killed themselves had been diagnosed with mental health issues by the time they were 8.

WHAT ABOUT THE KIDS LEFT BEHIND?

One of the many things we have to be careful of around teen suicide is the possibility of copycat suicides, as teens are very suggestible, especially when they're feeling down or distressed. While honouring a teenager's death with a web page might seem like a great idea, parents have to be cautious. Child psychologist Kimberley O'Brien points out that should teenagers who know the boy who has taken his life also be feeling depressed, lonely and rejected, then suicide may seem an attractive option for them as well.[3] Sadly there have been many instances which prove this very point. That's why after a suicide, schools are quick to offer counselling, and why responsible media outlets keep coverage of teenage suicides to the absolute minimum.

What you can do to support your son:

- *Ensure your home is a stable, nurturing environment for him.*
- *Be sure your son knows you love him unconditionally and are there for him.*
- *If you suspect there are problems, keep talking.*
- *Listen carefully to what he tells you.*
- *Make sure he understands you are listening.*
- *Reflect his feelings back to him without judgement or lecturing.*
- *Don't hesitate to talk to his teacher or your family doctor if you have ongoing concerns.*
- *Read ADHD by Dr Brenton Prosser.*
- *See www.living_withADHD.com.au and the ADHD pages of www.familydoctor.org*
- *Read* I Just Want You to Be Happy: Preventing and Tackling Teenage Depression *by professors Leanne Rowe, David Bennett and Bruce Tonge.*

Living in a violent world

Often when boys and violence are discussed, it's assumed boys are naturally violent. But is this so? Certainly some boys can be. The real question is how this violence emerges. Often our crude way of parenting boys doesn't help. We continue to smack or tell little boys off for crying or getting upset, forgetting how small they are. Then, as they grow, we encourage them to give as good as they get when they're facing conflict. Boys do need clear boundaries and discipline, but they also need to be heard, nourished, encouraged and protected. As we'll see, if a boy doesn't feel safe, he may end up being a danger to himself and others.

VIOLENT GAMES, VIOLENT BOYS

Violence has become a major form of entertainment for boys with violent video games and children's cartoons. In some of these games hurting people is seen as humorous, and killing them as exciting. In many online games, players get points for harming others. To play well they need to know the killing zones on the body. And the action heroes of these games solve difficult situations by exterminating people, and blasting whole buildings and landscapes out of existence. In these games violence is sometimes portrayed as sexy, and boys pick up on this.

'There's a ramping up of violent games. They're killing people every few minutes.' *Rebecca, mother and child protection worker*

Harvard professor of public health Deborah Prothrow-Stith doesn't accept that boys are inherently violent. She believes violence is learned. She reminds us that when a boy first witnesses someone being harmed, he is saddened by it. But if he sees that same act of violence over and over, numbness sets in.[1] With this numbness comes a drop in empathy, and a failure to fully comprehend the consequences of certain actions. When violence is presented as fun it desensitises boys, and can encourage them to imitate the behaviour they see onscreen.[2]

'Only a few years ago we were questioning boys playing with toy guns. Given what's now around, that seems laughable.' *Andrew Lines, father, teacher and founder of The Rite Journey*

SURROUNDED BY VIOLENCE

It's easy to underestimate how much violence children are exposed to as they grow up. By the time a boy is 18 he is likely to have witnessed 40 000 murders and 200 000 other acts of violence.[3] It's not just violent games that can be troubling to boys. Many also find the real world worrying. One study of TV violence indicated that two-thirds of the children interviewed were emotionally affected by violence on the news.[4] Reports of war and violent uprisings are particularly disturbing for kids, leaving them with the impression the world is a dangerous place. Boys need to feel safe before they start to push the boundaries during adolescence. They need parents who will show them how to deal with unpleasant situations by helping them find the best words and actions to use when they are in difficulty.

Today we've become nervous about talking about boundaries and discipline, because we don't want to appear uncool. But to be a functioning adult, we need boundaries and discipline. We need to know how *best* to relate to others. We can't achieve this in a vacuum. Boys need to learn strength, courage and endurance, and how families and communities work. Out of these qualities they begin to understand the value of being part of something bigger than themselves. It helps give them a genuine sense of belonging. Boys need to experience these qualities to mature. Without them, a boy is just in survival mode.

ARMED AND DANGEROUS

When a boy doesn't feel secure, he's a danger to himself and others. If he feels threatened, his first response is to fight back. This is one of the many reasons why more boys are carrying knives and other weapons to school, and why they join gangs. In New South Wales alone there's been a 17 per cent increase in school suspensions for using or possessing a weapon, a 20 per cent increase in teenagers suspended for violent behaviour, and 45 per cent increase in those suspended for serious criminal behaviour.[5] And a recent parliamentary committee in Britain found that children as young as 7 were carrying knives to school. Just under a third of kids aged between 11 and 16 admitted to carrying a weapon to school at some time.[6]

> **'Today all i've been doing is thinking about getting in fights and i've been getting an adrenaline rush just from thinking about it. oh and i learned today that people don't like to be around me because all i do is "raise hell" and you know what that's exactly how i like it.'** Colt 451[7]

Some of the teachers I spoke with are noticing a new breed of tougher risk-taking boys entering high school, determined to make their presence felt. Many older teens commented on this also. Teachers

245

suspect this is due to their increased exposure to violence on computer games and DVDs from a young age, as well as the need to prove they're grown-up. 'When we looked recently at the boys who were being suspended for violence, most were young for their year,' one teacher told me. 'They weren't coping. They were so angry, and were responding with violence. The kids entering high school are more violent. It's like they're trying to be the alpha group. They're violent in the way they behave and the way they talk to teachers.' There are a lot of angry, aggressive boys out there. Recent figures show almost 300 000 assaults have been committed by teen boys over two years. The largest proportion of offenders were aged 15 to 19. More than a quarter were repeat offenders.[8]

WHAT GROWN MEN DO MATTERS

How adult men behave also has a big impact on boys. Today's boys lack the excitement and empowerment of real-life adventure and exploration, which previous generations of boys enjoyed. They spend huge amounts of time immersed in popular culture instead. Boys are taking their cues from movie heroes, sports stars and Hollywood celebrities, whose dysfunctional behaviour is less than ideal. So it's hardly surprising that when Chris Brown bashed his girlfriend Rihanna, over half of those participating in a Boston survey said he was treated unfairly. Just under half felt Rihanna had it coming to her.

Everywhere boys look there are examples of grown-ups behaving badly. Fred Engh, president of the National Alliance of Youth Sports and author of *Why Johnny Hates Sports*, has been vocal in condemning 'sports rage'. When a father approached him about his son acting out, it transpired that at the boy's last game, the coach had taken his chair and thrown it across the room. The boy had picked up on this behaviour and had begun to behave violently too.[9]

WHERE ARE THE GOOD GUYS?

Due to heightened concerns about paedophiles, many men steer clear of boys, and our boys are poorer for it. Good men are great boundary-keepers for boys. When boys can look up to healthy male role models, they are more likely to modify their behaviour, because more than anything else they want to be men. Boys need men who can give them a new vision of themselves. Without this influence, too many lose their way, or fail to reach their potential.

> 'It matters what we say to them [boys]. It matters what we admire, and our behaviour matters.' Professor Prothrow-Stith, Harvard professor of public health[10]

CHARMING YET DEADLY

Boys can be very good at covering their tracks. A number of teachers spoke of kids who were utterly charming at school, but whose behaviour with peers was nothing short of scary. Sara told me of one of her students who was pleasant, sociable and attentive. Subsequently he was found to be severely beating up boys out of school.

> 'Movies like *Jackass* don't help. Boys think it's great entertainment to see them kicking each other in the groin, hitting each other in the head till someone passes out, setting themselves on fire. These are their heroes.' Sara, high-school teacher

A number of teachers also spoke of the lack of respect they get from boys, and also described how in some cases boys don't fear the consequences of their actions, because they see themselves as operating outside the rules. 'A new boy arrived at school,' explained Kayt, a high-school teacher. 'And, within a week, he was bullying other boys. When I pulled him aside, he went berserk and wanted to know who the kid was who'd said something, saying, "I'll really give him something to complain about." He wasn't at all worried about saying this to me.'

SETTING ON EACH OTHER

With the availability of phones, videos, cameras and texting, school violence and payback has become even more of a spectator sport. What would once have been a minor dust-up is now a major brawl. Lured by the possibility of five minutes of fame, increasingly kids are taking to each other with sickening brutality, spurred on by crowds. 'If there's going to be a fight, the details spread through the school in seconds,' Sara told me. 'Everyone turns up and records the fight, then it gets downloaded on to the internet. Then everyone writes their own comments about it. It's so dehumanising.'

> **'I ended up ventilated in intensive care after a bullying match. It saw me getting my head smashed into a brick wall repeatedly.'** *J*

Here again the lines between fantasy and reality blur, as violent acts are captured, then played back to peers as online entertainment. 'The big change I've noticed in the way violence is expressed is it now happens in gangs,' said Sara. 'Gone are the days when there was a one-on-one punch-up, then you got someone on the ground and it was all over. Now they talk about getting into someone as a group, then once he is on the ground stomping him and things, so they really hurt him. It's a different code. It doesn't tend to happen at school, but it's what they talk about after the weekends.' Now kids can phone and text each other to warn of a teacher approaching, it's difficult for teachers to know what's happening where.

FIGHT CLUBS

Teen fighting is now taking on new forms. Four months ago Stephen Luu, a teenage boy in Year 9, was punched to the ground during a 'fight club' meet in Sydney. Afterwards he felt dizzy, so his younger brother took him home. By late afternoon Stephen's condition had deteriorated. An ambulance was called. He was rushed to hospital, underwent emergency surgery for bleeding on the brain, and died a short time later. This was only one of a series of meets that had taken place over a few months. The number of boys organising their underground fight clubs here is recent and on the rise.

'This does seem a phenomenon of the *Mortal Kombat*, violent video game generation. The fight club offers the chance to bring those fantasies of violence and danger to life.' *Orin Starn, cultural anthropology professor*[11]

Some suggest this interest in fight clubs was sparked by the Brad Pitt movie *Fight Club*, where 'what happens at the fight club stays there'. Others blame the Ultimate Fight Championship (UFC), a mixed martial arts format of boxing, wrestling and martial arts for the rise in these fight clubs. Described by some as human cock fighting, within a few short years the UFC has become a billion-dollar industry. Its *Ultimate Fighter* and *UFC Unleashed* series are now screened in 36 countries. At one stage its violence caused such a public outcry that it was forced underground. Now it's back and stronger than ever.

'I just get a rush off it. I love it.' *Declan 18, underground fight club participant and organiser*

Police and health professionals are concerned about the growth of unofficial fight clubs because of the likelihood of boys sustaining serious injuries. Neurologists warn that critical head injuries aren't always immediately apparent, and may simply present as dizziness or fuzzy thinking, a headache or feeling a bit moody. While schools are aware of the emergence of these underground fight clubs, many are uncertain how to respond, as these activities tend to take place after school in secret locations. The more enterprising kids tape and edit the fights, put music behind them and post them on YouTube. Others sell the DVDs to teenage customers. Entry to the toughest fight clubs is by invitation only, and the spectators are also the fighters, so everything is kept under wraps.

'The attraction is the adrenaline of getting into a fight and trying to win.' Cody, 16

Fight clubs are not only capturing the attention of the underprivileged and the disposessed. 'We are seeing more fighting for entertainment, a heightened appetite for violence,' says Harvard professor Deborah Prothrow-Stith. 'We've tended to see this as a low-income, inner-city phenomenon, but now it's in the suburbs, it's crossing all lines.'[12] She reminds us that teen violence is an *adult* problem, and that boys need help in engaging in positive activities that allow them to take risks and stretch their boundaries. Father Dave Smith, who runs a neighbourhood Fight Club for at-risk boys, teaches them to box. When supervised and under a strict fitness regime, he finds the boys settle down. Confident they can handle themselves, they start to express themselves in a positive way. 'It's a natural thing inside boys. They need to rumble,' he explains, pointing out that there's a world of difference from being a warrior and a thug. 'While underground fight clubs are very dangerous, used properly the fighting sports can help boys gain control of their aggressive impulses, and make them strong and self-reliant.'

VIOLENCE TOWARDS PARENTS

Another worrying trend is the growing number of kids behaving violently towards their parents. This intimidation may be emotional, mental or physical and can include shoving, hitting and punching parents; frightening them; staying out all night; playing mind games; breaking things; threatening to run away, commit suicide or harm themselves; stealing money; making unrealistic demands; destroying the home or incurring debts. A number of parents have spoken of their anguish at being in this situation.

As this is a relatively new area of research, there's much more we need to know. However, between 2002 and 2006, Victoria reported a 23 per cent rise in teen domestic violence. One in ten domestic violence calls were prompted by teenage behaviour. The available details are sobering. Parents talk of sleeping with their bedroom doors locked, hiding knives and sharp objects, and never leaving their teenager with younger brothers or sisters. A New South Wales study revealed that half the women surveyed had experienced violence from their kids. Single, low-income mums were the most at risk. Where mothers were abused by their sons, often the boys have witnessed and experienced violence in the home, and have learning difficulties. The earlier the violence started in a child's life, the more violent they are likely to be. Sometimes parents don't know whether their teenager's behaviour is a one-off, or whether there's greater cause for concern. Again this behaviour isn't limited to kids in low-income areas. Homes with overworked parents eager to compensate for not being around can create this same situation by over-indulging their kids. [13]

GANGS

We are also seeing a growth in gangs across the western world. While we may assume it's only 'bad boys' who gravitate towards gangs, often the boys attracted to gangs are without adult male role models. Boys who live in difficult communities often seek out gangs to feel safe, as do risk-takers and those in need of excitement. While this safety comes at a price, it's a whole lot easier for a boy than trying to go it alone. Gangs give boys a tangible sense of belonging. Frequently these boys have already experienced violence or deprivation. School has little value to them, and with no-one to take an interest in them, they have few expectations. They see gang life as exciting and glamorous. Gangs are very attractive for boys with little else to aspire to.

Boys need to have a fresh perspective on violence, and there's no better place to create this than in the home. It's important to talk to boys about how ugly and self-defeating gang lives are, and how they inevitably end up badly.

Help your son navigate the violence he sees around him:

- *Be aware of the kinds of entertainment your son is exposed to.*
- *Provide him with positive risk-taking experiences.*
- *Set clear boundaries and expectations around behaviour.*
- *Discuss violence and macho behaviour in action movies.*
- *Ensure your son knows how good men behave.*
- *Surround him with good male role models he can look up to.*

When boys are vulnerable to violence

It's easy to forget that boys too can be vulnerable to violence. We've become so used to reports of boys getting beaten up, we don't tend to give it much thought, until it happens to someone close. How often do we hear of a boy out enjoying himself, alone or with a group of mates, or with his girlfriend, and suddenly finding himself a victim of attack? When we look at the Australian crime figures for 2007, over half the assault victims were male, and those aged 15 to 24 were most at risk. Male victims are most likely to be attacked by a stranger in a public place, and generally by another guy or group of guys.[1] Sometimes there may be provocation, and often there's alcohol involved. Too often it's simply the result of being in the wrong place at the wrong time. Frequently the injuries are severe, and may prove fatal. Boys need to know when they are vulnerable, and how best to deal with situations that may get out of hand, and to be wary of the times and locations where they are most at risk.

DATING VIOLENCE

Boys may also be victims of violence at the hands of their girlfriends. In the absence of local figures, it's interesting to note that in one major study of

American high school students in 2003, 8 per cent of both girls and boys suffered physical dating violence. The 2005 National Youth Risk Behaviour Study revealed that just under one in ten boys admitted to experiencing dating violence, which can include verbal abuse; hair-pulling; being slapped, punched, or stalked; experiencing unwanted touching; being blackmailed or being pressured to have sex.[2] Those boys who experience severe dating violence can be subjected to a range of situations from being thrown on the floor, to being kicked or attacked with a weapon.

As with many forms of abuse, violent girlfriends get at their victims in a number of ways, including a barrage of humiliating comments and threats. It's no surprise that a boy's confidence plummets. He may be left feeling trapped, embarrassed or depressed. Frequently abusers separate their victim from his friends, isolating him so as to have more control over him. Even when a boy continues to be abused he may be in denial, or may even try to defend his girlfriend whenever anyone tries to talk to him about her behaviour. It's important to stay close to a boy in this situation. Criticising his girlfriend won't help. Finding ways to talk non-specifically about abusive relationships and what they can do to people is a far better approach, as is maintaining the support of good friends, so as not to alienate the boy even further.

RAPE

While it's essential girls realise how sexually vulnerable they can be, we cannot neglect boys. They too need to know they can be victims of inappropriate sexual behaviour and rape. The tragic thing for men and boys is how rarely these things are discussed, and so even when they may have been violated, rarely do they speak out, let alone seek help. One night at a dinner I attended the subject of abuse came up. Out of eight people, four had suffered sexual abuse. Two of these had suffered abuse as boys. One had been raped by a family member. More often than not boys are abused by someone known to them. This is not a subject that gets much discussion, so often boys live with their pain, never speaking about what has taken place. These things continue to happen in homes and schools, at parties, and when boys are out enjoying themselves.

> 'From a boy you're taught not to be overpowering towards girls, but there's nothing about the vulnerability of men – you've just got to get on with it.' *Tony, 26*

GETTING REAL ABOUT SEXUAL ASSAULT

First and foremost sexual assault is about violence. Just because a boy is assaulted does not mean he's gay, though he may fear afterwards he is. He's likely to be left with a fear or distrust of men. As with a girl who is raped, the experience is terrifying and violating. And even if he experienced some sexual response to the attack, it does not mean he wanted it to happen. Boys suffer every bit as much as girls who are raped. Some suggest even more so, because there's not the same awareness that this can happen, or of the pain it causes. We still have a long way to go to discover the full extent of male sexual assault.

What we do know is that the early- to mid-teen period is when boys are most at risk. In one American study one in ten rape victims were found to be male. Another study found that more than seven out of ten male victims had been raped before they were 18.[3] Boys who are sexually assaulted also tend to experience physical violence during the sexual assault. Often boys remain silent because they're ashamed at being in this situation, or they fear they'll be labelled gay. Like other rape victims they may also suffer classic post-traumatic stress – flashbacks, nausea, loss of concentration and appetite, and difficulty sleeping. They need and deserve immediate professional attention.

Help protect your son against violence by:
- *Talking to him about the ways in which boys can be vulnerable.*
- *Encouraging him to come back to you with questions.*

- *Ensuring he understands being a victim does not mean someone is weak.*
- *Helping him to be street-savvy.*
- *Making him aware of times, situations and locations where he may be at risk.*
- *Ensuring he knows that he can talk to you about anything that concerns him.*

Why dads matter

It's a big journey from boyhood to adult life and, like mums, dads have much to contribute. 'For a boy a close relationship with his father is like gold,' explains Toby, 16. Boys need their dad's strength, comfort, guidance and protection. The boys I spoke with were in no doubt how much their dads meant. 'Having a father around means his presence empowers you and gives you something to strive for,' said Luca, 15. 'If you don't have this, you don't know how to act, except from your friends. Without your dad it's hard to know about your body and a whole lot of things.' Tom, 12, agrees. 'If a father lives with his son and is strong, he's like an anchor, one constant who models what they become.'

'If your dad is kind, loving and caring, it makes a great family life, and makes you kind, loving and caring. If he doesn't communicate then it's hard to know what you're meant to do.' *Zac, 15*

LEARNING ABOUT MEN

Boys also need their dads to help teach them about the world of men. Without this, it's very hard for boys to know who they are. According to Bryan Duke, who runs an adolescent regional mentoring program, often this confusion about what's expected leads to sadness in boys, a lack of hope about what the future will hold. Our boys also need to feel that their masculinity is valued. This just isn't happening nearly enough. They also need to know there are many ways to be a man in the world. That always appearing tough isn't a strength, and that expressing their emotions isn't a weakness. Educator Amrita Hobbs, who has facilitated workshops with adults and teenagers for more than three decades, agrees. 'I feel boys are in danger. The whole essence of masculinity is being challenged. If we have a whole lot of men who are uncertain of themselves, that's not going to work for women either.'

'[Fatherhood] is the single most creative, complicated, fulfilling, frustrating, engrossing, enriching, depleting endeavour of a man's adult life.' *Professor Kyle Pruett,* The Nurturing Father[1]

FATHER HUNGER

Many of the boys felt for peers who didn't have contact with their dads. 'I have a few friends without dads,' said Lyall, 12. 'They miss their dads in most cases, miss their support.' This was Tyler's experience also. 'I think it's very sad for the boys who don't have a dad around. They miss out on fun things, like going to the movies, arcades and shopping for stuff.' Flynn, 16, talked about how envious boys without a dad were of the boys who had good dads.

'For boys without dads it has a serious impact on how you can function, because you don't have a person you can base your personality on.' *Tommy, 12*

Boys whose dads aren't around clearly miss them. It was surprising to hear how often boys would confide this sense of loss to each other.

Even boys whose fathers were away for work a lot missed them. 'My best friend's dad was away four days every week. He missed his dad a lot. The high point of the week for him was when his dad would take him out on Saturday,' Tommy, 12, told me. Sometimes work demands make it impossible for dads to be at home during the week. The boys best able to deal with this absence had one-on-one time with their dad on the weekend, and shared joint activities.

WHEN RELATIONSHIPS FALL APART

One of the many reasons separations are very painful for boys is that it's often harder still for them to spend time with their dads. Sometimes fathers walk away and refuse contact, others do everything they can to ensure they stay close to their boys. However, the separated dads and boys I talked with spoke about how much they missed each other, and how they clung to the times they did share.

> **'Boys without their dads have to look around to see what they have to do.'** Lyall, 12

There are also single dads who, like single mums, strive hard to hold things together, often with little support. Whatever the circumstances, separated parents need to realise boys hurt as much as girls when their parents break up. Mothers also need to be very careful about the messages they give out about their ex and men in general, and dads need to be vigilant about the way they talk too. Kids should never feel that enjoying time with one parent is being disloyal to the other. Nor should they be asked to play spy or messenger. Both mums and dads have unique things to offer their boys. When this is understood, everyone wins.

'Being with Dad is about being around maleness and experiencing it in action. When Dad's not around a boy feels it emotionally. It leads to unhappy people deep down.' *Dave Mallard, father, senior executive and men's group facilitator*

After separations new relationships frequently develop, so boys can then have stepfathers and stepmothers to deal with. While there are many good stepdads out there, most of the boys I spoke with found the relationship with their stepfather particularly hard going. 'Me and my stepdad aren't very close. In the rare moments when we do communicate he does understand what I'm talking about, when Mum doesn't,' Angus, 17, told me. Tyler, 10, agreed. 'Some of my friends have two sets of dads. Sometimes their other dad isn't as loving as their real dad, or as trusting or forgiving.'

Sometimes parents don't realise the angst they create. Online teen forums spell this out, 'My dad has a girlfriend,' says 'Back to Grey'. 'I know him having a gf isn't wrong and it's not right of me to feel this way but I don't like it. My friend brought it up and I couldn't talk about it. I hate seeing them touch, I hate knowing that when he doesn't come home he's with her. I hate it. He deserves to be happy, I know he does, and yeah it makes me awful . . . but it's just bothering me. I hate it.'[2] Or as P puts it, 'I think my dad is upstairs getting laid by his girlfriend. Eww Seriously. I'm home, Wtf? And how does he get laid and I don't :(He's 50 for Christ's sake!'[3] Parents have the right to new relationships, but they need also to be sensitive about their kids, who can be left feeling as if they're second best, or exposed to intimacies they're just not ready for. Family time including the new partner is essential. So too is one-on-one time with their parents.

THE NEED TO COMMUNICATE

While boys want a good relationship with their dads, often there just isn't enough communication to foster a close relationship, or boys felt their dads were overly critical. Even now, many fathers are parenting their sons in the same way they were parented, but as Angus, 17, points out, today's boys are looking for more. 'My generation has changed. They're wanting to express their emotions.'

'A father must teach his son that masculinity and feelings can go hand in hand.' *Professor Kyle Pruett,* The Nurturing Father[4]

Boys need active encouragement, to be listened to, to question and to understand their alternatives. A lot of fathers still have a way to go in this area. 'Dads do put you down,' said Harrison, 15. 'They have an immense pride in you, but they're silent. They don't see the need to praise sons. Their "constructive criticism" can seem like an attack. It can leave you feeling persecuted and frustrated.' This was Mark's experience as well, 'Dads sometimes don't listen as much as they could do. They're a bit tougher.' Sometimes the opportunity to communicate gets lost in the huge expectations fathers have for their boys, as Angus, 17, explains, 'Some friends have dads who are overly stern and overbearing. They're the walk-in-my-shadow kind of person.' The boys who do have active encouragement are way ahead.

'My father is really important to me. We share a lot, talking a lot about things with him. It may be anything or nothing we talk about, but I realise how much my father has taught me, and how much I use what he's told me. I idolise my father.' *Toby, 16*

WHEN DADS AREN'T ENGAGED

There's so much boys need to know. If they don't get this from their dads, they have to look elsewhere. Flynn, 16, is spot on when he says, 'If a father isn't conveying a good message, then boys end up acting out bad stuff with their peers.' The boys who don't have dads who talk, or who don't talk about things that matter to them, expressed a real sense of loneliness. 'My dad doesn't talk to me about personal stuff,' said Mark, 15. 'I guess I would appreciate having someone.' Finding the time to talk can be hard. But even if there's not much time, letting boys know they're appreciated and under-stood can make all the difference. I was surprised at how often boys were aware of the many pressures their fathers were under, and appreciated whatever time they could find to chat. 'I don't talk to Dad as much as he's at work, but he's open-minded, which is great,' said Tim, 17.

'There's a beautiful openness in boys that is being closed down by well-meaning parents. Of course parents get frustrated, but they must always leave the door open for further discussion.'
Michael Waring, men's group facilitator, father and grandfather

Good communication is about more than talk. It's about shared activi-ties, hanging out together. It was wonderful to see how enthusiastic younger boys were when their dads took an interest. 'Dads take you bowl-ing and swimming and stuff,' explained Mark, 10, with great enthusiasm. 'Dads are really, really great, because they do sports stuff with you,' said Tyler, 10. Other good male role models in a boy's life can also help. Some boys appreciated being able to talk openly with male teachers. 'I spend a lot of time discussing things with my male teachers, so things don't bottle up. I think having a male teacher is much better for boys. They under-stand boys, what they're thinking and doing,' explained Lyall, 12. Teacher Andrew Lines gives us further insight into the world of boys. 'I'm always amazed at the end of the year how many boys come up and say, "Thank you for listening to me." There's a deep yearning to be heard.'

THE TEENAGE THING
As boys grow, keeping the lines of communication open isn't easy, espe-cially as teens begin to challenge parents. 'It's like a primal thing,' Dylan,

18, told me. 'You've got your father who's the leader. The young guy wants to get there, so there's tension. I stood up to my father earlier and told him to treat me differently. I was lucky though. I had the maturity and the height.' Breaking away from their dads is a necessary transition for boys, as they need to find their own way in the world. This is harder for some boys than others. 'When they're very young boys, they want to be like their dads,' Tommy, 12, told me. 'But then you want to be your own person, but a father has so much influence.' This does not mean dads no longer count, but as teens mature the relationship changes and is more complex. As Daryl, 17, put it, 'You want to beat your dad at this and that, but you also want the male influence. They're the benchmark to life, something to live up to. They give you the motivation to do stuff.'

'For most guys it's not your dad who's your role model. Until you're nine he's your hero. He does everything with you then it changes.'
Dylan, 18

DADS, NOT BEST FRIENDS

It's doubly challenging for today's sons and dads to have a close relationship as there's the overwhelming influence of peer and pop culture to deal with. So, how does a father stay relevant? Boys don't want trendy dads or best friends. They want fathers who are up-to-speed with the issues they're dealing with. As Dylan, 18, explains, 'Most dads don't realise the world has changed so much. You can't look at things the way they were when they were 17. It's so different now, like the rise in anorexia, depression and mental issues, and cutting. That wasn't happening when they were growing up.' The best starting-point is for fathers to realise the world has changed, then take the time to understand the current issues and opportunities their boys face. If they don't they'll get left behind. This takes effort, but it's time well spent. Dads need to be on the same page as their teenagers. 'Parents are struggling,' admits Jim, a father. 'We're not placing ourselves in a boy's world, so we don't know what it's like for them.' If parents don't make this transition they risk being seen as irrelevant.

DISCIPLINE

This doesn't mean dads should forget about discipline. The fathers who are clear about their expectations, give their boys a structure, and help them learn how to regulate their behaviour give their boys a head start. 'If a father says something you do it straight away,' said Flynn, 16. 'It's a big anchor. It keeps boys in line.' It was interesting to see how boys viewed what their fathers had to say. Flynn admitted his mum would often have to tell him three or four times before he'd do something, and Jacob, 17, admitted, 'Boys are more wary around dads. You try harder to impress your dad. If you get into trouble you're more scared of your dad than your mum.'

Fathers also need to get what's happening for their son, and respond accordingly. Switched-on dads recognise the need to take account of the changing world their son inhabits and to be flexible by continuing to discuss boundaries and reset them if necessary. 'I'm adjusting to my son's behaviour every day,' admits Frank. 'You can't come down on every aberrant thing he does. I've learned you have to choose how to react, and ask, "Will it create the right outcome at the time?"' This is not about dispensing with the boundaries, but relating them to today's world, not teen life three or more decades ago. When dads are clear about the rules and have discussed the consequences of stepping across the line, boys have a clearer sense of where they are. It's not a bad idea to have written agreements about family rules so there is no room for misunderstanding. Dads also need to make a habit of noticing when their boys do things right, and acknowledging them for the good stuff they do.

BOYS AND *THEIR* DREAMS

One of the areas that boys found hardest was the expectations their fathers had of them. 'Deep down a lot of guys want their boys to be like them,' said Gary, 17. 'It can be a little bit of a letdown for them if they're not, but it's an enormous pressure for their son – that thinking their dad knows best for them.' Angus, 17, agrees. 'A lot of teens have a lot of dreams, but fathers can be pretty hard on them.' This was Jacob's experience also. 'Dads think more logically, so if you talk about your aspirations, they're more bent on how you're going to achieve it, whereas mums are generally more encouraging. Sometimes the way dads respond can seem more of a deterrent than encouragement.'

Father–son relationships can be stretching, but dads can still be powerful role models. However, this new generation has been raised on information and collaboration. Boys want to voice *their* needs and perspectives. They want to be let in on the process, not simply lectured to or ordered about. The fathers who get it right enjoy a much stronger relationship with their sons.

SHARING THE LOAD

Dads don't have to do the masculine bit alone. As well as one-on-one time, an increasing number of dads are looking at valuable father–son experiences to share, seeing there are now some excellent programs around. Dave, a busy executive and father of two teenage boys, took his son to Pathways, a father-son retreat where men were open about all the issues that preoccupy teen boys, and where there was a real opportunity for boys to be heard. When I spoke with Dave's son, he described the experience as 'awesome'. For the first time in his life he realised he wasn't alone in the many teen challenges he faced. Hearing men be honest about their own vulnerabilities was also reassuring. Now he can't wait to support other boys to become men. These are powerful opportunities for our boys, and can have a huge impact on them

When both parents come to terms with the world today's boys are growing up in, and actively work together to support their boy in their journey to manhood, everyone wins.

As a dad, you can support your son by:

- *Doing things together that he enjoys.*
- *Telling him you love him.*
- *Listening to what he is trying to tell you.*
- *Having regular one-on-one time.*
- *Getting involved in school and out-of-school activities.*
- *Being honest about your own vulnerable times as a boy.*
- *Sending him affirming notes and texts.*
- *Encouraging a friendship with other good men.*
- *Getting a copy of Dr Bruce Robinson's DVD, What Kids Really Need from Their Dads, www.medicine.uwa.edu.au/go/tfp/about-us*

Role models and rites of passage

The sad thing is that with the overwhelming influence of peers and popular culture, today's boys are far less connected to adult men than were previous generations. Yet boys still need fathers and other good men to take a genuine interest and to help mentor them as much as they ever did. Rebecca, a child protection worker and mum, agrees. 'Young boys used to pick up a trade from their father, uncle or community member. I have a sense of boys maturing at a much slower rate, because they're interacting mainly with each other, instead of people of different ages.'

'Girls have all these teen magazines and fashion magazines and things, but boys don't really have role models. There are some good role models, but a lot that are not so good.' *Zac, 15*

QUESTIONABLE ROLE MODELS
If men are absent from a boy's life, then he'll find his own role models, who may be less than ideal. Boys look to the media and celebrity culture for what they're meant to be doing. While many of the examples they find there aren't great role models, in the absence of any real choice,

these are the ones they cling to. As Zac, 15, explains, 'Sports stars do have a big effect on boys. They mightn't consciously think some of the things they're doing are okay, but if you see it often enough on TV, you probably start to think it's okay.'

Too often we fail to provide boys with the support they need. Yet we're quick to criticise them when they go off the rails. 'We can't blame kids,' says Bryan Duke, who runs a regional mentoring program and is himself a father. 'What do they inherit? With the growth in technology, pornography and marketing they're inheriting a mall culture, an MTV culture.' Dave Mallard, a father, senior executive and men's group facilitator, agrees. 'For boys it's a tenuous path to manhood when they have to make it on their own. Growing up in a society that doesn't cherish and nurture boys for who they are works against the psychological health of boys. I think we've a long way to go.'

'With the growth in technology, pornography and marketing they're inheriting a mall culture, an MTV culture.' *Bryan Duke, father and mentor*

RITES OF PASSAGE

As they grow, boys do need to push their boundaries to glimpse what they're capable of. Helping boys set significant milestones helps prepare them for adulthood. Father, teacher and founder of The Rite Journey Andrew Lines has put together a powerful in-school program that does just this. 'The boys work with staff to devise their own challenges,' he explains. 'Often we start off with something simple like how many push-ups and sit-ups they can do. They do these at the beginning of class, and have a goal to reach by the end of term. They document their progress. Some boys struggle to get there, so we look at how pressure can sometimes help us to do better. Challenges include things like a high ropes course and long-distance running. In our program boys choose a male mentor. This helps them have a more positive relationship with adults, by getting a much deeper, personal understanding of what it's like to be an adult. We also try to instil in the boys that it's okay to fail, that sometimes the best learning comes from failures.'

'In term one they examine their relationship with themselves. We also work on "closing" their childhood, and calling them on a journey to be adults. In the second term we look at their relationships with others — at communication, friendship, sex, feeding their spirit, and in the third term we examine their relationship with the world — appropriate risk-taking, and their sense of purpose. We explore a lot of issues during the year, including things like thinking about the last time they cried.

'We also look at the principles of rock and water, which come from self-defence and martial arts. So when they're in a situation they are aware they have choices. They can respond with all their muscles tensed, or they can be more fluid like water, go with the situation and use their opponent's muscle to bring them down. We look at how this can play out in arguments with parents, where they can go in hard or move with the situation. At the end of the year they work up to a karate chop of a board. They prepare for this and also work on a vision for their future, so it's pretty powerful.

'The boys do solo work as well. They tell their story in front of a group of boys. They hold the talking stick. It has each of their symbols burnt into it, so it's a very powerful symbol for them. It's not easy for boys to talk about themselves. There's a drumming program, a singing program, juggling and so on. For too long the only help boys have had has focused purely on developing their physical prowess. The beauty of this program is that it isn't just about physical strength. It teaches boys about their emotional lives, how to feed their spirit.' The Rite Journey program in schools is now gaining momentum.

'The active involvement of good men in a boy's life is the most important factor in a boy's self-esteem, and in helping him make good decisions.' *Geoff Price, author and CEO of Pathways*

PATHWAYS

Another excellent program for adolescent boys is Pathways, which provides 13- to 15-year-old boys with the chance to spend five or six days with their dads, as well as other boys and their dads, and male mentors. In a bush camp setting this rite of passage program works on a boy's confidence and motivation by helping him understand more intimately what it means to be a boy and a man. 'It's the opportunity for fathers and mentors to nourish boys by providing them with a healthy transition from being a child to being an independent young man,' explains author and CEO Geoff Price. 'We also welcome boys into the male community, not because of their school marks or anything else, but for who they uniquely are.

'If there's one thing that boys want most, it's to be able to have open, honest and meaningful discussions with adults they can trust. So we provide a safe place for boys where honest stories can be told by boys and by the men, where adults are real, and where boys won't be judged. This way the boys get to explore their dilemmas and see their way forward. They gain from the wisdom offered them. It helps them understand themselves, and make good and wise decisions.' According to Price the presence of dads in the program is crucial. 'Having time with Dad here is extremely important for the boys. Research suggests that many fathers only have a minute a day with their sons. Other studies say it's eight minutes. Either way we're massively under-fathering and under-mentoring our boys.'

'When a boy is becoming a teen, give them tools. But let them take them, and don't force them. Let them take the next step. And if

they don't take it, offer them more opportunities to help them find their way forward.' *Luca, 15*

When you talk with boys about Pathways, they're in no doubt about what they got out of it. 'Pathways was awesome. I found it so relaxing to be with all the men. I just didn't care what I did when I got there – just spending a week with all the men and the boys,' Luca, 15 told me. One of the many benefits for Luca was realising that the issues he was dealing with were what boys his age grapple with. 'Now I know I'm not on my own,' he explained, adding, 'It was very hard before I knew that.' Luca is now looking forward to returning to Pathways to help mentor other boys through the process. 'As a leader it feels really good to help other guys, to hold the space and reassure them, and let them know what it's like, to help other boys become men.'

These are powerful opportunities for our boys. Every boy deserves to have the best of support and guidance in becoming a man. The men in our families and communities have a hugely important role in helping make this happen.

You can support your son in the following ways:

- *Make time for father/son weekends away with other good men and boys.*
- *Ensure your household is positive about men.*
- *Find memorable ways to celebrate your son's rites of passage, and to include him in significant moments for older family members.*
- *Encourage friendships with family and friends across the generations.*
- *Talk regularly about the qualities most admired in good men in a relaxed and engaging way.*
- *Make your home a place of interesting stories about men and boys from your own family history and beyond.*

When boys push the boundaries

From the time they are little, boys love to get physical and take risks. It's an important part of being a boy. But this doesn't sit well with our fear of boys hurting themselves, our fear of strangers and traffic, and lack of community. So, often when boys attempt to let off a bit of steam or play in public areas, we see them as nuisances. While we may even let them know exactly how we feel, we give little thought to creating safe and interesting places where they can hang out, push the boundaries and have fun. When we try to contain their enthusiasm often it comes out in inappropriate ways, or our boys spend their lives seeking adventure online or through other media. One father expressed this sense of isolation well. 'I went for a walk in a new housing development yesterday,' he explained. 'There was a boy skateboarding. He was weaving in and out, quite amazing, a beautiful boy. I could see he wanted me to take note. There was a real emptiness, a loneliness about him.'

SKATEBOARDING THAT WORKS
One of the many areas of contention around boys congregating in public places is the danger skateboarding poses to others. So what can we do

about this? We can ban skateboarding and other activities, or rise to the challenge. In the last couple of years youth worker on the north coast Terry Dolling has seen two skateboarding parks built in his local area. One was placed in an isolated area outside the community, and was soon trashed and quickly became a dangerous place to be. A second skateboarding park was built on the edge of a shopping centre, *inside* the community. Parents are able to drop their kids off here while they're shopping. The park is well used and often featured in the local newspaper. It's safe for girls, and has little graffiti. 'When boys feel part of the community, it's almost shocking when you see how much it means to them,' reflects Terry Dolling. He adds, 'It's sad because often they're living in a community that gives so little to them.'

CREATING COMMUNITY

Terry works actively with skateboarders and surfers to give them a greater sense of belonging. Every six months he gets kids together to look at the videos and photos they've taken of each other surfing and skateboarding. They also have a free monthly barbecue at the local skate park, where there are community awards for the best photos. The winners get their pictures framed, and there are frequent write-ups in the local paper. In less than a year the kids have created a strong sense of identity within the community. He's also had good feedback from parents. One father stopped Terry in the street to tell him how much more confidence his son has because of this recognition.

EXPRESSING WHAT MATTERS TO *THEM*

In encouraging boys to find activities that will stretch them, it's important they're given the chance to follow *their* passions. For example, the global Rock Eisteddfod Challenge, which is now almost two decades old, is perfect for boys into music. It's not an easy thing to get up and perform before hundreds of people, but a powerful milestone for a boy to achieve. Now more than 1 million kids have performed on stages from Aberdeen to Albany, Johannesburg to Dresden, Melbourne to Thursday Island, and it continues to grow. One study revealed that students who participated in the Rock Eisteddfod Challenge were more resilient and less likely to binge-drink or take drugs. Further research indicated that kids who performed in the eisteddfod were given 'unique opportunities to improve their psychological wellbeing'.

FEELING GENUINELY USEFUL

Some of today's boys have few opportunities to feel valued or take responsibility, so they grow up uncertain about who they are and where they fit in. Parents who include boys in small jobs around the home do them a big favour. This may begin with helping feed animals and tidy up. Then, as they mature, they can help Mum and Dad paint, mend garden hoses and bikes, concrete and put up garden fences. These kinds of jobs give boys confidence, practical skills and a sense of purpose. It helps them feel more prepared for adult life.

Too often we leave boys out, without realising what valuable life experiences they're missing out on. Including boys in jobs that need to be done can have unexpected benefits. The key is to *encourage* rather than force boys to participate. When recollecting the 1989 San Francisco earthquake, where thousands of people were injured, adolescent psychiatrist Dr Lynn Ponton observed that 'Teens in disaster-affected areas who were allowed, even encouraged, to participate in exhausting, yet at times exhilarating, disaster work were less likely to get involved in risky behaviour.'[1] Too often we fail to acknowledge that our teenagers have a lot to offer, and that they are valuable members of society.

Aware of boys' needs, principal Dr Timothy Hawkes of Kings School, Sydney, has put together a powerful four-year leadership course for boys which deals with everything from strategic planning to dealing with difficult people. Core life values such as honesty, truth and integrity are explored during the program. And, mindful of the fact that Hollywood has largely hijacked the stories our boys are exposed to, Kings boys now explore the lives of those who have made significant contributions through history, from liberator Simon Bolivar, after whom Bolivia was named, to Joan of Arc.

Dr Hawkes is also putting together a comprehensive Towards Manhood program. One of the most innovative aspects of the program is the opportunity for boys to learn first aid and car maintenance skills, as well as how to fix a washer, recycle and cook. 'Practical knowledge can give boys confidence to deal with life,' Dr Hawkes explains. 'This is really important as depression is one of the fastest growing issues for boys. Many lack social skills. These things help. It's about giving them capability and resilience in a society that's fragile.' Kings boys will also visit a whole range of locations from funeral parlours and graveyards to banks and courthouses. 'We've got to use the world as our classroom,' says Dr Hawkes. 'It has real and important resources.' Boys at Kings now also learn how to deal with solitude and the importance of thinking time, to balance the massive over-stimulation they often face. 'Presently we're concentrating on minds well-stuffed, not minds well-informed. To prepare boys for life they need time for problem-solving and critical thinking,' Dr Hawkes adds. 'There is a wealth of valuable information we can give our boys beyond popular culture. Without our help they may never access the material, or the insight and wisdom it offers.'

FAILURE IS VALUABLE

In amongst everything a boy experiences, it's essential he knows there will be failures along the way. Constantly shielding boys from disappointment doesn't make them strong. As Lynne Moten, director of service learning at Seymour College in Adelaide, points out, 'Kids have to take hard hits to grow emotionally.' Where better to learn how to deal with failure and disappointment than at home? Here parents can show a boy how to handle failure, learn from it and bounce back. So, be open about your own shortcomings. Model how to be gracious in defeat, and how best to get on with life. There will be times when a boy is determined to do something that isn't a good idea. As long as he's not likely to hurt himself or anyone else, it may be worth allowing him the experience, especially if it's followed by an open discussion about more fruitful approaches in the future.

When we give boys a genuine sense of themselves and what they may be capable of, they can achieve remarkable things. When he was a young boy Richard Branson's mother dropped him off in the countryside with instructions on how to get home, which, after a few false starts, he achieved. Celebrated author and teacher John Gatto tells of a former student, Roland Legiardi-Lura, whose parents both died and who had no finances to fall back on, yet as a young man he cycled across the United States by himself. 'Is it any wonder then that in manhood when he decided to make a film about Nicaragua, although he had no money and no prior experience with film-making, that it was an international award-winner — even though his regular work was as a carpenter?' John Gatto asks. Not all boys will achieve such dizzying possibilities, but when they have a firm foundation and a genuine sense of themselves they have a head start.

To thrive, our boys need:

- *A tangible sense of purpose.*
- *The chance to push their boundaries in positive ways.*
- *A father and/or other good men who will take a genuine interest in them.*
- *Access to stories and experiences that feed their minds, hearts and spirits.*
- *The opportunity to be useful.*
- *The chance to experience disappointment and failure.*

Building resilience

Boys need to know what they're capable of, and how to bounce back when things go wrong. This is especially important given the many challenges they will face as adults. Author and research psychologist Leonard Sax, who talks of 'the growing epidemic of unmotivated boys', believes that today's boys are less resilient and less ambitious than they were only two decades ago.[1] By the time they're adults, boys need to know how to deal with everything from difficult people, unfamiliar situations and pressure to how to make their own way and handle disappointment and failure. However, with their shrinking life experience and friendships largely confined to peers, it's much harder for boys in many ways. With their vulnerabilities around peers, possessions and presentation, and the lack of positive role models, today's boys don't get much of a chance to learn these life skills.

Often we assume boys are more resilient than girls, but studies suggest otherwise. In many situations, particularly emotional crises, girls are clearly more resilient. We don't help boys bridge this gap by expecting them to be strong and independent without showing them how. It's also important we don't mistake empowering our boys with indulging

277

them. As author and psychologist Michael Carr-Gregg points out, every week he sees teenagers in his practice 'who are "empowered" to the point where adults in their lives feel helpless and ineffectual'.[2] International resilience expert professor Michael Ungar stresses the importance of 'enlightened self-esteem', where a boy's self-worth is more grounded, and fed in part by what he can offer his family and community.[3] He also encourages us to expose boys to 'managed risk' – *positive* situations which take boys out of their comfort zones and help them develop powerful life skills. To help boys mature we need to expose them to physical, emotional and social challenges.

SOCIAL CONFIDENCE

Part of preparing a boy for the future is in helping him relate to others and feel confident in a variety of situations. This makes it easier for him to make friends, empathise with others, and adapt to whatever situation he finds himself in. Parents have an important role to play in creating a wider sense of community in and around the home. Assigning boys specific jobs at family picnics and barbecues, including taking care of certain guests, helps them be a valuable part of what's going on. It's so much more engaging and fun to have a job to do when there's a big event such as a wedding or funeral. When boys are a genuine part of these events, their social confidence skyrockets. Get-togethers with family and friends are something to look forward to.

FRIENDSHIPS ACROSS THE GENERATIONS

Boys who only mix with their peers miss out on different points of view and life experiences. They don't know what to expect as adults. This changed for one group of teen boys when they got involved in a weekend project to help elderly people. Over the weekend these boys began to see elderly people as real people with their own lives, losses and achievements. They learned to go at a different pace and assist them with meals and other everyday concerns. 'It's very sad,' said one boy, describing what it was like to be with people so old and frail. 'It puts everything into perspective, like family stuff.'

As they got closer to the old folk, a number of boys opened up. They asked their elderly friends tender questions about relationships and other issues that were troubling them – questions they probably wouldn't ask anyone else. They were also interested in how, for example, these old people tackled relationship upsets – the loss of partners to war, terminal illness and dementia. Some boys were keen to stay in touch and write to their new friends, wanting to invite them to significant events in their own lives. One of the most powerful aspects of this time together was when the elderly people told the boys how special they were, how much they appreciated their help, and that they were nothing like media reports. Warmed by this appreciation, the boys had a new sense of themselves, and the old people felt cared for. Everyone benefited.

Having friendships across the generations, from family, friends and neighbours to local shopkeepers, helps give boys a much richer sense of belonging and *complements* what peers bring to their lives. The boys who had access to grandparents spoke warmly about their contributions to their lives. They clearly cherished these relationships and felt very protective of them, because they clearly mattered.

EMOTIONAL INTELLIGENCE

Not everything in life is fun or easy, but when boys are supported through difficult situations, they're more likely to benefit from the experience. As Bob Reitemeier, who runs The Children's Society, an independent British research body which campaigns on behalf of kids and rescues at-risk kids, points out, 'Perhaps the dreams we should be encouraging our children to follow are about the good life well lived, based on values which help unite us rather than emphasising individualism.'[4]

MEN IN THE MAKING

Lynne Moten, director of service learning at Seymour College, Adelaide, has worked with boys for some years. She devised a project to take boys aged 16 to 18 with her to India for a few weeks to work in Mother Theresa's organisation, where they worked with intellectually and physically disabled kids, dressing and playing with them, feeding them and helping them with their exercises. 'One of the things boys miss out on is the opportunity to be challenged emotionally, so they don't grow emotionally,' she explains. 'When you challenge them you have to do so with support. When you do, you see their confidence and resilience grow, and often you see them step up to something even higher.' After their days boys would have time out to rest, debrief and write up their journals so they could make sense of their experiences.

At first the boys were so challenged by the disabled children they saw, they couldn't bear to be in the same room. By the end of their week together the boys were holding and feeding the disabled kids. In just a few days these boys had learned how to connect meaningfully with those who are different from them. They then went on to a remote school where the tribal people had rarely seen westerners, again helping and encouraging the local kids. The local kids sang and danced their tribal dances, and the boys then got up and sang and danced too. This was very liberating for the western boys as they don't get much chance to do this.

During their visit the boys played cricket with the local kids, who had no protection when they played, no shoes and very basic equipment. The local boys, who were very skilful at cricket, won every match. 'It's a great lesson for our boys who have all those resources,' Lynne Moten explains. The final part of their month in India was at a school with kids who were even more severely disabled. Again this proved life-changing as the boys helped these kids with their daily routines.

'When boys go to India they become free, because they're not worried about being judged there,' Lynne Moten reflects. Sometimes the return is hard at first, because boys see western values with very different eyes. 'On one side in the plane I had a boy saying it was all over too soon,' she explains. 'He was crying. The other was angry. He belted the arms of the seat saying that everything they were going back to was the same old bullshit of what car you drive, what your postcode is.' On their return the boys saw their lives differently. They realised how much they had to be grateful for. It was coming up to Christmas, and one boy said he didn't want any Christmas presents, because he already had so much. These boys returned with a much greater vision of who they were and were excited about the future, as they now had a stronger sense of what they were capable of as adults.

LIVES CHANGED THROUGH VOLUNTEER WORK

Another excellent program in which thousands of high school students now participate each year is World Challenge.[5] With a mix of volunteer work and trekking in developing countries, boys and girls have the opportunity to challenge themselves in new ways. With guidance, the boys begin by working on their itineraries, while fund-raising and undergoing fitness training. Their trip may result in altitude trekking in Cambodia, working in an orphanage teaching the children basic English, digging wells and other needed activities.

As well as camping and trekking, one school group helped build a recycling plant in the foothills of the Himalayas. Sam, 16, went for a month with his team of thirteen to Nicaragua and Costa Rica. In their six-day hike they had twenty-seven river crossings, and trekked up to 20 kilometres a day. They then went on to work in an impoverished community, helping restore their primary school and assist with planting and wildlife conservation. One of the hardest challenges for Sam was fund-raising the $6900 required to go on the trip. 'It's a bit of a buzz when you've paid it off,' he explained. 'Overall it was a pretty full-on experience' that he wouldn't be without. He's returned with many insights and life skills. Most important to Sam is the work ethic he's gained, and a realisation that if you want something to happen you have to work hard for it.

According to Hannah Cross of World Challenge, the boys and girls who undertake the challenge come home with greater confidence and more empathy for those less fortunate. As they are each in charge of an aspect of the trip from the budget to food or transport, they all get to experience leadership. Living out of a backpack for a few weeks, they learn to be more team-oriented and resilient. Most of all, these life-changing experiences and insights provide a powerful entry into adult life, fine-tuning this new generation's values and aspirations.

BOYS HELPING OUT IN UGANDA

Every two years volunteers from Sydney's St Luke's Grammar School go to Uganda to help at the Watoto Christian Mission Orphanage. Returning home, the boys speak of really appreciating what they have, including their education, of how happy the Ugandans are although they have little, and of wanting to give something back. What impressed principal Jann Robinson was the way the boys were so willing to open up and share their experiences on their return. One boy spoke of holding a baby at the orphanage, and suddenly realising this little baby would grow up without a mother or father. Like him, the baby was going to want to be a man, but the boy was aware how much further this little one would have to travel to get there. While there was a new iPod out, another boy said he didn't need it.

During their time at the orphanage, the boys built two houses for the teachers at Watoto's school. The boys also went to church, which made some think about their faith. Many boys reflected on how much love there was in the orphaned families, even though they weren't blood relatives. They also saw how happy the Ugandans could be without having to drink alcohol. As well as helping out at the orphanage, the boys got to climb Mount Kenya. At the end of the trip they had an African adventure, a visit to a game park and white water rafting down the Nile. The whole school was involved in raising money for the building project, so they got to share in the experience as well. Jann Robinson is now exploring opportunities for St Luke's boys to work with the underprivileged within Australia. 'The program helps privileged kids see the world in perspective,' she explains, adding, 'where kids can do something meaningful, it does wonders for their resilience.'

SUPPORT NETWORK

Boys can only enjoy a rich journey to adulthood when they have strong support at home and school. Our boys also need to know they're valuable members of their home and community, and that we *enjoy* having them around. Exposing them to experiences that matter helps also. When we nurture our boys in this way, even though they may not have immediate solutions to the challenging situations life brings, they will be confident they'll find a way through, because they've been *encouraged* to think about situations and how to handle them. Backed up by their parents' beliefs, an increase in responsibility over time, and knowing the importance of seeking help should they need it, they're able to be strong and to test their resilience. And, should a boy be lucky enough to have a wider friendship base, while he mightn't always come to his parents for advice, he has other supportive adults he can go to as well.

OUR BOYS *ARE* THE SOLUTION

International resilience expert Bonnie Benard stresses the need to see our kids not as problems, but as wonderful resources who are well able to contribute to their families, schools and communities. Social analyst Richard Eckersley agrees. His research reveals, 'Young people value the opportunity to discuss the future with each other and with adults; they need to be given more of these opportunities, including in schools, families and communities, as part of making sense and meaning of the world and their lives; and they deserve a greater voice on matters of most concern to them. Creating more spaces for dialogue would increase their engagement and capacity to act in the face of daunting challenges.'[6]

When we include boys in finding solutions, remarkable things can happen. As author and teacher John Gatto points out, 'Kids can be asked to help solve [problems] in exchange for the respect and attention of the total adult world. Good for kids, good for all the rest of us.'[7] In the course of my work in schools, and frequent approaches I get from students preparing assignments based on issues raised in my research, I emphasise the role teenagers play in finding solutions to their issues. They get very excited about this. As we've seen, there are many ways we can excite boys about what *they* have to offer in the home, their school and community, and their nation.

To help build your son's resilience:

- *See him as a resourceful person, not a problem.*
- *Encourage him to be at ease socially by helping him build good social networks.*
- *Develop a 'giving' culture in the home by contributing to charity and community events.*
- *Know his passions and help him find ways to express them.*
- *Stretch him by giving him increased responsibilities and freedoms over time.*
- *Encourage him to be adventurous and have a go.*
- *Balance the imposition of boundaries and understanding of consequences with your son's need to mature.*
- *Make sure he understands that failing and making mistakes can be really valuable.*
- *Remember there's no one way to be a man – allow your son to forge his own unique path to adulthood.*

Where to now?

There are real challenges to raising boys right now, but some wonderful opportunities also. This is not the time to sit back, or to abandon our boys to the marketers now shaping their values and aspirations. It's uncomfortable to admit that the fragilities our boys struggle with mirror our own, and that in large part their values are our values.

We need to face up to the ways in which our rampant consumerism is depriving boys of their individuality and imagination, their opportunity for rich life experiences and a wider world view. Each and every one of us must work actively to change the status quo by the values we espouse, the way we spend our leisure time and the goals we seek. It's essential we speak out against material we find objectionable, and strive for tighter regulation of advertising and marketing to our young.

Unless we want boys to grow up anxious, bored and immature, we must walk alongside them, and understand their twenty-first-century world intimately. We also need to appreciate boys more, to allow them to feel good about being boys. It's time we paid more attention to their emotional lives, and recognised how hard it is to be emotionally confident in a world that doesn't acknowledge your feelings.

Boys do need clear boundaries and discipline. However, they must also be heard, encouraged and protected. To grow up to be strong, empowered men, they also need to be around as many good men as possible. This means respecting how much men have to offer boys on their journey to manhood. Without a positive masculine influence, it's hard for our boys to have a vision of what is possible, so they turn instead to the dysfunctional role models churned out by the media and marketers.

If we don't want boys lost in virtual, often violent, fantasy worlds, real life must be more appealing. We need more community activities for boys and more locations *within* our neighbourhoods where they can safely let off steam. Boys also need to feel wanted and valued, to be given a more profound sense of belonging than they currently experience.

Childhood and teen life has changed radically in a few short years, and we must face up to this. When we view current issues through our own early experiences, we can so easily get it wrong. It's not enough to provide boys with drug and alcohol education and smart ad campaigns. We need to know what deep inner ache makes substance abuse and driving dangerously so attractive, and fully understand how action movies and the lives of celebrities feed these problems.

As we too have become desensitised to the sexually saturated world we inhabit, often we fail to realise just how vulnerable this material can make boys. It's vital we provide boys with good, engaging information, and with insight into the sexualised landscape, so they don't end up in situations they regret. We are right to be concerned by the numbers of boys, some of whom are at primary school, accessing porn, because in cyberspace boys get to experience both the best and worst of life. We don't know yet the full impact of a boy's early exposure to porn, but there are growing concerns that we could be creating the next generation of abusers purely from their internet experiences. Our boys cannot traverse these countless worlds within worlds on the net without direction, guidelines and a clear understanding of the dangers and consequences.

We also need to face the growing issues around boys and body image. Now marketers have boys in their sights, the anxiety boys are experiencing around looks and presentation is likely to escalate. Unless we want our boys to grow up constantly worried about their appearances, we need to work actively to give them a far greater sense of self.

Teenagers turn to their peers because they're there for them constantly and because they *understand*. Many boys wish they could discuss their issues with their parents, but are at a loss as to where to start. As most mums and dads are out of touch with teen life, often boys have no choice but to give up on their parents and go elsewhere for information. We need to stay relevant to our boys by keeping up to date with their world, so that the much-needed discussions of their issues can take place in the home.

Some of the material in this book is disturbing. That's why boys need parents to be there for them, just as much, if not more than ever before. It's important we remember this hyper-sexualised, fast-moving, often violent and confronting world is what boys are experiencing day in, day out. To safely navigate their way through, they need us to talk frequently with them so they have a clear sense of how best to respond.

As educator Ken Robinson reminds us, our task is to educate our children's *whole* being so they can face the future and make something of it.[1] To achieve this we need to balance education for careers with education for twenty-first-century life. Our boys also need good discussions around the kitchen table, in the car and out walking. They need friendships across the generations so they can access lifetimes of experience. They also need to feel useful, to be given opportunities to stretch themselves, to push their boundaries in positive ways, to serve their communities, to give back, and to experience just how special it is to touch someone else's life. When we achieve these things, we nurture a boy's humanity. We also teach him how to feed his spirit, so that in the years to come he can then mentor others.

While we may struggle with aspects of contemporary life, it's important we're optimistic about the challenges ahead, as much of the media is not. When we tell boys *they* are the reason we're looking forward to the future, we remind them of the important role they have to play in shaping their world. When we as adults can be engaged, informed and inclusive, we help empower boys and awaken their imagination and vision. Then they can achieve all we wish for them, and more besides.

For Maggie's talks schedule, reading group notes, or feedback, please see her website www.maggiehamilton.org

Further reading

Adams, Gerald, ed., *Adolescent Development: The Essential Readings*, Blackwell Publications, Oxford, 2000.

Adler, Patricia A. with Adler, Peter, *Peer Power: Preadolescent Culture and Identity*, Rutgers University Press, New Brunswick New Jersey, 1998.

Apter, Terri, *The Myth of Maturity: What Teenagers Need From Parents to Become Adults*, W.W. Norton and Co, New York, 2001.

Biddulph, Steve, *Manhood: An Action Plan for Changing Men's Lives*, Finch Publishing, Sydney, 1994.

Biddulph, Steve, *Raising Boys: Why Boys Are Different and How to Help Them Become Happy and Well-Balanced Men*, Finch Publishing, Sydney, 1997.

Brazelton, T. Berry et al, editors, *Affective Development in Infancy*, Ablex Publishing, Norwood, New Jersey, 1986.

Buckingham, Jennifer, 'Boy Troubles: Understanding Rising Suicide, Rising Crime and Educational Failure', *Centre for Independent Studies Policy Monographs 46*, St Leonards, 2000.

Carr-Gregg, Michael, *The Princess Bitchface Syndrome*, Penguin, Melbourne, 2006.

Cross, Gary, *Kids' Stuff: Toys and the Changing World of American Childhood*, Harvard University Press, Cambridge, Massachusetts, 1997.

Dillon, Paul, *Teenagers, Alcohol and Drugs: What Your Kids Really Want and Need to Know About Alcohol and Drugs*, Allen & Unwin, Sydney, 2009.

Doidge, Norman, *The Brain That Changes Itself: Stories of Personal Triumph from the Frontiers of Brain Science*, Penguin, London, 2007.

Eckersley, Richard, *Well and Good: Morality, Meaning and Happiness*, Text Publishing, Melbourne, 2004.

Eckersley, Richard, *Never Better or Getting Worse: The Health and Wellbeing of Young Australians*, Australia 21, Canberra, 2008.

Farrell, Warren, Ph.D., *The Myth of Male Power: Why Men Are the Disposable Sex*, Random House Australia, Sydney, 1994.

Gratch, Alon, *If Men Could Talk: Here's What They'd Say*, Little Brown and Company, New York, 2001.

Gurian, Michael, *Mothers, Sons and Lovers: How a Man's Relationship with His Mother Affects the Rest of His Life*, Shambhala, Boston, 1995.

Hamilton, Maggie, *What Men Don't Talk About*, Viking, Melbourne, 2006

Hüther, Gerald, Ph.D., *The Compassionate Brain: How Empathy Creates Intelligence*, Shambhala Publications, Boston, 2006.

Kasser, Tim, Ph.D., and Kanner, Allen D., Ph.D., *Psychology and Consumer Culture: The Struggle for a Good Life in a Materialistic World*, American Psychological Association, Washington, 2003.

Kelsey, Candice M., *The Secret Cyber Lives of Teenagers: Parenting in the Age of MySpace.com*, Marlowe & Company, New York, 2007.

Kindlon, Dan Ph.D. and Michael Thompson Ph.D., with Teresa Barker, *Raising Cain: Protecting the Emotional Life of Boys*, Ballantine Books, New York, 1999.

Lamb, Michael E., ed., *The Role of Fathers in Child Development*, Third Edition, John Wiley and Sons, New York, 1997.

Lashlie, Celia, *The Journey to Prison: Who Goes and Why*, HarperCollins, Auckland, 2002.

Lindstrom, Martin with Seybold, Patricia, B., *BRANDchild: Remarkable Insights Into the Minds of Today's Global Kids and Their Relationships with Brands*, Kogan Page, London, 2003.

Lindstrom, Martin, *buy.ology: Truth and Lies About Why We Buy*, Doubleday, New York, 2008.

Miedzian, Myriam, *Boys Will Be Boys: Breaking the Link Between Masculinity and Violence*, Anchor, Bantam, Doubleday, New York, 1991.

National Health and Medical Research Council, *National Youth Suicide Prevention Strategy: Setting the Evidence-Based Research Agenda for Australia: A Literature Review*, March, 1999.

Palmer, Sue, *21ˢᵗ Century Boys: How Modern Life Is Driving Them off the Rails and How We Can Get Them Back on Track*, Orion, London 2009.

Petre, Daniel, *Father Time: Making Time for Your Children*, Pan Macmillan, Sydney, 1998.

Phillips, Katharine A., *The Broken Mirror: Understanding and Treating BDD*, Oxford University Press, New York, 1996.

Pollack, William, *Real Boys: Rescuing Our Sons From the Myths of Boyhood*, Random House, New York, 1998.

Ponton, Lynn E., M.D., *The Romance of Risk: Why Teenagers Do the Things They Do*, Basic Books, New York, 1997.

Pope, Harrison G. Jnr., Katharine A. Phillips, and Roberto Olivardia, *The Adonis Complex: How to Identify, Treat and Prevent Body Obsession in Men and Boys*, Simon & Schuster, New York, 2002.

Postman, Neil, *Technopoly: The Surrender of Culture to Technology*, Vintage Books, New York, 1992.

Price, Geoff, *Puberty Boy*, Allen & Unwin, Sydney, 2005.

Quart, Alissa, *Branded: The Buying and Selling of Teenagers*, Basic Books, New York, 2003.

Ritchie, Karen, *Marketing to Generation X*, Lexington Books, New York, 1995.

Rowe, Leanne et al, *I Just Want You to Be Happy: Preventing and Tackling Teenage Depression*, Allen & Unwin, Sydney, 2009.

Rutter, Michael and David J. Smith, eds., *Psychosocial Disorders in Young People: Time Trends and Their Causes*, Academia Europa, John Wiley and Sons, Chichester, 1995.

Sauers, Joan, *Sex Lives of Australian Teenagers,* Random House, Sydney 2007.

Siegel, David L., *The Great Tween Buying Machine: Capturing Your Share of the Multibillion Dollar Tween Market,* Dearborn Trade Publishing, Ithaca NY, 2001.

Sax, Leonard, *Boys Adrift: The Five Factors Driving the Growing Epidemic of Unmotivated Boys and Underachieving Young Men*, Basic Books, Philadelphia, 2007.

Shneidman, Edwin, *Suicide as Psychache: A Clinical Approach to Self-Destructive Behaviour*, Jason Aronson, Northvale, New Jersey, 1993.

Silverstein Olga, and Beth Rashbaum, *The Courage to Raise Good Men*, Viking, New York, 1994.

Tanenbaum, Joe, *Male and Female Realities: Understanding the Opposite Sex*, Candle Publishing Company, Sugar Land, Texas, 1989.

Thomas, Susan Gregory, *Buy, Buy Baby: The Devastating Impact of Marketing to 0-3s*, Houghton Mifflin, Boston, 2007.

Ungar, Michael, *Too Safe for Their Own Good: How Risk and Responsibility Help Teens Thrive*, Allen & Unwin, Sydney, 2008.

Ungar, Michael, *Turning the Me Generation Into the We Generation: Raising Kids That Care,* Allen & Unwin, Sydney, 2009.

Notes

INTRODUCTION

1 'Consuming Kids: The Commercialisation of Childhood', *Media Education Foundation*, DVD, 2009.
2 Robert McChesney, 'Merchants of Cool: What's This Doing to Our Kids?', transcript, *Frontline*, PBS Radio, www.pbs.org/wgbh/pages/frontline/shows/cool/themes/doingtokids.html
3 Mark Crispin Miller, 'Merchants of Cool', transcript, *Frontline*, PBS, www.pbs.org/wgbh/pages/frontline/shows/cool/interviews/crispinmiller.html

BILLION-DOLLAR BABIES

1 Barbara F. Meltz, 'Marketers See Babies' Noses as Pathway to Profits', *The Globe*, 19 May 2005, www.frankwbaker.com/marketers_babies_profits.htm
2 Ibid.
3 Ibid.
4 Ibid.
5 Martin Lindstrom, *buy.ology: Truth and Lies About Why We Buy*, Doubleday, New York, 2008, p147.
6 *Campaign for a Commercial Free Childhood*, Judge Judy Baker Center, www.slideshare.net/ccfc/ccfc1
7 Helen Signy, 'Billion Dollar Baby', *Essential Baby Parenting Australia*, 6 December 2007, www.essentialbaby.com.au/parenting/toddler/billion-dollar-baby-20080506-2bhl.html?page=2
8 James McNeal, *The Kids Market: Myths and Realities*, Paramount Market, New York, 1999, p201.

9   Neo, 'Marc Jacobs for Bugaboo: Out in All Black!', *Trends Update*, 21 November 2008, http://trendsupdates.com/marc-jacobs-for-bugaboo-out-in-all-black

10 Susan Gregory Thomas, *Buy, Buy Baby: The Devastating Impact of Marketing to 0–3s*, Houghton Mifflin, Boston, 2007, p 91.

11 Erin E Clack, 'What a Tween Wants . . . Now: Market Research Experts Reveal What's New in This Important Demographic', *Children's Business*, 1 April 2004.

12 Susan Linn, *Consuming Kids: Protecting Our Kids From the Onslaught of Marketing and Advertising*, Random House, New York, 2004, p 54.

13 Susan Gregory Thomas, *Buy, Buy Baby: The Devastating Impact of Marketing to 0–3s*, Houghton Mifflin, Boston, 2007, pp 88–91.

14 Jay Giedd, 'Inside the Teenage Brain', transcript, *Frontline*, PBS, www.pbs.org/wgbh/pages/frontline/shows/teenbrain/interviews/giedd.html

15 'AAP Discourages Television For Very Young Children', News Release, *American Academy of Pediatrics*, 2 August 1999, www.aap.org/advocacy/archives/augdis.htm

16 Susan Gregory Thomas, *Buy, Buy Baby: The Devastating Impact of Marketing to 0–3s*, Houghton Mifflin, Boston, 2007.

17 Frederick Hecht, M.D. and Barbara K. Hecht, Ph.D., 'Attention Problems Due to TV Before 3', *MedicineNet*, 5 April 2004, www.medicinenet.com/script/main/art.asp?articlekey=31871

18 Sue Palmer, *21st Century Boys: How Modern Life Is Driving Them Off the Rails and How We Can Get Them Back on Track*, Orion, London 2009, p37.

WHAT BABY BOYS NEED TO THRIVE

1   Joe Tanenbaum, *Male and Female Realities: Understanding the Opposite Sex*, Candle Publishing Company, Sugar Land, Texas, 1989.

2   Gerald Hüther, Ph.D., *The Compassionate Brain: How Empathy Creates Intelligence*, Shambhala Publications, Boston, 2006, p74.

3   Gerald Hüther, Ph.D., *The Compassionate Brain: How Empathy Creates Intelligence*, Shambhala Publications, Boston, 2006, p73.

4   'Turn Down the Noise to Encourage Baby's Language Development', *playonwords.com*, 28 October 2007, http://playonwords.com/articles/category/tv-and-videos/

5   'Practice Builds Brain Connections For Babies Learning Language, How To Speak', *Physorg.com*, 11 July 2006, www.physorg.com/news71809173.html

6   Rebecca Smith, 'Children's Language Skills Harmed by TV', *The Daily Telegraph*, 2 June 2009, p14.

7   www.ccrctulsa.org/inf_tod_files/InternationalInfantToddlerConferencefinal.pdf

SHRINKING CHILDHOOD

1 James McNeal, *The Kids Market: Myths and Realities*, Paramount Market, New York, 1999, pp 14–15.
2 Zoe Williams, 'The Commercialisation of Childhood', *Compass,* http://clients. squareeye.com/uploads/compass/documents/thecommercialisationofchildhood. pdf, p5.
3 Barbara F. Meltz, 'Marketers See Babies' Noses as Pathway to Profits', *The Globe*, 19 May 2005, www.frankwbaker.com/marketers_babies_profits.htm
4 Dan S. Acuff, Ph.D. with Robert H. Reiher, Ph.D., *What Kids Buy And Why: The Psychology of Marketing To Kids*, Simon & Schuster New York, 1997.
5 John W Whitehead, 'The Hostile Takeover of Childhood', *The Huffington Post*, 16 June 2009, www.huffingtonpost.com/john-w-whitehead/the-hostile-takeover-of-c_b_215547.html
6 Mark Stackpole, 'Playing with Dad: Can Roughhousing Go Too Far?', *Dadstoday.com*, www.dadstoday.com/articles/play-time/playing-with-dad-600/3/
7 Sandy Fazio, 'How to Help Boys Read and Write', *Supernanny.co.uk*, www.supernanny.co.uk/Advice/-/Learning-and-Education/-/4-to-13-years/ How-to-help-boys-to-read-and-write-.aspx

A TWEEN'S WORLD

1 Ron Harris, 'Children Who Dress For Success', *Los Angeles Times*, 12 November 1989, A1.
2 Dawn, Chmielewski, 'Disney to Target Boys With Rebranded Cable Channel', *Los Angeles Times*, 7 October 2008, http://articles.latimes.com/2008/aug/07/ business/fi-disney7
3 'Special Issues for Tweens and Teens: The Tween Market', *Media Awareness Network*, www.media-awareness.ca/english/parents/marketing/issues_teens_ marketing.cfm
4 Martin Lindstrom, *buy.ology: Truth and Lies About Why We Buy*, Doubleday, New York, 2008, pp 82–83.
5 'Consuming Kids: The Commercialization of Childhood', *Media Education Foundation*, DVD, 2009.
6 http://directory.leadmaverick.com/Kid-Club-Marketing/ProvidenceNew- BedfordFall-River/RI/10/4323/index.aspx
7 www.livepositively.com/my_coke_rewards_for_schools
8 Eric Schlosser, *Fast Food Nation: The Dark Side of the All-American Meal*, Penguin Books, New York, 2002, p45.

TWEEN BOYS, FOOD AND FASHION

1   Eric Schlosser, *Fast Food Nation: The Dark Side of the All-American Meal*, Penguin Books, New York, 2002, p47.

2   Ibid.

3   Gary Ruskin, 'Why They Whine: How Corporations Prey on Children', *Mothering Magazine*, Number 97, Nov/Dec 1999, www.commercialalert.org

4   Michael Pollan, 'You Are What You Grow', *The New York Times*, 22 April 2007, www.nytimes.com/2007/04/22/magazine/22wwlnlede.t.html?pagewanted=1&_r=1

5   'Fast Food Salt Levels "Shocking"', *BBC News*, 18 October 2007, http://news.bbc.co.uk/2/hi/health/7050585.stm

6   Martin Lindstrom, *buy.ology: Truth and Lies About Why We Buy*, Doubleday, New York, 2008, p148.

7   Jane Bainbridge, 'Men's Toiletries – Altered Image', Sector Insight, *Marketing Magazine*, 10 May 2006, www.marketingmagazine.co.uk/news/558310/Sector-Insight-Mens-toiletries-Altered-image

8   'Breaking News On Cosmetics Formulation and Packaging: North America', *Cosmeticsdesign.com*, www.cosmeticsdesign.com/Prodicts-Markets/Tween-boys-the-new-niche-market

9   Tiffany B, 'Fall and Winter Fashion Trends for Young Boys', *Associated Content*, 2 October 2008, www.associatedcontent.com/article/1055599/fall_and_winter_fashion_trends_for.html?cat=46

10 Theresa, 'Plaid Okkie Pant', *Upscale Baby Blog*, 14 July 2009, www.blogcatalog.com/blog/upscale-babyblog/e18796ceb7ba2a53d46cfa435fcf6ef8

11 http://askville.amazon.com/SimilarQuestions.do?req=hot+trends+backpacks+pre+teen+boys+clothing+shoes+year

12 Zoe Williams, 'The Commercialisation of Childhood', *Compass*, http://clients.squareeye.com/uploads/compass/documents/thecommercialisationofchildhood.pdf, p6.

13 Martin Lindstrom with Patricia B Seybold, *BRANDChild: Remarkable Insights into the Minds of Today's Global Kids and Their Relationships with Brands*, Kogan Page, London 2003, p196.

14 Ibid.

LOSING TWEEN BOYS TO VIRTUAL WORLDS

1   David Kushner, 'The Neopets Addiction', *Wired Magazine*, Issue 13, 12 December 2005, www.wired.com/wired/archive/13.12/neopets.html

2   'Is Modern Life Ruining Childhood?', *BBC News*, 12 September 2006, http://news.bbc.co.uk/1/hi/uk/5338572.stm

3   Professor Neil Postman, 'Informing Ourselves to Death', *German Infomatics Society*, www.frostbytes.com/~jimf/informing.html

RECLAIMING CHILDHOOD

1   A.L., Duckworth & M.E.P. Seligman, 'Self-Discipline Outdoes IQ in Predicting Academic Performance of Adolescents', *Psychological Science, 16(12),* 2005, pp939–944.
2   John W. Whitehead, 'The Hostile Takeover of Childhood', *The Huffington Post*, 16 June 2009, www.huffingtonpost.com/john-w-whitehead/the-hostile-takeover-of-c_b_215547.html

YOUNG BOYS IN NEED OF GOOD BLOKES

1   Celia Lashlie, *Journey to Prison: Who Goes to Prison and Why*, Harper Collins, Auckland, 2003.
2   Christine Ford, 'Teaching Boys Self-Confidence: Father Figure or Male Role Model', *Kaboose.com*, http://parenting.kaboose.com/behavior/emotional-social-development/teaching-boys-self-confidence-5.html

THE IMPACT OF THE STORIES WE TELL

1   Joe Tanenbaum, *Male and Female Realities: Understanding the Opposite Sex*, Candle Publishing Company, Sugar Land, Texas, 1989.

EARLY SEXUALISATION

1   Des Houghton, 'Sex Attack Seen as Childhood Experiment at Queensland School', *The Courier Mail*, 12 September 2008.
2   Martin Lindstrom, *buy.ology: Truth and Lies About Why We Buy*, Doubleday, New York, 2008, p192.
3   Melinda Tankard-Reist, ed. *Getting Real: Challenging the Sexualisation of Girls*, Spinifex Publishers, Melbourne, 2009, p163.
4   Cheryl Critchley, 'Mums Outraged Over Saucy Messages on Infant Clothes', *The Herald Sun*, 22 July 2009, www.news.com.au/heraldsun/story/0,21985,25817531-662,00.html
5   Michael Flood, 'The Harms of Pornography Exposure Among Children and Young People', *Child Abuse Review*, Vol 18, pp384–400.
6   P. Doherty, 8.30 a.m, ABC Radio 774, 4 October 2001.
7   Sgt Dale Yates, 'The Dark World of Child Porn', *90th Space Wing Public Affairs*, 2 February 2007, www.warren.af.mil/news/story.asp?id=123039750
8   Maggie Hamilton, *What's Happening to Our Girls?* Penguin, Melbourne, 2008, p53.
9   'Internet Watch Foundation', *Annual and Charity Report 2006*, www.iwf.org.uk/documents/20070412_iwf_annual_report_2006_(web).pdf, p8.

PUBERTY SUCKS

1 Maggie Hamilton, *What Men Don't Talk About*, Penguin, Melbourne, 2006, p49.
2 Jay Giedd, 'Inside the Teenage Brain', transcript, *Frontline*, PBS, www.pbs.org/wgbh/pages/frontline/shows/teenbrain/interviews/giedd.html
3 Deborah Yurgelun-Todd, 'The Teen Brain Is a Work in Progress', transcript, *Frontline*, PBS, www.pbs.org/wgbh/pages/frontline/shows/teenbrain/interviews/todd.html
4 Ibid.

BOYS AND THEIR NEED FOR POSSESSIONS

1 Tim Ingham, '360 Global Sales Surpass Original Xbox', *MCV.com*, 24 November 2008, www.mcvuk.com/news/32449/360-global-sales-surpass-original-Xbox
2 Nanette Byrnes, 'Secrets of the Male Shopper', *Business Week*, 4 Sept 2006, www.businessweek.com/magazine/content/06_36/b3999001.htm
3 John Byrne and Nanette Byrnes, 'Secrets of the Male Shopper', podcast, *Mefeedia,* 24 August 2006, www.mefeedia.com/entry/secrets-of-the-male-shopper/6967619
4 Nancy Pekala, 'Teen Tribes: Affiliation and Attitudes Drive Teen Shopping Patterns', *Marketing Power*, 27 October 2008, www.marketingpower.com/ResourceLibrary/Pages/Marketing%20Matters/MarketingMattersNewsletter102708/Teen_Tribes_Affiliation_and_Attitudes_Drive_Teen_Shopping_Patterns.aspx

WORRIES ABOUT BODY IMAGE

1 Interview 29 July 2005.
2 Interview 9 July 2009.
3 Interview 9 July 2009.
4 'Body Dysmorphic Disorder Drives Teens to Supplements', *Aphrodite: Women's Health*, 5 August 2005, www.aphroditewomenshealth.com/news/20050705015144_health_news.shtml
5 'Males and Eating Disorders: Some Basic Facts and Findings', *International Eating Disorder Referral Organisation,* www.edreferral.com/males_eating_disorders.htm
6 Kay Hawes, 'Is Bigger Better?' *National Collegiate Athletic Association News*, 24 September 2001, www.ncaa.org/news/2001/20010924/active/3820n27.html
7 Dr Robyn J.A. Silverman, 'Body Image and Boys: The Adonis Complex and Steroid Abuse among Teens, *Dr Robyn Silverman's Blog*, 25 June 2008, http://drrobyn.wordpress.com/2008/06/25/body-image-and-boys-the-adonis-complex-and-steroid-abuse-among-teens/

8 Aaron Patnode, 'Many Body-Conscious Teens Use Supplements to Improve Physique', *Medical News*, 1 August 2005, www.medicalnewstoday.com/articles/28439.php

9 www.golivewire.com/forums/peer-ynnbopb-support-a.html

10 Caroline Marcus, 'Adam's Descent Into Hell: 130 Kg At 15, 45 kg and Desperate at 23', *The Sun-Herald,* 22 March 2009.

11 http://tilt214.tripod.com/id7.html

12 www.prettythin.com/apps/blog/

13 Julie Robotham, 'Children Prove Thicker Skinned', *The Sun-Herald*, 1 March 2009.

14 Erin O'Dwyer, 'Tackling Childhood Obesity: Get Mum Fit Too', *The Sydney Morning Herald,* weekend edition, 7–8 February 2009.

PEER PRESSURE

1 'Peer Pressure', *Children's Parliament on the Environment*, Spring 2002, www.la21.org.uk/cp2002/pressure.html

2 Ibid.

3 'Resisting Peer Pressure: New Findings Shed Light on Adolescent Decision-Making', *ScienceDaily*, 27 July 2007, www.sciencedaily.com/releases/2007/07/070725093605.htm

THE BULLYING THING

1 Alex McDonald, 'Teased So Much He Wanted to Die', *The Sun-Herald*, 1 February 2009, p33.

2 Dr Jean B. Healey, 'Peer Abuse as Child Abuse and Indications for Intervention in Schools', *Self Concept Enhancement and Learning Facilitation Research Centre*, University of Western Sydney, www.aare.edu.au/05pap/hea05418.pdf

3 'Cyber Bullying: Statistics and Tips', *2004 I-Safe-America Survey*, I-Safe.org, www.isafe.org/channels/sub.php?ch=op&sub_id=media_cyber_bullying

4 'Putting U in the Picture: Mobile Bullying Survey 2005', *Tesco Mobile and the National Children's Home*, www.filemaker.co.uk/educationcentre/downloads/articles/Mobile_bullying_report.pdf

5 www.blogsafety.com/thread.jspa?threadID=1100000219

STRESSED-OUT BOYS

1 Anna Ferguson, 'Burnout: How Much Is Too Much for Today's Busy Teenager?', *North Virginia Daily*, 10 April 2006, www.cleaninc.org/press/Burnout.htm

2 'Body Story, Teen Dreams: Emotions', *Channel 4,* www.channel4.com/science/microsites/B/bodystory/teen_emotions.html

3 Fred Engh, 'Sports Rage: Adults Losing Control at Kids' Sporting Events', *ABC News*, 11 September 2000, http://abcnews.go.com/US/story?id=94468

4   'Decision Making: A Series of National Surveys of Teens About Sex', *Kaiser Family Foundation* and *seventeen*, September 2000, http://74.125.153.132/ search?q=cache:euj8jHN9BtMJ:www.kff.org/youthhivstds/loader. cfm%3Furl%3D/commonspot/security/getfile.cfm%26PageID%3D13538+kais er+foundation+boys+pressure+sex&cd=1&hl=en&ct=clnk&client=safari, p3.

UNDERSTANDING A BOY'S FEELINGS

1   Ernesto, 'Emotions: Dealing With Feelings', abouthealth.com, www.abouthealth. com/t_topicX.htm?topic=50
2   Dan Kindlon, Ph.D. and Michael Thompson, Ph.D., with Teresa Barker, *Raising Cain: Protecting the Emotional Life of Boys*, Ballantine Books, New York, 1999.
3   www.golivewire.com/forums/peer-ynnspii-support-a.html
4   Ibid.
5   Ibid.

MUMS AND THEIR BOYS

1   Joanna Murray-Smith, 'To My Beautiful, Unknowable Boy, All the Things Unsaid', *The Age*, 3 February 2009, www.theage.com.au/opinion/to-my-beautiful-unknowable-boy-all-the-things-unsaid-20090202-7voy.html
2   www.golivewire.com/forums/peer-ynnabap-support-a.html
3   Ibid.

WHY BOYS LOVE THEIR COMPUTERS

1   Stacey Waters, 'Cyber Bullying and the NET Generation: Bullying-Related Research', *Child Health Promotion Research Centre*, Edith Cowan University http://72.14.235.132/search?q=cache:rD3oGZHHXDAJ:www.aisnsw.edu.au/ PD/LinkClick.aspx%3Flink%3DConferences%252FStacey%2BWaters%2B-%2BCyber%2BBullying.pdf%26tabid%3D1001%26mid%3D1931+stacey+wate rs+bullying+presentation&cd=3&hl=en&ct=clnk&client=safari, p27.
2   Julie Tullberg, 'Computer Addiction: A Growing Problem', *The Age*, 7 December 2007, www.news.theage.com.au/national/computer-addiction-a-growing-problem-20071207-1flm.html?page=2
3   Stacey Waters, 'Cyber Bullying and the NET Generation: Bullying-Related Research', *Child Health Promotion Research Centre*, Edith Cowan University http://72.14.235.132/search?q=cache:rD3oGZHHXDAJ:www.aisnsw.edu.au/ PD/LinkClick.aspx%3Flink%3DConferences%252FStacey%2BWaters%2B-%2BCyber%2BBullying.pdf%26tabid%3D1001%26mid%3D1931+stacey+wate rs+bullying+presentation&cd=3&hl=en&ct=clnk&client=safari, p27.

4   Julie Tullberg, 'Computer Addiction: A Growing Problem', *The Age*, 7 December 2007, http://news.theage.com.au/national/computer-addiction-a-growing-problem-20071207-1flm.html?page=2

5   Nick Galvin, 'Social Notworking', Icon, *The Sydney Morning Herald*, 12 May 2009, p20.

NOT ENOUGH SLEEP

1   Mary Carskadon, 'Inside the Teenage Brain', transcript, *Frontline*, PBS, www.pbs.org/wgbh/pages/frontline/shows/teenbrain/interviews/carskadon.html

2   Ellen Connolly, 'Unhealthy Love of SMS', *The Sunday Telegraph*, 7 September 2009.

3   Siri Carpenter, 'Sleep Deprivation May Be Undermining Teen Health', *Monitor On Psychology*, Vol. 3, No. 9, October 2001, http://www.apa.org/monitor/oct01/sleepteen.html

4   'Sleep Deprivation', *Apollo Health*, www.apollolight.com/new_content/circadian%20rhythms_disorders/sleep/sleep_deprivation.html.

5   'Nighttime Computer Users May Lose Sleep', archive, *WebMD*, 19 June 2003.

THE WEIRD WORLD OF CYBERSPACE

1   'Web Friend Conned into Murder Bid', *BBC News*, 28 May 2004, http://news.bbc.co.uk/2/hi/uk_news/england/manchester/3758209.stm

2   Andrew Nott and Don Frame, 'Internet "Murder" Boys Told: Never See Each Other Again', *The Manchester Evening News*, 29 May 2009, www.manchestereveningnews.co.uk/news/s/118/118226_internet_murder_boys_told_never_see_each_other_again.html and Helen Carter, 'Boy Arranged His Stabbing Via Internet', *The Age*, 30 May 2004, www.theage.com.au/articles/2004/05/29/1085641761298.html.

3   www.blogsafety.com/thread.jspa?threadID=1200001380

4   www.blogsafety.com/thread.jspa?threadID=1200001504

5   www.blogsafety.com/thread.jspa?threadID=1200001344

6   Amanda Lenhart et al, 'Teenage Life Online: The Rise of the Instant-Message Generation and the Internet's Impact on Friendships and Family Relationships', *Pew Internet and American Life Project*, 20 June 2001, www.pewinternet.org/~/media//Files/Reports/2001/PIP_Teens_Report.pdf, p5.

7   Amanda Lenhart et al, 'Teenage Life Online: The Rise of the Instant-Message Generation and the Internet's Impact on Friendships and Family Relationships', *Pew Internet and American Life Project*, 20 June 2001, www.pewinternet.org/~/media//Files/Reports/2001/PIP_Teens_Report.pdf, p4.

8   Bonnie Ruberg, 'Peeking Up the Skirt of Online Sex Work: Topless and Proud', *villagevoice.com*, 28 August 2007, www.villagevoice.com/2007-08-28/columns/peeking-up-the-skirt-of-online-sex-work/

9   Dan Goodin, 'Student Charged After Alerting Principal to Server Hack: Intentional Criminal Act?', *The Register*, 28 October 2008, www.theregister.co.uk/2008/10/28/student_charged/

10 John Leyden, 'Teen Hacker Charged With Nasa Attacks: Intel Hackers Smoked Crew Claim Cracker as One of Their Own', *The Register*, 14 March 2001, www.theregister.co.uk/2001/03/14/teen_hacker_charged_with_nasa/

11 Larry Neumeister, 'Two Arrests Made in NASA: Student, Man Charged for Breaking Into NASA Computers', *ABC News*, 13 July 2000, Hacking http://abcnews.go.com/Technology/story?id=119677&page=1

12 Dan Goodin, 'Teen Hacker Confesses Three-Year Crime Spree', *The Register*, 19 November 2008, www.theregister.co.uk/2008/11/19/dshocker_pleads_guilty/

13 'Number of Teen Gamblers in the US Rise Significantly', *PBS News Hour Extra*, 20 June 2005, www.pbs.org/newshour/bb/youth/jan-june05/gambling_6-20.html

14 Ibid.

15 Alison Branley, 'Teens Bet Mobiles, Virginity', *The Sydney Morning Herald*, 18 August 2009.

16 Monica Villavicencio, 'As More Teens Gamble, Experts Urge Public Education', *News Hour Extra*, PBS, 25 April 2005, www.pbs.org/newshour/extra/features/jan-june05/gambling_4-25.html

17 Catherine Donaldson-Evans, 'Junior Jackpot: Teen Gambling on the Rise', *Fox News*, 17 May 2006, www.foxnews.com/story/0,2933,195751,00.html

THE SECRET LIVES OF BOYS

1   Amanda Lenhart et al, 'Teenage Life Online: The Rise of the Instant-Message Generation and the Internet's Impact on Friendships and Family Relationships', *Pew Internet and American Life Project*, 20 June 2001, www.pewinternet.org/~/media//Files/Reports/2001/PIP_Teens_Report.pdf.pdf, p15.

2   Ibid.

3   Ibid.

4   Tracy L. Doerr, 'A Wangled, Wired Web: What You Need to Know About Online Cheating', *iParenting.com*, www.teenagerstoday.com/articles/back-to-school-headquarters/a-wangled-wired-web-1039/

5   Jill Tucker, 'More High-Tech Cheating – and Rationalizing', *SFGate.com*, 19 June 2009, www.sfgate.com/cgi-bin/article.cgi?f=/c/a/2009/06/19/MNPT189R9I.DTL Shallow knowledge – bytes of information

6   www.urbandictionary.com/define.php?term=suck+my+cock

7   Michael Carr-Gregg, *The Princess Bitchface Syndrome*, Penguin, Melbourne, 2006, p.xv.

ADDICTED TO GAMING

1   http://au.gamespot.com/pages/forums/show_msgs.php?topic_id=26482661
2   Amanda Woodward, 'Game Faces', *Sunday Life Magazine*, *The Sun-Herald*, p17.
3   Matt Vella, 'Grand Theft Auto Rakes in Record Sales Innovation Column', *Business Week*, May 2008, www.businessweek.com/innovate/gamesinc/archives/2008/05/grand_theft_aut.htm
4   Blake Snow, 'Mainstream Criticism of Grand Theft Auto IV Begins . . .,' *Gamepro.Com*, 30 April 2008, www.gamepro.com/article/news/181488/mainstream-criticism-of-grand-theft-auto-iv-begins/
5   Jason Rybka, 'Grand Theft Auto San Andreas Hot Coffee Mod: A Look at the So-Called Murder Simulators and Sex-Sims Within Videogames', *About.com,* http://vgstrategies.about.com/od/basictips/a/gta3hotcoffee.htm
6   Posting 14 June 2005, www.spike.com/video/hot-coffee/2673401
7   Bill Costello, 'Video Games for Christmas? Perhaps Not for Boy's Education', *News.org*, 12 November 2008, www.ednews.org/articles/31802/1/Video-Games-for-Christmas-Perhaps-Not-for-Boys/Page1.html
8   Ibid.
9   'Boys and Computer Games: Advice to Facilitators', Information Notes, *Education Department*, Queensland, http://74.125.153.132/search?q=cache:Gb7GypoDJ5sJ:education.qld.gov.au/students/advocacy/equity/gender-sch/docs/issues-games.doc+Give+senseless+violence+that+comedy+feel&cd=1&hl=en&ct=clnk&gl=au
10 Chris Kohler, 'Red Steel Hands-On: Officially Awesome', *Game Life,* 25 October 2006, http://blog.wired.com/games/2006/10/red_steel_hands.html
11 'Boys and Computer Games: Advice to Facilitators', Information Notes, *Education Department*, Queensland, http://74.125.153.132/search?q=cache:Gb7GypoDJ5sJ:education.qld.gov.au/students/advocacy/equity/gender-sch/docs/issues-games.doc+Give+senseless+violence+that+comedy+feel&cd=1&hl=en&ct=clnk&gl=au
12 'Violent Video Games Affect Biological Systems', press release, Stockholm University, 13 November 2008, www.su.se/english/about/press/press_releases/violent_video_games_affect_biological_systems?page=2
13 Craig A Anderson et al, 'Violent Video Games Effects on Aggression, Empathy, and Prosocial Behavior in Eastern and Western Countries: A Meta-Analytic Review', *Psychological Bulletin*, American Psychological Association, proof of forthcoming article, 2010
14 Craig A Anderson, transcript, Violent Video Games Increase Aggression and Violence', presentation to *US Senate Commerce Committee hearing on 'The Impact of Interactive Violence on Children',* 21 March 2000, p3

15 Karen E Dill, 'Violent Video Games Can Increase Aggression,' press release, *American Psychological Association*, 23 April 2000

16 Jim Reed, 'Thailand Bans Grand Theft Auto IV', *BBC News*, 4 August 2008, http://news.bbc.co.uk/newsbeat/hi/technology/newsid_7540000/7540623.stm

THE ALCOHOL GENERATION

1 'CASA 2003 Teen Survey: High Stress, Frequent Boredom, Too Much Spending Money: Triple Threat That Hikes Risk of Teen Substance Abuse', press release, *National Center on Addiction and Substance Abuse*, Columbia University, www.casacolumbia.org/absolutenm/templates/PressReleases.aspx?articleid=348&zoneid=46

2 Buddy T, 'Teen Drinking – Not Just a Phase: Teens Who Start Early Have Later Problems', About.com, http://alcoholism.about.com/cs/teens/a/aa010108a.htm

3 Shari Roan, 'Educators Disagree on Minimum Legal Drinking Age', *The Missourian,* 11 September 2008, www.columbiamissourian.com/stories/2008/09/11/educators-disagree-minimum-legal-drinking-age/

4 Ralph W Hingson et al, 'Age at Drinking Onset and Alcohol Dependence: Age at Onset, Duration, and Severity', *Archives of Pediatrics and Adolescent Medicine,* Volume 160, 2006, http://archpedi.ama-assn.org/cgi/content/full/160/7/739, pp739–746.

5 Leslie B Synder et al, 'Effects of Alcohol Advertising Exposure on Drinking Among Youth', *Archives of Pediatric and Adolescent Medicine,* 2006, Issue 160, http://archpedi.ama-assn.org/cgi/content/short/160/1/18, pp18–24.

6 C. Pechmann, et al., '*Journal of Public Policy and Marketing* 24, 2005, pp202–221.

7 Buddy T, 'Teen Drinking – Not Just a Phase: Teens Who Start Early Have Later Problems', About.com, http://alcoholism.about.com/cs/teens/a/aa010108a.htm

THE DRUG SCENE

1 Paul Dillon, *Teenagers, Alcohol and Drugs: What Your Kids Really Want and Need to Know About Alcohol and Drugs*, Allen & Unwin, Sydney 2009, pp119–120.

2 Jonathan Owen, 'Heavy Cannabis Use by Teens Is More Dangerous Than Alcohol', *The Independent*, 22 April 2007, www.independent.co.uk/life-style/health-and-families/health-news/heavy-cannabis-use-by-teens-is-more-dangerous-than-alcohol-445742.html

3 Ibid.

4 Paul Dillon, *Teenagers, Alcohol and Drugs: What Your Kids Really Want and Need to Know About Alcohol and Drugs*, Allen & Unwin, Sydney 2009, p114.

5   Kate Benson, 'Ice Users Risk Brain Shrinkage', *The Sun-Herald*, 23 November 2008, p24.
6   Julie-Anne Davies, '4000 Kids Under 10 on Mood Drugs', *The Australian*, 3 December 2008, www.theaustralian.news.com.au/story/0,25197,24743413-2702,00.html
7   Angela Saurine, 'Kid's Home Drug Parties', *The Daily Telegraph*, 11 October 2008, p9.
8   Joseph Califano, National Center on Addiction and Substance Abuse.
9   Maggie Hamilton, *What Men Don't Talk About*, Penguin, Melbourne, 2006, p55.
10 'Herbal Remedy: Teens Often Use Cannabis for Relief, Not Recreation, Study Finds', *Science Daily*, 24 April 2009, www.sciencedaily.com/releases/2009/04/090422191724.htm
11 Maggie Hamilton, *What Men Don't Talk About*, Penguin, Melbourne, 2006, p52.
12 Laurie Wilmot, 'Raising Drug Free Teenagers', *Drugrehabtreatment.com*, www.drugrehabtreatment.com/raising-drug-free-teens.html

BOYS AND CARS

1   Professor George Patten, 'Teens and Young Adults Most at Risk of Death', press release, Murdoch Children's Research Institute, 11 September 2009.
2   Diana Smart et al, 'In the Driver's Seat: Understanding Young Adults' Driving Behaviour', Australian Institute of Family Studies, Research Report 12, 2005, www.aifs.gov.au/institute/pubs/resreport12/introduction.pdf, p4.
3   Ibid.
4   *Australian College of Road Safety*, Issue 1, September 2003, www.acrs.org.au/srcfiles/September-03---Issue1.pdf, p2.
5   Christine Mulvihill et al, 'Development of a Model Resource for Parents as Supervisory Drivers', Monash University, Accident Research Centre, September 2005, Report No. 243 www.monash.edu.au/muarc/reports/muarc243.pdf, p7.
6   Ibid.

THE SEX LIVES OF TEEN BOYS

1   AAP, 'Oral Sex Is on the Rise', *Sydney Morning Herald*, 16 September 2008.
2   Rob Stein, 'Increase in Cancer Rates Linked to Oral Sex', *Sydney Morning Herald*, 11 May 2007, p9.
3   David McCowen, 'Students Pledge to Respect Women', *St George and Sutherland Shire Leader*, 24 September 2009, p3.

BOYS INTO PORN

1 Caroline Sullivan, 'Internet Traders of Child Pornography: Profiling Research', October 2005, www.dia.govt.nz/

2 Sgt Dale Yates, 'The Dark World of Child Porn', *90th Space Wing Public Affairs*, F.E. Warren Air Force Base, 2 February 2007, www.warren.af.mil/news/story.asp?id=123039750

3 Professor Max Taylor, 'Combating Paedophile Information Networks in Europe', *COPINE Project*, University College, Cork, March 2003.

4 Gail Dines, 'Childified Women: How the mainstream porn industry sells child pornography to men', from Sharna Olfman, ed., *Sexualisation of Childhood*, Praeger Publishers, Santa Barbara, 2008.

5 'Give me gape: adult video news', September 2004, p58. Quoted in Gail Dines, 'Childified Women: How the mainstream porn industry sells child pornography to men' from Sharna Olfman, ed *Sexualisation of Childhood*, Praeger Publishers, Santa Barbara, 2008.

6 Internet Watch Foundation, *Annual and Charity Report*, 2006, www.iwf.org.uk/documents/20070412_iwf_annual_report_2006_(web).pdf, p8.

7 Cassell Bryan-Low, and David Pringle, 'Sex Cells: Wireless Operators Find That Racy Cellphone Video Drives Surge in Broadband Use', *The Wall Street Journal*, 12 May 2005.

8 Rebecca Leung, 'Porn in the USA, Steve Kroft Reports on a $10 Billion Industry', *60 Minutes*, CBS News, 5 September 2004, www.cbsnews.com/stories/2003/11/21/60minutes/main585049.shtml

9 Ibid.

10 Ibid.

11 Ibid.

12 Editorial, 'Protecting Kids Online', *Washington Post*, 1 July 2004.

13 Michael Flood, 'Exposure to Pornography Among Youth in Australia', *Journal of Sociology*, 2007, Vol 43 (1), p48

14 Ibid.

15 Bev Betkowski, 'Study Finds Teen Boys Most Likely to Access Pornography', *Folio,* University of Alberta, 2 March 2007, www.ualberta.ca/~publicas/folio/44/13/09.html

16 'McAfee, Inc. Research Reveals Mothers Rate Cyber Dangers as High as Drunk Driving or Experimenting With Drugs', Press Release, *McAfee Inc. Research*, 22 October 2008, www.mcafee.com/us/about/press/corporate/2008/20081022_095000_x.htm

17 Internet Watch Foundation, *Annual and Charity Report*, 2006, www.iwf.org.uk/documents/20070412_iwf_annual_report_2006_(web).pdf, p8.

18 Michael Flood, 'Exposure to Pornography Among Youth in Australia', *Journal of Sociology*, 2007, Vol 43 (1), p58

19 Michael Flood, 'The Harms of Pornography Exposure Among Children and Young People', *Child Abuse Review*, Vol 18, 2 November 2009, p390

20 Michael Flood, 'The Harms of Pornography Exposure Among Children and Young People', *Child Abuse Review*, Vol 18, 2 November 2009, p393

21 Norman Doidge, *The Brain That Changes Itself: Stories of Personal Triumph from the Frontiers of Brain Science*, Penguin, London, 2007, p103.

22 Ibid.

23 'One in Three Boys Heavy Porn Users, Study Shows', *Science News, ScienceDaily*, *25 February 2007*, www.sciencedaily.com/releases/2007/02/070223142813.htm

CAMBOY

1   Kurt Eichenwald, 'Through His Webcam, A Boy Joins a Sordid Online World', *The New York Times*, 19 December 2005, www.nytimes.com/2005/12/19/national/19kids.ready.html

WHEN SEX BECOMES SEXUAL ASSAULT

1   Dr. Michael Rich, 'Sexual Health in a Climate of Sexual Confusion', *Family Strengths Conference*, American Academy of Pediatrics' Media Matters Campaign, 28 October 2003, www.delko.net/sexual%20development%20slides.pdf

MENTAL HEALTH ISSUES

1   Richard Eckersley, 'Never Better – Or Getting Worse? The Health and Wellbeing of Young Australians', Australia 21, Canberra, 2008.

2   Mary Carskadon, 'Inside the Teenage Brain', transcript, *Frontline*, PBS, www.pbs.org/wgbh/pages/frontline/shows/teenbrain/interviews/carskadon.html

3   Matt Bachl, 'Suicide "Craze" Could Hit Australia', *Nine News*, 25 January 2008, http://news.ninemsn.com.au/article.aspx?id=371672

LIVING IN A VIOLENT WORLD

1   Deborah Prothrow-Stith, 'Do "Fight Clubs" Reflect America's Violent Culture?', transcript, *NPR News and Notes*, 17 August 2006, www.npr.org/templates/story/story.php?storyId=5663321

2   Ellen Wartella, 'Media and Problem Behaviours in Young People', *Psychosocial Disorders in Young People: Time Trends and Their Causes,* edited by Michael Rutter and David J. Smith, Academia Europa, John Wiley and Sons, Chichester, 1995.

3   'Children and Media Violence Fact Sheet', *National Institute on Media and the Family*, www.mediafamily.org/facts/facts_vlent.shtml

4   Peter Sheehan, 'Perceptions of Violence on Television', www.aic.gov.au/
    publications/aust-violence-1/Sheehan.pdf
5   Linda Silmalis, 'Guns, Knives in Our Schools', *The Sunday Telegraph*, 26 April
    2009, p9.
6   Nick Britten, '7-Year-Olds Carrying Knives in "Arms Race"', *The Daily Telegraph*,
    p12.
7   www.golivewire.com/forums/peer-ynbnbba-support-a.html
8   Evelyn Yamine, 'Teen Boys Are Our Worst Criminals, ABS Figures Show,'
    The Daily Telegraph, 28 August 2009, http://wl.news.com.au/dailytelegraph/
    story/0,22049,25990979-5005941,00.html
9   Fred Engh, 'Sports Rage: Adults Losing Control at Kids' Sporting Events', *ABC
    News*, 11 September 2000, http://abcnews.go.com/US/story?id=94468
10 Deborah Prothrow-Stith, 'Do "Fight Clubs" Reflect America's Violent Culture?',
    transcript, *NPR News and Notes*, 17 August 2006, www.npr.org/templates/story/
    story.php?storyId=5663321
11 Michael McCarthy, 'Illegal, Violent Teen Fight Clubs Face Police Crackdown',
    USA Today, 1 July 2006, www.usatoday.com/news/nation/2006-07-31-violent-
    fight-clubs_x.htm
12 Deborah Prothrow-Stith, 'Do "Fight Clubs" Reflect America's Violent Culture?',
    transcript, *NPR News and Notes*, 17 August 2006, www.npr.org/templates/story/
    story.php?storyId=5663321
13 Sherrill Nixon, 'Alarming Rise in Teen Abuse of Parents', *The Sydney Morning
    Herald*, 15 August 2008, p8.

WHEN BOYS ARE VULNERABLE TO VIOLENCE

1   'Assault', *Australian Institute of Criminology*, 2007, www.aic.gov.au/statistics/
    violent%20crime/assault.asp
2   R.B., 'Physical Dating Violence Affects U.S. Teen Boys and Girls Equally,
    Study Shows', Health and Wellness, *Associated Content*, 24 November 2007,
    www.associatedcontent.com/article/453152/physical_dating_violence_
    affects_us.html?cat=5
3   'Male Rape', *National Center for Victims of Crime*, www.ncvc.org/ncvc/main.aspx?d
    bName=DocumentViewer&DocumentID=32361

WHY DADS MATTER

1   Kyle D. Pruett, *The Nurturing Father: Journey Towards the Complete Man*, Warner
    Books, New York, 1987, chapter 15.
2   www.golivewire.com/forums/peer-yntnyin-support-a.html
3   Ibid.

4   Kyle D. Pruett, *The Nurturing Father: Journey Towards the Complete Man*, Warner Books, New York, 1987, chapter 9.

WHEN BOYS PUSH THE BOUNDARIES
1   Lynn E. Ponton, MD, *The Romance of Risk: Why Teenagers Do the Things They Do*, Basic Books, New York 1997, p30.

BUILDING RESILIENCE
1   Leonard Sax, *Boys Adrift: The Five Factors Driving the Growing Epidemic of Unmotivated Boys and Underachieving Young Men*, Basic Books, Philadelphia, 2007.
2   Michael Carr-Gregg, *The Princess Bitchface Syndrome,* Penguin, Melbourne, 2006, pxiv.
3   Michael Ungar, *The We Generation: Raising Socially Responsible Kids*, Allen & Unwin, Sydney, 2009, p208.
4   'The Good Childhood Inquiry: What You Told Us About Lifestyle', *The Children's Society*, www.childrenssociety.org.uk/resources/documents/good%20childhood/6294_full.pdf
5   www.worldchallenge.com.au
6   Richard Eckersley, Australia 21, www.australia21.org.au/youth.htm
7   John Taylor Gatto, 'Acceptance of New York City Teacher of the Year Award' 1990, http://momelo.wordpress.com/2009/04/17/a-great-speech-to-read-from-john-taylor-gatto/

WHERE TO NOW?
1   Sir Ken Robinson, 'Do Schools Kill Creativity?' *TED*, Monterey, California, February 2006.